The
Double
in
Literature

The Double in Literature

A Psychoanalytic Study of

by Robert Rogers

Wayne State University Press, Detroit 1970

Published simultaneously in Canada
by The Copp Clark Publishing Company
517 Wellington Street, West
Toronto 2B, Canada.

Library of Congress Catalog Card Number: 76–100975
Standard Book Number: 8143–1415–5

Contents

for Joanne

who knows a holotype
from a schizotype—
and much more

Preface

Several months ago my three-year-old acquired an imaginary friend of his own age named Gary. Gary keeps him company when he feels lonesome, performs daring exploits beyond his reach at present, and often commits minor sins which call for reprimand. Such fictive companions, harmless at this age in most cases, can contribute to a child's development by helping him master anxiety. Not only does the literary artist sometimes create comparable figures, doubles, for some of his characters, he often does so without knowing it. Neither he nor his reader grasps that two or more apparently autonomous characters in a story may be component portions of a psychological whole. While doubling in literature usually symbolizes a dysfunctional attempt to cope with mental conflict, there is nothing abnormal or malign about this phenomenon considered as part of the artistic process. On the contrary, enormous formal gains can result when endopsychic conflict presents itself in the guise of a relationship between ostensibly independent characters in fiction.

The purpose of this book is to provide an account of the psychological framework of doubling—more for its heuristic value than its intrinsic interest. Though I draw on the commentary of others, my own analyses of literary works constitute the bulk of illustrative material. I hope that many of these analyses will illuminate the works they study over and above what the remarks contribute to the argument of the book. At the same time I trust it will be understood that these analyses are subordinate portions of a larger discussion and are not intended as comprehensive interpretations of individual works. Certain other limitations of scope ought to be indicated here. The selection of works for discussion is partly arbitrary, partly dictated by the amount and kind of material required to illustrate certain aspects of the subject, and partly a reflection of my relative familiarity with particular works and authors. While doubling is sporadic rather than omnipresent in literature, the incidence is great enough to make it impossible for anyone to mention all occurrences of it. I have not even attempted to give a complete account of it in the works of any single author, but I have tried to treat doubling in enough different writers to suggest that it is a basic literary process reflecting fundamental tendencies of the human mind and not just an aberration on the part of a few authors.

It is a pleasure to acknowledge the support this project has received from various quarters. For permission to draw on earlier versions of the discussion of "The Jolly Corner" (chapter 4), *Billy Budd* (chapter 8), and *Othello* (chapter 4), I am grateful to the editors of *American Imago, Literature and Psychology,* and *Shakespeare Quarterly,* respectively. The Research Foundation of State University of New York has generously provided me with extra time in the form of three Faculty Fellowships. Dr. Frederick Wyatt, Chief of the Psychological Clinic at the University of Michigan, introduced me to the possibilities of psychoanalytic criticism. If I have not made good use of them, he is in no way responsible. My students at Buffalo in English 423–424 endured my divarications on the subject of doubles and stimulated me by their questions to work out many of the ideas in this book. To friends and colleagues at Buffalo who made contributions to this study, Jerome Mazzaro, Benjamin Townsend, Howard Wolf, Angus Fletcher, John Ogden, and Herbert Schneidau, I am most grateful, especially to Terry and Herb for their aid with the entire manuscript version. They saved me many blunders. Norman Holland has enriched my professional life in many ways. I wish to thank him, Roger Porter, Dr. Mark Kanzer, and Simon O. Lesser for the encouragement they offered and for reading portions of the manuscript. To my good editorial father figure, Leonard F. Manheim, and to Eleanor Manheim, I owe a lasting debt for warm support over a period of many years. I am mindful also of an enduring obligation to the late Richard Chase for his guidance and example. My wife never hesitated to put aside her

Preface

own work to proofread for me, but I dedicate this book to her for other, more important reasons.

Buffalo, New York   R. R.
September 1969

Introduction

Lucretius tells us that "there never were, nor ever can be, Centaurs —creatures with a double nature." Nor were there ever such monstrous hybrids as Scylla, "half sea-monster, with a girdle of mad dogs," nor such composites as Chimaera, "with three bodies rolled into one, in front a lion, at the rear a serpent, in the middle the she-goat that her name implies, belching from her jaws a dire flame born of her body." While Lucretius argues his view of the nature of things with vigorous common sense, modern science gives us pause. Common sense no longer seems adequate now that we are accustomed to thinking of space as curved, or of light as having weight and moving both as waves and particles. Simple assertions are suspect in an age when we know myth has meaning, when we can read the riddle of the Sphinx, another preposterous composite creature. We exist in a century when, as Norman O. Brown suggests, we can understand almost as much about psychic fission as about nuclear fission.

If monsters, as well as gods, are made in the image of man, perhaps the mind of man is not altogether unlike the composite body of the Sphinx. Hence it may be that Photius, the Byzantine lexicographer, speaks with deep insight in his life of Pythagoras: "For every other creature is guided by one principle; but we [man] are pulled in

1

different directions by our different faculties . . . . towards the better by the god-like element . . . towards the worse by the domination of the bestial element within us." In the quasi-scientific allegory of modern metapsychology one might speak instead of a tug-of-war between man's superego and id. No matter what terms are used, we can argue that man does have a double—or multiple—nature. We need not be mystified along with Walt Whitman when he says, "I cannot understand the mystery, but I am always conscious of myself as two." Nor will we think Maupassant completely mad for having seen his hallucinatory double sit at the other side of a desk, dictating what he should write. We are familiar with the double, or doppelgänger, both as a common literary motif in works like Poe's "William Wilson" and a recurrent phenomenon in psychopathology, as in the instance of the inimitable Mr. G., a patient who, when he saw his double a few feet away in space, not only remained calm but discountenanced the rogue by changing his facial expressions so rapidly that the alter ego could not keep pace with the transformations.

Casual familiarity with the double in literature has bred a strange mixture of contempt and awe, contempt for what seems like a facile device of melodrama and awe at the uncanny feelings which exposure to doubles can evoke. The conventional double is of course some sort of antithetical self, usually a guardian angel or tempting devil. Critics oriented toward psychology view the diabolic double, which predominates, as a character representing unconscious, instinctual drives. Despite the intriguing features of these anti-social doubles, the device has been used so often that the double in literature as it is usually understood borders on being a stereotype, yet the term "double" provokes confusion. Albert J. Guerard asserts that "no term is more loosely used by casual critics of modern literature. As almost any character can become a Christ-figure or Devil-archetype, so almost any can become a Double."[1] To eradicate this confusion we need a broad, generic definition of the psychological double and a taxonomy of the numerous subtypes. Even more important, we need to understand in psychological terms why authors portray doubles in their works. Above all we want to comprehend how major authors enhance the dramatic effect of their work by doubling.

Walt Whitman oversimplifies when he speaks of the mystery of his consciousness of himself as two. We find not two, but many selves and masks in his poetry—the autobiographical Walt, Walt the

2

Introduction

Prophet-Poet, Walt the Body, Walt the Soul, Walt the American, Walt the Cosmos.

> Do I contradict myself?
> Very well then I contradict myself,
> I am large, I contain multitudes.

Another writer with a sense of the multifaceted nature of the artist is F. Scott Fitzgerald: "There never was . . . a good biography of a good novelist. There couldn't be. He's too many people if he's any good." If he is any good, it might be added, these "people" may become various characters in his works, characters who appear as autonomous artistic entities and yet are fragments of some other characterological whole, as perhaps Jay Gatsby and Nick Carraway are. A psychiatrist, in discussing the writer's problem of identification in the portrayal of characters of the opposite sex, asserts that "the artist projects his ego in polymorphous transformations into his work, that is, he projects his inner experiences into an imagined outer world."[2] Schiller is quoted in this connection as saying, "All creatures born by our fantasy, in the last analysis, are nothing but ourselves." This does not mean that every character of every work of fiction is some sort of double of the author. Nor does every personage in a dream represent some aspect of the dreamer. A more appropriate focus for commentary on doubles is this statement in Wellek and Warren's *Theory of Literature:* "The novelist's potential selves, including those selves which are viewed as evil, are all potential *personae* . . . . Dostoevsky's four brothers Karamazov are all aspects of Dostoevsky. Nor should we suppose that a novelist is necessarily limited to [outward] observation of his heroines. '*Madame Bovary, c'est moi,*' says Flaubert."[3] While Flaubert's remark highlights the tendency of writers to reify portions of themselves in their characters, Madame Bovary cannot be considered as a true "double" as the term will be defined in this study unless some other character in the novel represents a complementary aspect of either the author or the human psyche in general. As it happens, Simon O. Lesser shows that Flaubert identifies with both Emma and her husband, Charles—Madame Bovary corresponding to Flaubert's id and Charles to "his hoodwinked ego."[4] So Madame Bovary is a double —of Charles.

As for the fragmentation of Dostoevsky's soul in *The Brothers Karamazov,* Hanns Sachs comments:

All four of them [Dmitri, Ivan, Alyosha, Smerdyakov] are Dostoevsky himself. Each is a part of his mind, of his affects and most of all, of his own unconscious. . . . Every one of the four is a perfect absolutely complete human being; with none of them we get the impression that he is only a part or particle of an individual. . . . Yet while all these figures are complete individualities as far different from each other as human beings can be, there is still a mysterious bond between them; we feel that they have in spite of all diversities a hidden identity which becomes manifest in their common urge for parricide.[5]

A similar statement comes from Selma Fraiberg: "We can also argue that the three brothers Karamazov and Smerdyakov were the external representatives of an internal conflict within one man."[6]

Four distinctions about the nature of the psychological double can be made based on the example of *The Brothers Karamazov*. First, the fragmentation in this novel is implicit, not explicit. We may sense this division, but it is not mentioned by the author, and none of the characters exhibits any direct awareness of it. By analogy to levels of expression in dreams, the fragmentation is *latent* rather than *manifest*. Most commentary on the double has been confined to overt, or manifest, examples, such as in Dostoevsky's celebrated short novel *The Double* in which the clerk, Golyadkin, encounters his alter ego, also named Golyadkin, who appears to be his mirror image in many respects.

The second distinction involves terminology. In the case of the Karamazov brothers the fragmentation is not dual but multiple. Clearcut examples of such splitting into three or more fragments are harder to identify and more difficult to deal with than the more common dual split. Both dual and multiple fragmentation can be described satisfactorily by the term "decomposition," but this concept is not well known outside of psychoanalytic writings and not even used consistently in them. This study, therefore, will use the terms doubling, splitting, fragmentation, and decomposition as synonymous. In particular, the term "double," which already has wide currency in literary criticism, will often be used as synonymous with the more inclusive phrase "composite character." Context may normally be relied upon to make clear whether the word "double" refers to one-half of a duality (a "component character"), to a pair, or to one of a group of interdependent, interrelated characters. These terms generally will refer to characters which may be thought of, from a psychological point of view, as directly portraying, or indirectly generated by, conflict which is essentially intrapsychic or endopsychic.[7]

A third distinction is made between doubling by multiplication and doubling by division. In the latter case (of which the four Karamazov brothers would be an example) the division involves the splitting up of a recognizable, unified psychological entity into separate, complementary, distinguishable parts represented by seemingly autonomous characters. Illustrative of doubling by multiplication would be the appearance in a story of several characters, all of whom are father figures representing a single concept of, or attitude toward, the father. Doubling by division of father figures occurs in cases where the characters are complementary, for example, the "good" father and the "bad" father. This kind of representation typically expresses ambivalent feelings, the conjunction of which (particularly when hostility is repressed) is so intolerable that the ambivalence is dealt with defensively by decomposing the loved and hated father into two separate and seemingly unrelated persons.

Doubling may be subjective or objective. Both represent conflict, but subject doubling represents conflicting drives, orientations, or attitudes without respect to their relation to other people, whereas object doubling displays inner conflict expressed in terms of antithetical or incompatible attitudes toward other people. In *The Brothers Karamazov* Father Zossima represents doubling by division of an *object;* he figures as the idealized, pure, revered, dignified, understanding, and loving father in contrast to Karamazov *père,* the cruel, tyrannical, despicable, sexual father of the flesh and fact.

The phenomenon of decomposition in literature has its origins in so fundamental a stratum of mental activity that it has analogs in other quite different realms of human concern. At the level of common experience few people escape the impulse to put on a false front at times. Another ordinary experience is that of hearing someone excuse behavior with the remark, "I'm not myself today." Such instances demonstrate the occasional disparity between what is assumed to be one's true identity and some kind of false or alien identity. The theme of confusion about one's identity crops up in *Alice in Wonderland*. "Who are you?" asks the Caterpillar. "I—I hardly know, Sir," answers Alice, having in mind her changes of size. When the Caterpillar challenges her to explain herself, she says, "I can't explain *myself,* I'm afraid, Sir . . . because I'm not myself, you see." Earlier in the story we are told that "this curious child was very fond of pretending to be two people." It is not surprising to hear a critic suggest that "the character of Lewis Carroll reverses at every point the behavior which was so well known in Professor Dodgson, bachelor don at Oxford College."[8]

Unless we are like Arthur Casebeer, Jr.—a stupid character in Lionel Trilling's "Of This Time, Of That Place" who is very sure of who he is and where he is going in life—all of us share a measure of confusion about who we are, and all of us seek to establish a firm identity. That Thoreau was on such a quest when he went to live at Walden Pond can be seen in this remark: "It will be a success if I shall have left myself behind." The infinite pathos of Kafka's failure—or sense of his failure—to consummate a similar quest is revealed when he asks, "What have I in common with the Jews when I have scarcely anything in common with myself?" A humorous aside on the subject of personal identity is voiced by J. D. Salinger's Zooey, who believes that "half the nastiness in the world is stirred up by people who aren't using their true egos" and who mocks his Madison Avenue employer by saying, "He *has* no ego any more—if he ever had one. He's split it up into *hob*bies."

The inclination of the racist to make an invidious division of all people into superior whites and inferior blacks presumably stems not so much from simple-mindedness as from an inner, emotional split, an ambivalence generated out of his own confusion about his identity. The racist adopts social myths as a mode of dealing with his own inner tension and insecurity, just as the neurotic does. Similar dichotomous tendencies prevail among competing social, political, and economic ideologies.

In Christian demonology the devil appears as the evil opposite, or double, of God. G. Rattray Taylor comments on the psychological process of decomposition by way of accounting for the nature of the devil: "The way in which the devil is made to provide a mirror image of the Deity is quite striking. He has his Mass, his churches, his disciples (who go about in twelves, or, with their leader, thirteen); he has great power and knowledge; he descends into hell. Not for nothing has the devil been called God's Ape." Taylor argues that

> men make gods in their own image, and if the Deity was an image of their better selves, the Devil was an image of their worse selves. He engaged in just those forbidden sexual acts which tempted them: and this is why he was so frequently accused of sodomy. (In some accounts, he is equipped with a forked penis, so that he can commit fornication and sodomy at the same time.) But it is also true that the Deity is a father

figure, and it therefore follows that his counterpart, the Devil, is a projection of many of the aspects of a father. Not only has he great knowledge and power, not only is he extremely old, but he also obstructs one's plans and must be circumvented by cunning. Despite his wisdom, he is often outwitted. Like a father, he can often be induced to help one, especially in return for promising to do what he says; he is quite grateful for cooperation, and seems genuinely concerned about injustice.[9]

The comparable evil counterpart of the Virgin Mary in church history, according to Taylor, is the witch, the antithesis of the pure and compassionate elements in the mother: "The witch is the bad mother, and . . . the witch's main function, psychologically speaking, was to have intercourse with the bad father. This explains why it was such an essential dogma that all witches had had intercourse with the devil."[10]

Analogs to psychological doubles of particular significance can be found in primitive man's conceptions about the nature of the soul.[11]

Since the so-called savage accounted for the processes of inanimate nature by assuming that living beings caused these processes, it was natural for him to make a similar explanation of animate nature: "If a man lives and moves, it can only be because he has a little man or animal inside him who moves him. The animal inside the animal, the man inside the man, is the soul." Huron Indians assumed the soul to have arms and legs; it was a model of the man himself. Malays think of the soul as a little man "mostly invisible and of the bigness of a thumb, who corresponds exactly in shape, proportion, and even in complexion to the man in whose body he resides." Thus it is supposed that there can be souls which are long or short, thin or fat, and so on. The soul of a sleeping person is widely supposed to venture forth from his body and visit the places, see the persons, and perform the actions of which he dreams. Naturally it could be fatal in such a case if the soul failed to return to the sleeping body; hence "it is a common rule with primitive people not to waken a sleeper, because his soul is away and might not have time to get back." If a man's soul quits his body when he is awake, the result is sickness, death, or insanity. It follows, of course, that demons and sorcerers can cause these events by abducting a man's soul.

Of special interest is the widespread belief that shadows, reflections, and portraits of the body are the same as souls, or are at least vitally linked with the well-being of the body. If a man's shadow is struck or stabbed, he will feel the injury and may even die. A man's shadow must avoid things, places, and people which are taboo for him; thus it is not surprising that an Australian native "once nearly died of fright because the shadow of his mother-in-law fell on his legs as he lay asleep under a tree." A man's reflection can be subject to danger. The Basutos contend that a crocodile can kill a man by dragging his reflection underwater, and the prevalent folk custom of covering mirrors or turning them to the wall after someone has died in a house is based on the idea that the soul reflected in the mirror may be seized by the ghost of the departed. It is especially dangerous for sick people to see themselves in a mirror. Even today people occasionally suffer from catoptricophobia—fear of mirrors and reflections—and a well-known superstition maintains that breaking a mirror will cause seven years of bad luck. What holds true for shadows and reflections obtains as well of portraits. Aborigines often refuse to have their photograph taken because they assume that their photographic image is an extension of themselves. Portraits can be dangerous, too, as in the gothic novel.

Another group of related beliefs involves the concept of the external soul.[12] The major idea, which is the reverse of the assumption that it is dangerous for the soul to be absent from the body, is that if the safety of the external soul can be insured, the body to which it belongs remains invulnerable. Frazer cites the Norse story of "the giant who had no heart in his body" as an example. The typical tale involves a perdurable ogre who holds a beautiful princess in thrall until he is finally defeated by the handsome hero who destroys the soul located in a remote place, for example, within a bird, within a cage, within a circle of palm trees in a thick jungle in a distant land. Various folk customs reflect the supposition that the external soul may reside in inanimate things, plants, and animals. In Southern Celebes, for example, the doctor who attends a woman in childbirth keeps in his own abode something made of iron, such as a chopping-knife, which is brought to him and which represents the woman's soul; he returns it after the confinement is over and the danger past.

A. E. Crawley furnishes interesting details concerning primitive ideas about duplication and the double.[13] To begin with, two was often considered a sacred number, especially in Samoa. Another belief assumed a connection between diet and conception, the idea being that a woman will bear twins if she eats anything double such as a double banana or a double cherry. There is a group of customs in which the chief performer is attended or represented by duplicates. The Egyptian bridegroom walks between two friends dressed just as he is; the Abyssinian bride's sister accompanies her, attired exactly as she is. Even more striking is the custom of employing mock kings.

Both birth and death are associated with doubles. It was commonly believed that any man who saw his double, or "wraith," was about to die. It was also commonly believed that the child was a duplicate of the father, and the minute size of the soul was necessary in order that it be capable of entering the woman's body. Thus, as Crawley points out, the principle of duplication "serves as a theory of the soul and of future existence. It also serves as a theory of biological reproduction and of physical evolution generally." In addition, of course, it functions as a primitive theory of personal identity.

Figures resembling the primitive soul-double are ghosts, revenants, vampires, werewolves, the dolls of necromancy, the golem (and his modern counterpart, the robot), the mannikin, the thumbling, and the homunculus.[14] These figures of magic and superstition, which can be thought of as appearing at a somewhat "later" stage in the development of personifications of psychic forces, are usually malignant, threatening figures, whereas most primitive soul-doubles are merely second selves and not antagonists.

Bridging the gap between primitive and modern psychology is the metapsychology of Plato, which resembles Freud's in several striking particulars.[15] Especially important is Plato's inclination to divide the psyche into component parts (or functions), the way Freud does, as compared to the monistic conception of the soul among primitives. The following table correlates the system of psychology (and its analogs) which Plato discusses in *The Republic* with Freud's later formulation of the makeup of the psyche:

Freudian psyche	*Image of the Soul*	*Principles of the Soul*	*Three Classes*	*Virtues of the Soul*	*Soul of the Lover* (Phaedrus)
ego	man	reason	rulers	wisdom	charioteer
superego	lion	passion	warriors	courage	noble horse
id	monster	(spirit)	commoners	temperance	evil horse
		appetite			
		(desire)			

In Book IX of *The Republic* Socrates tries to demonstrate that no man respecting the nobility of his soul can prefer injustice to justice by projecting an "image of the soul," the three components of which are man, lion, monster. To allow the monster to rule over the man would constitute injustice. Man, or the rational principle of the soul, must rule over the concupiscent monster with the aid of the "lionheart." By the same token, rulers of the state must in their wisdom govern the commoners with the help of the courageous warriors. Elsewhere, in *Phaedrus,* Plato suggests that conflict in the soul of the lover resembles the contest between the charioteer and his good horse, on the one hand, and the bad, temperamental, licentious horse on the other.[16] However rough the correspondences may be, it is fairly obvious that Plato's concept of the soul resembles Freud's, the ego being the rational component, the id being the appetitive one. Less clear is the relationship between the superego and Plato's spirited lion. If it is remembered that the superego is fundamentally nonrational, embodying as it does the more or less arbitrary dictates of parents and society, then the correspondence between Freud's superego and Plato's spirit will appear to be relatively close. In any case, what is important is that Plato's analysis of the nature of the inner forces in man sees those forces as sometimes in conflict, as always in need of being balanced or harmonized, and as susceptible of being conceptually isolated into component parts. Only in the light of such a psychology, ancient or modern, can the phenomenon of decomposition in literature be understood and described effectively.

Other analogs to psychological decomposition can be found in philosophy. Among the best known examples of philosophical dualism are the dichotomies of *yin* and *yang* in Chinese cosmology, body and soul in Plato, body and mind in Descartes, and perceiving mind and perceived object in Locke. All reflect in philosophical terms what will have to be dealt with in psychological terms. In the case of the division of body and soul the implications are at once obvious and yet so complex as to block further discussion at this point. The *yin* and *yang* dichotomy parallels splitting of characters along bisexual lines, a telling literary example of which can be seen in Virginia Woolf's *Orlando.* Body-mind dualism suggests, among other things, the dissolution of the body image which is so often encountered in people suffering from autoscopic hallucinations. As for the perceiving mind and perceived object of Locke, it will be apparent that when we deal with delusions, hallucinations, and the various kinds of projection so characteristic of decomposition, the objective "reality" of things seen and events taking place is unimportant. Their subjective reality is all-important.

Introduction

Psychoanalytic commentary has long been concerned with the process of doubling. The first significant observations come from Freud himself. As early as *The Interpretation of Dreams* (1900) Freud mentions that the ego sometimes appears in dreams together with other people who prove, on analysis, simply to be further representatives of the ego ("ego" here meaning "self").[17] The self, he says, can achieve multiple representation either directly or by virtue of its identification with other personages in the dream. A few years later Freud applies this insight to literature in "The Relation of the Poet to Day-Dreaming" (1908) by emphasizing that the hero stands as a representative of the ego (self) and by remarking upon "the tendency of modern writers to split up their ego by self-observation into many component-egos, and in this way to personify the conflicting trends in their own mental life in many heroes."[18]

The first truly complex application of the psychoanalytic concept of decomposition appeared in Otto Rank's *The Myth of the Birth of the Hero,* originally published in 1909.[19] In this brilliant study Rank correlates a number of myths about such heroes as Sargon, Moses, Oedipus, Paris, Gilgamesh, Tristan, Romulus, Hercules, Jesus, Siegfried, and Lohengrin. Rank singles out the recurrent motifs in these stories and then explains the typical features in psychoanalytic terms. He formulates the standard saga, or paradigm of the hero, as follows:

> The hero is the child of most distinguished parents, usually the son of a king. His origin is preceded by difficulties, such as continence, or prolonged barrenness, or secret intercourse of the parents due to external prohibition or obstacles. During or before the pregnancy, there is a prophecy, in the form of a dream or oracle, cautioning against his birth, and usually threatening danger to the father (or his representative). As a rule, he is surrendered to the water, in a box. He is then saved by animals, or by lowly people (shepherds), and is suckled by a female animal or by a humble woman. After he has grown up, he finds his distinguished parents, in a highly versatile fashion. He takes his revenge on his father, on the one hand, and is acknowledged, on the other. Finally he achieves rank and honors.[20]

Rank assumes that the characteristic duplication of parental figures corresponds to the so-called "family romance" fantasy encountered often in neurotics, the fantasy that one's parents are actually substitutes for one's "real" parents, who are of high and distinguished station in life (in myth, they are of royal blood). In myth the royal parents are usually also the tyrannical, persecutory parents, while the humble parents are kind and sustaining. The hostility of the father in the myths reflects a projection of the son's hostility toward him; the theme of the mother's humble station—or animal nature—reflects "a separation of the mother into the parts of the child-bearer and the suckler." Gilgamesh is rescued by an eagle, Lohengrin is carried ashore by a swan, and Romulus (and Remus) is first suckled by a she-wolf and later raised by the wife of a swineherd. Not only are the parents duplicated but so is the hero as well on occasion. For instance, Tristan's career repeats some features of the life of his father, Riwalin. According to Rank, the often complex array of personages in most of these myths actually represents only various relationships subsisting within the nuclear family: the hero and his parents. To illustrate Rank's theories in the case of Oedipus, it would appear that in addition to his true parents, Laius and Jocasta, and his royal foster parents, Polybus and Merope, the shepherd who rescues the outcast and the messenger who carries him to Polybus and Merope also serve in the capacity of parents. Since Teiresias and Creon have been accounted parental figures in a recent critical study, the principal characters in Sophocles' version all appear to share familial roles from a psychoanalytic point of view.[21]

Soon after Rank's application of the concept of decomposition to mythology came Ernest Jones's use of the idea in the 1910 version of his famous study of *Hamlet:*

> The most interesting of these mechanisms [aiding repression] in myth formation is that of "decomposition" (*Auseinanderlegung*), which is the opposite to the "condensation" (*Verdichtung*) mechanism so characteristic of normal dreams. Whereas in the latter process attributes of several individuals are fused in the creation of one figure, much as in the production of a composite photograph, in the former process various attributes of a given person are disunited and several individuals are invented, each endowed with one group of the original attributes. In this way one person, of complex character, gets replaced by several, each of whom possesses a different aspect of the character that in a simpler form of the myth was combined in one being; usually the different individuals closely resemble one another in other respects, for instance in age.[22]

Hamlet himself, says Jones, appears as a decomposed part of a whole, for he represents in part the rebellious son of patricidal and incestuous impulses, while Laertes depicts the loyal, obedient, submissive son. There are, moreover, three "fathers" in the play—Hamlet's actual father, Polonius, and Claudius—who are objects, respectively, of various attitudes toward the hypothetical father-in-general—love and pity; hatred and contempt; and "conscious detestation coupled with unconscious sympathy and identification."[23]

Jones implies that the mechanism of condensation is more commonly found in dreams than in myth and that the opposite is the case with decomposition. The same generalization applies to fiction and dreams; that is, the incidence of decomposition in fiction is far greater than in dreams and condensation occurs less often in fiction than in dreams.[24] Melville's whale might be cited as an example of condensation. Moby Dick is associated, both directly and indirectly, with good and evil; God and the Devil; theism and atheism; paternity and maternity; and at various points with strength, beauty, nature, masculinity, castration, terror, light, knowledge, the unknowable, and the womb.[25] In this study condensation will be discussed only when it casts light on the process of decomposition—as would be the case we were to analyze Ishmael and Ahad in *Moby Dick* as alter egos.[26]

Decomposition remains a minor concept in psychoanalytic theory. Because of the early abandonment of hypnosis in psychoanalytic treatment on the grounds that it tended to weaken rather than strengthen the ego, cases of autoscopic vision and multiple personality—the principal counterparts of decomposition in clinical practice—have not been encountered by practitioners of classical psychoanalysis.[27] The integrative goals and dynamic emphasis of psychotherapy do not provoke decomposition as a defense in patients. Psychoanalysts have remained aware of the presence of decomposition in literature, however, as is shown by such instances as Freud's commentary on the relationship between Macbeth and Lady Macbeth and Ernst Kris's analysis of Shakespeare's Henry IV plays. But most recent studies of decomposition have been made by eclectic psychiatrists and psychologists.

A special case is that of Otto Rank. Significantly, the bulk of his commentary on the double was produced after his break with classical psychoanalysis. Most of it does not appear to grow logically out of his earlier concern with decomposition in *The Myth of the Birth of the Hero*.[28] The later works do have value, of course, and what cannot be ignored is his emphasis on doubling as a narcissistic phenomenon and his stress on the connection between doubling and paranoia insofar as the mechanism of projection is common to both. What may be ignored are Rank's Rousseauesque attempt in *Beyond Psychology* to rediscover "the natural self of man" and such statements as the following: "The primitive and modern material concerning the Double . . . will show how a positive evaluation of the Double as the immortal soul leads to the building up of the prototype of personality from the self; whereas the negative interpretation of the Double as a symbol of death is symptomatic of the disintegration of the modern personality type."[29] Whatever the merits of Rank's case for the double as immortal soul, his remarks are militantly beyond the pale of psychoanalysis and hence beyond the scope of the present discussion.

As for Rank's stress on paranoid features of doubling, a recent study by Lawrence Kohlberg has called it into question, specifically with reference to Rank's assessment of Dostoevsky's *The Double* as being a classic portrayal of a paranoid state.[30] On the contrary, says Kohlberg, any awareness of an evil second self is alien to the paranoid state because the typical paranoid thinks of himself as completely innocent and unjustly blamed or persecuted by others. Kohlberg argues that Dostoevsky's doubles present the classic symptoms of an obsessive-compulsive character. The decomposition is not a splitting of selves but "an obsessive balancing or undoing of one idea or force with its opposite." This suggestion that doubling in Dostoevsky's works constitutes an obsessive balancing or undoing will be seen to have application to other authors as well.

Although literary critics must exercise scrupulous care to distinguish the mimetic from the actual, it seems clear that one clinical counterpart of the manifest double in fiction is the visual hallucination of the physical self, an event known as "autoscopy." If autoscopy and decomposition are not the same, they are at least so similar that they may be treated, *mutatis mutandis,* as identical, and in fact a recent psychiatric study of the double by Todd and Dewhurst utilizes a mixture of clinical and literary examples of autoscopic phenomena without apology. Todd and Dewhurst endeavor to distinguish between certain factors likely to produce visual hallucinations in general and specific factors tending to induce visual hallucinations of the self. The four major factors are (1) narcissism, (2) supernormal powers of visualization, (3) "archetypic thinking," and (4) disturbance of function in somatognostic areas of the brain.[31] The authors contend that factors "such as narcissism and irritative lesions in the somatognostic areas play a specific role as etiological agents underlying autoscopic hallucination," whereas "such a motley group of conditions as anxiety, fatigue, addiction to drugs or alcohol, cerebral lesions (not confined to somatognostic zones), psychoses, etc., are non-specific factors" which tend to produce visual hallucinations of any kind. Specific and general factors may act in concert, and some factors, such as "archetypic thinking," may be general or specific. Autoscopic hallucinations vary in kind and "quality": they may be of the whole body, or present just a bust or an arm, and they may be either solid or insubstantial, clear or misty. They may even be nonvisual in character, sometimes merely kinesthetic and sometimes simply "psychological" in the sense of a "felt presence" in the darkness.[32] Lukianowicz classifies autoscopic phenomena into two etiological groups: symptomatic, or organically caused autoscopy, and idiopathic, or pschogenically determined autoscopy, the latter involving some psychodynamic mechanism of a compensatory, or self-defensive, or wish-fulfilling kind.[33] This study will be confined to the latter type.

Less often linked with doubling than autoscopy is the more dramatic phenomenon of dissociation, known better by its result, the dual or multiple personality. Stevenson's *Dr. Jekyll and Mr. Hyde* presents the classic example in literature. Morton Prince's *The Dissociation of a Personality* and Thigpen and Cleckley's *The Three Faces of Eve* describe celebrated cases encountered in clinical practice.[34] Compared to autoscopy, multiple personality involves behavioral dissociation in time, whereas autoscopy involves visual "dissociation" in space. While dissociation may be either dual or multiple, autoscopic vision is normally dual only. Dissociation resembles latent decomposition in literature more closely than autoscopy does, and autoscopy resembles manifest decomposition more closely than dissociation does.

Decomposition in literature and the related phenomena of dissociation and autoscopy in clinical practice always reflect psychosexual conflict, however obliquely, with the sole exception of organically caused cases of autoscopy. Stanley M. Coleman arrives at essentially the same conclusion: "In both the male and the female, a conflict between libidinal and other aims is a fundamental factor for the postulation of doubles."[35] At times this libidinal factor can be perceived with relative ease, as in the case of the hysterical attack observed by Freud in which the patient acted out simultaneously the roles of raping man and attacked woman by pressing her dress with one hand while endeavoring to rip it off with the other.[36] But most of the time the psychosexual genesis of doubling lies so deeply buried that only profound analysis will unearth it.

A recent theory of importance which bears on the subject of decomposition is the generative hypothesis formulated in Angus Fletcher's *Allegory: The Theory of a Symbolic Mode*.[37] Fletcher suggests that the allegorical hero may be said to "generate" secondary personalities which constitute partial aspects of himself, agents who react with or against him in a "syllogistic manner." He likens allegorical heroes to people who in actual life "project" in the psychological sense by ascribing fictitious personalities to other people. We can determine what is occurring in the mind of an imaginative projector by analyzing the projections: "If the reader wants a sketch of the character of Redcrosse in Spenser, he lists the series of adventures and tests undergone by Redcrosse, not so much for the pleasure of seeing *how* Redcrosse reacts in each case, as to see, literally, what aspects of the hero have been displayed by the poet." Thus Redcrosse imagines Sansfoi, Sir Guyon imagines Mammon and his cave, Sir Calidore imagines the Blatant Beast. The most common agents of allegory, the subcharacters, may be said in this sense to be generated by the main protagonists. Fletcher's discussion of the fragmentation of the composite allegorical hero will be considered at length in Chapter 8 in connection with the dramatic gains which ensue when psychological decomposition takes place.

Some of the dichotomies which result when splitting occurs, such as consciousness and unconsciousness or sanity and insanity, have already been mentioned. It must be emphasized that these psychological antinomies are many and varied. When Freud speaks of the susceptibility of the ego to being split, he offers this analogy: "If we throw a crystal to the floor, it breaks; but not into haphazard pieces. It comes apart along its lines of cleavage into fragments whose boundaries, though they were invisible, were predetermined by the crystal's structure."[38] It follows that since there are many kinds of crystals, there are many kinds of defects in personality structure and hence many ways in which the personality may split up under stress. The fissures which are apt to develop have in common their genesis in psychic conflict but are rather bewildering in their variety. Such fissures may be said to develop between love and hate; heterosexuality and homosexuality; ego libido and object libido; the Eriksonian categories of autonomy and dependence; masochism and sadism; acitivity and passivity. Fissures may also be said to appear between the psychic constellations of id, ego, and superego, or between the oral, anal, and phallic stages of libidinal development as compared to mature genital development, or between the pleasure principle and the reality principle. If a man splits, he splits along the grain. When the grain is gnarled and knotty, the split is not a smooth one, that is, it does not follow easily predictable lines. This seems to be the case with Dostoevsky's Golyadkin, whose double represents both qualities he hates in himself and attributes he lacks and desires to have. Adding to the complexity of the situation is the fact that the doubles in this work represent a veritable potpourri when regarded from a clinical point of view. One of the objects of the present study, therefore, is to convey an idea of the full range of possible patterns which doubling may take in order that simplistic notions embodied in such impressionistic rubrics as "devil double" will no longer be accorded more than their due.

Freud's analogy also indicates that to the naked eye a polished crystal may have no discernible structure or observable "faults" along which lines the crystal will fracture when subject to stress. Similarly, when we are confronted by latent doubles in literature, the fracture between them is not ordinarily apparent to the reader's conscious mind. More precisely, there are two pieces of crystal which can be placed together in such a way that the perfect congruence of their surfaces proves that a fracture has in fact taken place. While such latent doubles are of much greater interest than manifest ones, we begin with the latter group because by examining the fit of what are obviously two pieces of a ruptured whole we can better discern more subtle instances of decomposition later on.

The Mirror Image

Hallucinations of seeing oneself constitute a special category, one to be distinguished sharply from hallucinations of anything or anyone else because delusions of encountering one's own self betray a morbid preoccupation of the individual with his own essence. These visions of the self can be characterized without exception as narcissistic, and a consideration of such cases must be founded on an understanding of the nature of narcissism.

Narcissism is a kind of love, but it is misleading to translate the concept into what is known commonly as "self-love." Self-love in the everyday sense of "egotism" is a metaphorical expression. In narcissism the self-love is literal. The only difference between this kind of love and the erotic love of another person is in the object. Narcissism paradoxically involves a relationship, a relationship of self to self in which one's self is regarded as though it were another person. Freud stated the paradox in a way which emphasizes the connection between narcissism and decomposition:

> The ego is in its very essence a subject; how can it be made into an object? Well, there is no doubt that it can be. The ego can take itself as an object, can treat itself like other objects, can observe itself, criticize itself, and do Heaven knows what with itself. In this, one part of the

ego is setting itself over against the rest. So the ego can be split; it splits itself during a number of its functions—temporarily at least.[1]

Such a taking of the ego as object is a libidinal taking, an erotic process. Elsewhere, in his essay "On Narcissism," Freud emphasizes the libidinal nature of narcissism when it occurs as a component of states which do not, at first glance, seem characterized by self-love, such as physical illness, often marked by regression and withdrawal; sleep, which like illness "implies a narcissistic withdrawal of the libido away from its attachments back to the subject's own person"; dreams, the dreamer himself always being the central figure or observer; and hypochondria, where the body of the patient (specifically, its imagined hurts) receives the attention of the libido.[2] The results of the taking of one's own ego as an object can be seen in their most morbid form in the psychoses, with their radical megalomania and marked withdrawal of interest in the external world. Since narcissism involves an investment of libido in the ego, it is always in some sense pleasurable, though it may not be felt as such. Thus even the paranoid's characteristic sense of being watched or spoken to is considered by Freud to be a delusion of observation which results in a narcissistic gratification for the ego-ideal.[3] Another form of narcissistic gratification is that obtained by the homosexual in seeking out objects more like himself.

In examining a number of literary works displaying manifest doubling of the self, particular stress will be laid upon the presence of narcissistic complications and the esthetic limitations of manifest doubling.

A special genre of the manifest double is the mirror image, the projected self being not merely a similar self but an exact duplicate. A special case of the mirror image can be seen in the celebrated story of Narcissus, whose behavior has given us a name for a basic psychological concept. One sign of morbidity in Narcissus' preoccupation with himself is that he has trouble discriminating between the "me" and the "not-me." "Am I the lover / Or beloved?" he asks (in Ovid's version).[4] Like the victim of autoscopy, Narcissus is at least partly aware that his vision is not completely real in the sense of being corporally separate from himself. For the most part, however, the myth presents the mirror image in the pool as a symbol of Narcissus' unawareness that what he sees is only a reflection of himself. Another sign of morbidity in the hero is the sexualization of his self-love. In fact, erotic behavior per-

19

vades the tale. Not only does Narcissus *love* himself, this child of passion is born of the rape of Liriope by Cephisus. He is loved by the rejected young swain whose curse, "O may he love himself alone . . . yet fail in that great love," is carried out by Nemesis. He is also loved by Echo, whose passion seems undisguisedly sexual: she throws herself in his arms and is described as being like "sulphur / At the tip of torches, leaping to fire / When another flame leans toward it." That the love of Narcissus for himself transcends mere admiration or egotism, that he wants in a literal way to possess himself sexually, is symbolized by his attempt to kiss his image in the pool.

One facet of his erotomania can be seen in his compulsive flirtatiousness:

> The way Narcissus had betrayed frail Echo,
> Now swift, now shy, so he had played with all:
> Girls of the rivers, women of the mountains,
> With boys and men.

This passage points to another feature of psychological interest, the homoerotic element. Narcissus flirts with males, loves his own sex in loving himself, and performs a traditionally feminine ritual of grief in beating his breast with his "pale hands," the same action which his sisters perform as they grieve for him. The metamorphosis of Narcissus into a flower confirms the presence of a feminine strain in him, and intimations of his psychosexual impotence are contained in the two references to loss of sight in Ovid's version: we are told that neither food nor sleep can lure him away from the pool as he lies there "until sight failed," and at the end "death shut fast the eyes that shone with light / At their own lustre." Given his psychological makeup, it is not surprising that he rejects the lovely Echo: "May I be dead / Before you throw your fearful chains around me."

One of the most charming tales on the theme of the mirror image is Hawthorne's whimsical "Monsieur du Miroir." The tone of light irony is sounded at the very beginning of the fantasy sketch: "Than the gentleman above named, there is nobody, in the whole circle of my acquaintance, whom I have more attentively studied, yet of whom I have less real knowledge, beneath the surface which it pleases him to present." Hawthorne's easy, punning humor seems at first to belie any awareness of the gravity of his theme. He speaks of his subject as involving "grave reflection" and concludes the sketch by doubting that

M. du Miroir is the wiser for all his meditation, though his whole business is "reflection." He jokes about there being reasons for supposing M. du Miroir to be a near relative except for his French name, which obliges him to disclaim all kinship. He chides his mirror double, who moves his lips but makes no sound, for being a "dumb devil." He notes that M. du Miroir shares his own taste in clothes to the last detail and all his moods and feelings, even to the point of simulating a swollen jaw when Hawthorne has a toothache. M. du Miroir, something of a wag, thrusts his head into a bright new warming pan in the hardware store and paddles, in full dress, "from one mud puddle to another . . . plunging into the filthy depths of each."

But beneath the surface levity of Hawthorne's style lurks the troubling theme of narcissism. M. du Miroir shares Narcissus' fondness for water. He is often seen in the ballroom "in my age of vanities." Even his impish omnipresence reflects an exaggerated awareness of the self. At one point Hawthorne says directly, "I loved him well," speaking of his youth when "Monsieur du Miroir had then a most agreeable way of calling me a handsome fellow"—a compliment which Hawthorne is careful to return to the image in the mirror. The intimate connection between the physical image and the image of the artist in his own eyes is sounded when Hawthorne wonders if M. du Miroir will haunt his grave after death, lingering "to remind the neglectful world of one who staked much to win a name."

Though it is couched in light irony, serious notes creep into the sketch again and again. The mirror image is a conjurer, capable of passing through brick walls and bolted oaken doors. Twice the demonic motif appears, once when the image is referred to as a "dumb devil" and once when it is criticized for lacking the common sense to know that Hawthorne "would as willingly exchange a nod with the Old Nick" as greet him in public. It seems ominous, too, when Hawthorne —who hid himself away from people for many years—admits that even when isolated in his chamber, with the key turned, withdrawn, and the keyhole stuffed with paper, he cannot escape the haunting presence of his other self. Remarks concerning the speaker's relations with the opposite sex, which occur sporadically in the sketch—seemingly without any important connection—actually form a consistent pattern. "Whenever I have been in love," we are told, "Monsieur du Miroir has looked passionate and tender." At the lady, we wonder, or at his counterpart in front of the mirror? During one tender moment the mischievous imp "stole into the heaven of a young lady's eyes; so that, while I gazed and was dreaming only of herself, I found him also in my dreams." In a similar vein we hear Hawthorne jokingly insist that when the "intrusive intimate" follows him into his bedchamber, "I should prefer—scandal apart—the laughing bloom of a young girl to the dark and bearded gravity of my present companion." In each instance, love of a woman is either blended with or partly obstructed by narcissism, a pattern which bears out Freud's suggestion that a kind of reciprocity exists between ego-libido and object-libido such that "the more that is absorbed by the one, the more impoverished does the other become."[5] In any case, there can be little doubt concerning the profundity of Hawthorne's comparison of the attempt to escape his M. du Miroir with "the hopeless race that men sometimes run with memory, or their own hearts, or their moral selves, which, though burdened with cares enough to crush an elephant, will never be one step behind."

Just such a hopeless race with memory, heart, and moral self is run in Wilde's *The Picture of Dorian Gray,* a tale which implies that the worship of one's own physical beauty is more hazardous for men than for women. The novel presents a young man ravished by a painting of himself (the portrait double being but a variation of the mirror-image double). Dorian Gray's first glance at the canvas teaches him to love his own beauty and to know that "when one loses one's good looks . . . one loses everything." The name of Narcissus is invoked in the text, and the protagonist says of the portrait, "I am in love with it . . . It is part of myself." Sad at the thought that the image in the portrait will remain young and handsome while he grows old and ugly, Dorian Gray expresses the fateful wish that the situation be reversed. And so it happens: the face in the diabolical painting, hidden away, reflects over the years the passions, crimes, and physical age of the subject, while the living Dorian Gray appears untouched by time, at least until the protagonist, hounded by guilt, decides to stab the portrait. This symbolic act magically causes his actual death, whereupon his servants discover him, withered and loathsome beyond recognition, beside the handsome "original." With respect to the dangers of narcissism, the tale speaks for itself. Almost as obvious to the modern eye is the epicene atmosphere of the novel. One need not make any inferences from Oscar Wilde's life to perceive the androgynous nature of Dorian Gray and the homoerotic attraction which he has for his friends, Lord Wotton and the painter of the portrait, Basil Hallward. Given this context, Gray's declaration that he cannot love because "I am too much concentrated on myself" occasions no surprise.[6] What may not be apparent in the novel is that the painter, Basil Hallward, is a latent double of Dorian Gray. "I have put too much of myself into it," Hallward says, to which Lord Wotton replies, "Too much of yourself . . . Basil, I didn't know you were so vain." What seems to have happened in psychological terms is that Hallward, himself perhaps an allegorical artist-surrogate of Oscar Wilde, has projected his narcissistic ideal into the painting; in any case, Hallward's goodness and integrity are complementary to Dorian Gray's corruption and hypocrisy.

The complementarity of personality traits typical of a man and his double obtains in Hans Christian Andersen's "The Shadow," a droll tale about a wise and humble Learned Man who loses his shadow only to have it return to him, sassy and presumptuous, with pretentions of having an independent existence. The shadow proposes that the real man serve as traveling companion and supposed shadow of the shadow. Having visited the abode of Poetry, about which the Learned Man is curious, the shadow claims to know everything and to be privy to all men's secrets. As a result he has become extraordinarily vain, even to the point of insisting that the Learned Man not *tutoyer* him, though when the man becomes the shadow's servant the shadow says "thou" to the man. In a curious variation on the theme of the incompatibility of narcissism with romantic love, the shadow presumes to win the hand of a princess. When the Learned Man threatens to expose the fraud for what he is, a mere shadow, the shadow has the man declared insane and executed, and the story ends with the marriage of the shadow and the princess. The shadow seems to symbolize the narcissistic hazards of too much knowledge, the dangers of a Faustian yearning for worldliness, and the ill fortune that portends when a man sees his shadow.

Alfred de Musset, one of a number of authors who actually saw their own doubles, presents an equally narcissistic version of the mirror image in his "La Nuit de Décembre."[7] In the first part of the poem the speaker describes various mournful crises in his life when, alone, he saw a figure dressed in black which "resembled me like a brother." The shadowy figure always mirrors the poet's current melancholy mood. He is invariably alone at these moments, and it turns out that when the vision speaks at the end of the poem he personifies Solitude:

Je ne suis ni dieu ni démon,
Et tu m'as nommé par mon nom
Quand tu m'as appelé ton frère;
Où tu vas, j'y serai toujours,
Jusques au dernier de tes jours,
Où j'irai m'asseoir sur ta pierre.

Le ciel m'as confié ton coeur.
Quand tu seras dans la douleur,
Viens à moi sans inquiétude.
Je te suivrai sur le chemin;
Mais je ne puis toucher ta main,
Ami, je suis la Solitude.

Though Musset presumably did not intend it that way, the vision seems to represent the spirit of sentimental Self-Pity more than Solitude. This is in keeping with the theme of narcissism pervading the work. Since most of the sad moments stem from disappointed love, we are confronted once again with the evidence of the conflict between self-love and love of others.

The proclivity of phantom doubles to show up only when the subject is in solitude can be seen in one of Maupassant's stories: "But if there were two of us in the place, I feel certain that he would not be there any longer, for he is there just because I am alone, simply and solely because I am alone!" So ends "He?"—in which the narrator explains to a friend that though he feels more than ever incapable of loving one woman alone "because I shall always adore all the others too much," he intends to marry, a very ordinary girl as it happens, in order to insure that when he wakes in the middle of the night, he will not be alone and hence subject to a visitation of the unidentified "he." Although the monstrous presence christened "The Horla" in Maupassant's story of that title is never directly identified as a double, passages such as "He is becoming my soul" and the scene in which the maddened narrator fails to perceive his reflection in a mirror just after he has "felt" the Horla reading over his shoulder leave little doubt that he is a double, even though elsewhere he is thought to be a suffocating, soul-sucking vampire. Having failed to kill the visitant by the expedient of burning his chateau to the ground, the victim concludes that to destroy the Horla he must kill himself—as Maupassant tried to do in his final madness. The narrator in "The Horla" appears to live alone except for servants and no love interest is mentioned, but

the drift of "He?" when matched with Maupassant's notorious saty-
riasis leads to the supposition that the Don Juan impulse in him
amounted to a defensive reaction-formation against the feeling of being
unable to love at all.[8] If so, it would follow that the persecutory double
in both stories is a superego projection which hounds the guilty
protagonists. Extreme anxiety plagues the heroes of both tales.

One of the most representative superego doubles appears in Poe's
"William Wilson." Here the narrator emphasizes his own evil proclivities in contrast to the good advice and cautionary whispers of his
"guardian angel" double, who resembles him in name, feature, age,
and so forth. Indicative of the burden of unconscious guilt borne by the
narrator is the seemingly shameless young decadent's confession that
"an intolerable weight of anxiety" is lifted from him when the other
William Wilson spoils his attempt to cheat a fellow Oxford student at
cards. Except for cheating at cards and excessive drinking, the various
"debaucheries" are with one exception unspecified. In this disparity
between the relatively innocuous nature of the protagonist's crimes and
the extreme baseness by which they are characterized in the story itself,
the tyrannical severity of the superego finds expression. Poe's own
gambling and wine-bibbing at the University of Virginia, which
caused his tightfisted foster father to refuse him further support,
despite Poe's success as a student, appear in exaggerated form in the
narrative, at least according to Marie Bonaparte, who stresses that the
double in this story represents, quite in conformity with psychoanalytic
theory, "the introjection of the repressive father system" in the son.[9]
The only "crime" involving women in the story is the implied but
unspecified plan to seduce "the young, the gay, the beautiful wife of
the aged and doting Di Broglio." This plot, in which oedipal overtones
are obvious, is foiled by the double. Enraged, the protagonist challenges
the double to a duel and ends by realizing as he looks into a mirror
that he has stabbed himself—a rather stereotyped ending perhaps
borrowed from E. T. A. Hoffmann's "Story of the Lost Reflection." No
pronounced narcissism appears to possess William Wilson, but Bonaparte suggests that the ambivalence toward the self portrayed in this
story may be regarded as a defensive reaction against narcissism.[10]

Perhaps the most famous and certainly the most influential of all
double stories concerns the adventures of Peter Schlemihl, who sells his
shadow to a remarkable man in a gray coat in exchange for unlimited
riches. Chamisso's tale is a feeble variation of the Faust legend, with

25

Peter Schlemihl cast as Faust and the man in the gray coat as Mephistopheles. Despite the inexhaustible riches Schlemihl gets in return, he becomes a pariah, avoided by all who perceive him to be without his soul-shadow. His Helen of Troy is the beautiful Minna, whom he cannot marry if he does not have a shadow.

Several passages in the narrative point to narcissism as the source of Schlemihl's problem. He says concerning his feeling for the lovely Franny, "My vanity was only intent on exciting hers to make a conquest of me; but although the intoxication disturbed my head, it failed to make the least impression on my heart." He is flattered at being mistaken for the King of Prussia. And when he meets Minna, it is significant that he thinks that "she lived but in me, her whole soul being bound up in mine regardless what her own fate might be." Since shadows are invariably gray and since the man in the gray coat leads Schlemihl to "the pleasures of the world," old Graycoat functions as a bad angel or devil double of Schlemihl; that is, he in effect replaces the shadow which Schlemihl sells. That Graycoat can be overcome only by conscience ties in with the protagonist's statement early in the story that he has sacrificed his conscience for riches and his remark elsewhere that he has long been "a rigid censor" of himself and has nourished in his heart "the worm of remorse." Yet Peter Schlemihl, who uses his riches primarily for display and commits no really nefarious acts, cannot be called an evil figure. His real problem seems to be that his narcissism is even more inexhaustible than his riches. That is the true reason why he cannot marry Minna.

Along with Chamisso many other writers in the period of German romantic literature shared a penchant for portraying doppelgänger in their works, among them Goethe, Tieck, Fouqué, Heinrich von Kleist, E. T. A. Hoffmann, and Jean Paul Richter, who introduced the term doppelgänger.[11] For the most part, according to Tymms, "the romantic of the early period used the theme as a straightforward device for humorous, or grisly, misunderstandings in the tradition of the farce of mistaken identity or of folklore."[12] Of all these authors Hoffmann is best known for his portrayal of doubles.

Hoffmann, who experienced autoscopic hallucinations, once rewarded the praise of his hostess in the bitterness of his old age with the sarcastic comment that she mistook him, the Councillor Hoffmann, for Hoffmann the writer, a man of such genius that he could not deem her invitation worthy of notice.[13] This split between artist and practical man, resembling that between fantasy-maker Lewis Carroll and mathematician Lutwidge Dodgson, is the theme of Hoffmann's "The Doubles." The two doubles, alike even in their birthmarks, undergo a series of mysterious experiences in a plot worthy of Plautus or Shakespeare in its variations on mistaken identity. These experiences culminate in Deodatus Schwendy's being recognized as heir to the late prince, while his counterpart, painter George Haberland, dedicates himself anew to the life of the artist. The familiar pattern of frustrated love emerges in the renunciation that both men must make of the beautiful Nathalie, who cannot choose between them. Schwendy, the true prince, is left with the responsibilities of administering a realm, while Haberland has the task of idealizing Nathalie in his art.

Freud provides some important remarks about decomposition in his analysis of another of the many tales by Hoffman which deal in doubles, "The Sandman."[14] The story begins with the student Nathaniel's anxiety about his encounter with an itinerant optician, Coppola. The encounter reminds him of his childhood fears of the Sandman, a bogyman whose function, according to Nathaniel's nurse, was to throw handfuls of sand in the eyes of children when they refused to go to bed, making their eyes jump out of their heads. Coppola resembles the lawyer Coppelius, who used to visit Nathaniel's father after the boy went to bed and whom Nathaniel believed responsible for his father's death in connection with certain alchemical experiments. The rest of the action of the story, in brief, involves Nathaniel's obsessive love for Olympia, an automaton doll fabricated by Professor Spalanzani with the help of Coppola; his rejection of his betrothed, Clara; his madness; his recovery; his ultimate relapse into madness when he attempts to murder Clara; and his eventual suicide. In the sequel Clara eventually marries, finding a domestic happiness which Nathaniel, "with his tempest-tossed soul," could never have given her. Although Nathaniel does not see his double in any direct fashion, Clara suggests—and at one moment of temporary insight Nathaniel accepts—that Coppelius and Coppola exist only in his mind and are phantoms of his own self.

Freud's analysis stresses that the main motif in the story concerns the tearing out of children's eyes by the Sandman. He explains that "morbid anxiety connected with the eyes and with going blind is often enough a substitute for the dread of castration," citing Oedipus' blinding of himself as a parallel. Why, asks Freud, does Hoffmann make such an intimate connection between the father's death and anxiety about eyes, and why does the Sandman interfere with love each time he appears (dividing Nathaniel from Clara and from his best friend, her brother; destroying Olympia; and later driving Nathaniel to suicide just when he has regained Clara)? "Things like these and many more seem arbitrary and meaningless in the story so long as we deny all connection between fears about the eye and castration; but they become intelligible as soon as we replace the Sand-Man by the dreaded father at whose hands castration is awaited." Freud goes on to explain that Nathaniel's father and Coppelius represent a split of the father imago generated by the child's ambivalence; one threatens to blind (castrate) him while one intercedes for his sight. The repressed wish for the death of the father is symbolized in the narrative by the father's accidental death. In Nathaniel's student days Professor Spalanzani and Coppola reproduce the split father imago: "Just as before they used to work together over the fire, so now they have jointly created the doll Olympia; the Professor is even called the father of Olympia." Another castration equivalent in the story, the fantasied unscrewing of Nathaniel's arms and legs by Coppelius, helps to explain what Olympia really represents. "She, the automatic doll, can be nothing else than a personification of Nathaniel's feminine attitude towards his father in his infancy." This inference enables us to understand the otherwise mysterious assertion that the optician, Coppola, has stolen Nathaniel's eyes in order to set them in the doll. Olympia is, then, "a dissociated complex of Nathaniel's which confronts him as a person, and Nathaniel's enslavement to this complex is expressed in his senseless obsessive love for Olympia. We may with justice call such love narcissistic." In this connection Freud might well have quoted the reverie Nathaniel has after the ball given by Professor Spalanzani: "Upon me alone did her [Olympia's] loving glances fall, and through my mind and thoughts alone did they radiate; and only in her love can I find my own self again."

Thus the story embodies all of the elements which Freud singles out in his essay as pertaining to uncanny experiences: the revival of repressed infantile complexes by some chance impression; the confirmation of primitive beliefs; animism; magic and witchcraft; the omnipotence of thoughts; repetition-compulsion; man's attitude toward death; and the castration complex.[15] Elsewhere in the same essay Freud emphasizes that the primitive conception of the double as a second self and immortal soul springs from the soil of man's primary narcissism, the unbounded love for himself originating in infancy, and he links the defensive reduplication of the self with the similarly defensive representation of castration anxiety in dream language by multiplication of genital symbols.[16]

These examples of manifest doubling in literature provide a basis for considering what common ground literary versions of decomposition share with actual hallucinations of one's mirror image. The most obvious inference is that case histories of autoscopy confirm the psychological validity of subject doubling in fiction. When an author portrays a protagonist as seeing his double, it is not simply a device or gimmick calculated to arouse the reader's interest by virtue of the strangeness of the episode but is, in fact, a result of his sense of the division to which the human mind in conflict with itself is susceptible.

An equally obvious inference to be drawn is that when an author wishes to depict mental conflict within a single mind a most natural way for him to dramatize it is to represent that mind by two or more characters. Such a technique is a natural one whether the author is aware of what he is doing or not. It must also be insisted that when a man sees an image of himself a few paces away and when an artist doubles or splits up a coherent psychological entity into two or more seemingly autonomous characters, both the neurotic and the artist are "thinking" archaically, that is, their mental operations in this matter are not logical and in accordance with objective reality. This kind of mental activity is what Todd and Dewhurst call "archetypic thinking" in their discussion of autoscopy in life and literature.[17] They mean that the mental processes of neurotics and psychotics who see visions of themselves resemble in their content the magical conceptions of "primitive" superstition as seen in myth and folklore. In psychoanalysis such mental processes, occurring characteristically in neurosis, psychosis, narcosis, extreme inebriation, dreams, and in the fantasies of children, are known technically as "primary process thinking."[18] While artistic creation, in literature and other media, may involve critical, ratiocinative, ego-oriented thinking (the secondary process), it should be borne in mind—though the fact cannot be demonstrated here—that id-oriented primary process mentation in the artist is largely responsible for the concreteness of symbolic representation which so distinguishes the literary imagination from that of the analytical, discursive thinker. Where a philosopher might speak of conflicts between body and spirit, for example, a literary artist would be likely to conjure up representative characters: a Sancho Panza and a Don Quixote, let us say. In short, autoscopy and decomposition always involve archaic thinking.

Three other features of autoscopic hallucinations which have counterparts in literature are the double as a conscience figure, as a projected wish-fulfillment, and as a reflection of the subject's narcissism. Mr. G., the patient who succeeded in outpacing the facial expressions of his double by changing his own faster than the alter ego could, spoke of his mirror image as a conscience trying to "put me right" and called it a "copycat" with no original ideas of its own, except when it scolded him.[19] We have already seen in "William Wilson" the conscience or superego double *par excellence* and can discern in Dorian Gray's portrait and the shadow of Peter Schlemihl sections of the self which, when missing, leave the rest without moral control. Wish-fulfillment finds expression in some of the other cases cited by Lukianowicz: Mrs. A. feels her double to be more alive and warm than she is herself; Mr. B., who had lost his right leg, is visited by a double resembling him in all respects except that it wears no prosthesis; Mr. C., apparently a would-be musician, sees himself conducting an orchestra. Correlative examples of wish-fulfillment in stories discussed are numerous. One might single out in particular the patent wish elements in the Narcissus myth, in Dorian Gray's desire for permanent youth and beauty, and in Peter Schlemihl's yearning for riches and beautiful women. The narcissistic aspects of autoscopic phenomena would seem to be self-evident. A curious instance of the narcissism involved in autoscopy can be seen in the comical example of the dream spectacle of a homosexual who "always dreamed of committing mutual masturbation *with a man very similar in appearance* to himself."[20] As narcissism has been stressed in the stories analyzed, further instances need not be repeated. Still another parallel between art and life is the general apprehension—if not positive fear—which vision of the self excites in the beholder, such as in the stories by Maupassant. As for the love life of patients who experience autoscopic hallucinations, the studies drawn upon do not mention it, but the patients probably experienced marked difficulties in romantic object relations with the opposite sex.

While the mere psychological authenticity of manifest doubling in literature can be confirmed by virtue of its resemblance to the phenomenon of autoscopy, what of the merit of decomposition, of the overt sort, as a vehicle for the imaginative rendering of psychic conflict?

Such merit, which may appear to have been assumed all along, hardly seems to be supported by the prevailing quality of the stories so far discussed. And if the quality of stories analyzed are not representative of the best that might have been chosen, what works presenting palpable doubles are? While no one would disparage the artistic might of Ovid and Hawthorne, the Narcissus passage and "Monsieur du Miroir" cannot by themselves bear the full weight of these authors' artistic reputations, and the other authors discussed in this chapter belong to the secondary and tertiary ranks of world writers, however popular they may be as tellers of tales. Thus we are left with the inference which Tymms makes in the first sentence of *Doubles in Literary Psychology:* "Superficially, doubles are among the facile, and less reputable devices in fiction." But by "doubles" Tymms refers solely to manifest doubles. His statement does not hold true for latent doubling.

The reader's response to stories portraying manifest doubles may be presumed to be akin to his reaction to such figures as Virtue and Vice in the old morality plays. As Leslie Fiedler might put it, Archetype becomes Stereotype; that is, the archetypal potential of the demonic in man degenerates all too often into the stereotype of The Diabolical Other Self. Such work possesses all the worst features of melodrama, the author resembling to some extent an amateurish prestidigitator who either moves with clumsy slowness or fails to distract his audience from the bare mechanics of his act with an obfuscating line of patter.

The literary deployment of the manifest double involves several inherent limitations which can be stated in psychological terms. A crucial drawback lies in the reader's awareness that some kind of decomposition is being represented. The lack of esthetic distance resulting from this transparency allows incipient guilt and anxiety feelings in the reader to inhibit deep identification with the characters. Where decomposition is latent, the reader can identify with the protagonist consciously and with the antagonist unconsciously, but where decomposition is manifest, the reader's awareness that the "bad guy" is somehow part of the "good guy" tends to block his identification with both of them. A corresponding factor operates in the mind of the composing artist which deters free and spontaneous play of his fantasy powers. This assumption is based on the concept known in ego psychology as "flexibility of repression." The artist's special talent for

31

temporarily reducing repression in order to dredge up id material and then subsequently manipulate such material in a relatively conscious, critical, ego-oriented fashion without awareness of its unconscious significance is handicapped when he deals in manifest doubles. A third factor, related to the other two but dynamic in its essence, concerns the relative absence of shifts in psychic distance by both reader and writer stemming from an insufficiency of ambiguity in the work. Such works are relatively static and esthetically uninteresting.[21] Only when the work is surcharged with ambiguity, as Hawthorne's sketch, can these limitations inherent in the use of the overt double be partially overcome. The drawbacks may be presumed to operate regardless of the merit of the artist employing the device.

James Hogg's novel-length treatment of the motif in *The Private Memoirs and Confessions of a Justified Sinner* illustrates the esthetic limitations of the mode. In this satire of theological extremism growing out of the Reformation, George Colwan, laird of Dalchastel, marries a religious prude beguiled by the doctrines of her Protestant minister, Robert Wringham, a righteous Calvinist certain that he numbers among the Elect of God. A son, George, is born of the match. He is a generous, warmhearted, aristocratic young man. Another son, privately disowned though publicly acknowledged by the laird, is borne by the mother and is given the name of the minister. When this son, Robert, is eighteen, his minister foster-father (and implied father-in-the-flesh) tells him that he, too, numbers among the Elect. Shortly thereafter the righteous young Robert sees his double, whom we are led to understand is Satan in masquerade, and is tempted to perform certain crimes by this double and duplicitous friend whom Robert idolizes. For practice, as it were, he kills a good minister. Then begin the machinations of haunting and finally murdering his brother George. Later on, after becoming laird of Dalchastel upon the death of the old laird, Robert commits a number of other crimes. They include murdering his mother and his sweetheart, though Robert professes he has no recollection of doing these latter deeds (which seem to have been performed during fugue periods). Finally driven from his lands, Robert commits suicide, believing himself—as he reveals in the memoirs which constitute the second portion of the novel—a "justified" sinner to the last, that is, justified in the dogmatic sense of the term (the doctrine of justification by faith alone as opposed to good works).

The devil-double is an obvious projection of Robert's evil inner impulses, which are released from the bonds of conscience when the minister informs him that he is one of the Elect (and hence beyond good and evil). In a more subtle way, both young Robert and his double function as latent doubles of George in an oedipal matrix, George being the normal, healthy, heterosexually orientated son of a warm, normal, lusty father and Robert being the sick, corrupt, homosexually oriented son of a cold, doctrinaire, and seemingly prudish father. Robert's matricide can be construed as symbolic incest.[22] The murder of his sweetheart is at once consonant with and contradictory to his self-confessed misogyny: he declares that he despises and abhors "the beauty of women," regarding it as "the greatest snare" to which mankind is subject, but he shows himself capable of obtaining narcissistic satisfaction through a woman's devotion to him: "I felt a sort of indefinite pleasure, an ungracious delight in having a beautiful woman solely at my disposal." While the psychology of the work is much more complex than it appears on the surface, Hogg emphasizes the overt relationship between Robert and his clearcut devil-double for satirical purposes—to the neglect of the covert relationship between Robert and George as complementary parts of the composite son. The characterization of the main figures is crude, and melodrama bulks large in the action of the story, so much so that one can only account for André Gide's unrestrained enthusiasm (in the introduction which he wrote for a recent edition of the book he calls the personification of the Devil in the novel "the most ingenious ever invented") by assuming that the author of a work like *Les Faux-Monnayeurs* entertained a special fondness for the theme of the double.[23] Hogg's really choice touches in the novel, such as the wonderful treatment of local color in the dialect and folk wisdom of the servant class, and his shrewd satire of the doctrines of election, predestination, and so forth, bear little relation to his pedestrian management of the psychological elements of the work.

The novel presents us with the paradox of a study which dwells on the subject of evil, largely in psychological terms, yet fails to involve our emotions deeply because of the way in which evil is accentuated and isolated in a diabolical other self. Just as the principal character projects his malevolent impulses onto his double, thereby disclaiming any responsibility for such impulses, so is the reader easily able to shunt off the guilt he unconsciously shares with the evil protagonist. As a result, the novel does not provide that balanced appeal to the principal parts of the human psyche which Simon O. Lesser regards as characteristic of great fiction.[24] Hogg's *Justified Sinner* circumvents true involvement of the superego by offering the reader a villain to hang in effigy; hence the manifest doubling tends to undercut rather than support the dramatic effect.

Dostoevsky's *The Double,* on the contrary, is a marked exception to the meretricious effects of decomposition nakedly presented. The intricacy of the narrative line, the complexity of the double figure, the richness of psychological detail, and the ambiguity which pervades all features of the novella enable the reader to respond in a less guarded fashion to the piteous spectacle of a petty, weak, rather obnoxious man who clutches at any straws—including nonexistent ones—in his futile attempt to save himself from humiliation and madness. Enhancing the ambiguity of the work is the inability of the reader to know which of the events depicted actually occur and which are only figments of Golyadkin's autistic and diseased imagination. But the most saving ambiguity stems from the fact that Golyadkin Jr., the double, has no simple, easily discernable value.

The "real" Golyadkin is a dreamer given to creating his triumphs out of the whole cloth of fantasy, whereas the double is a man of action, all of it successful. Golyadkin Sr. is a loner, a queer fellow of schizoid tendencies who has no friends, preferring like the Underground Man whom he so much resembles to cut himself off from society (though he simultaneously yearns to be a part of it) in spite of his doctor's advice that he indulge in amusements, visit friends, and cultivate cheerful company. Golyadkin Jr. is a highly sociable creature with a talent for ingratiating himself with other people. Golyadkin Sr. is insecure, anxious, unsuccessful, inarticulate, and awkward, while Golyadkin Jr. is quite the opposite and takes over Golyadkin Sr.'s position in the bureaucracy with ease by showing a preternatural efficiency. Filled with a sense of unworthiness and insignificance, except when in his rages he endeavors to secure what he believes to be his "rights," Golyadkin Sr. imagines his double has unlimited confidence and self-respect. The irasible, truculent, rebellious Golyadkin Sr., who dotes on his imagined independence and straightforwardness, depicts Golyadkin Jr. as a servile toady and lickspittle, though in fact Golyadkin Sr. is always humble in the presence of his superiors and is much given to the guile and innuendo he claims he hates in others, especially in Golyadkin Jr. Golyadkin Sr. constantly feels humiliated by others and writhes in the embarrassment which he experiences at the hands of his shameless double. Nevertheless, Golyadkin Sr. likes to be haughty and cruel, as he is with his servant, Petrushka, and other inferiors in the social and bureaucratic hierarchies. It is clear that Golyadkin Sr., who entertains a romantic, idealistic attitude toward women, represses his instinctual impulses; he sees his double as a lecher. Golyadkin Sr. professes religious orthodoxy and believes his double to be an agent of the devil. Most significant of all, Golyadkin Sr. believes himself subject to all sorts of conspiracies, his double being his principal and most unrelenting persecutor. In general Golyadkin Jr. combines all the traits and accomplishments Golyadkin Sr. desires, and at the same time the double embodies all those Golyadkin fears or claims to despise.

Why, then, does Golyadkin see his mirror image? The first episode of autoscopy follows Golyadkin's presumptuous attempt to crash the birthday party of the beautiful and socially prominent Klara Olsufyevna and his humiliating ejection from the festivities. Seeing his double offers him an escape. He is "fleeing from his foes, from persecution, from a hailstorm of fillips aimed at him," and looks "as though he wanted to hide somewhere from himself, as though he were trying to run away from himself." The appearance of the double amounts to wish-fulfillment. After first seeing the stranger double, Golyadkin fears him but knows he will see him again: "Oddly enough, he positively desired this meeting, considered it inevitable." Once Golyadkin has conjured up his double he has an explanation for all of his problems. His weakened contact with reality and his feeble ego identity provide grounds for the split. After seeing his double he begins "to doubt his own existence" and pinches himself, as he does repeatedly, to see if he is really "there"—just as a schizophrenic will pinch himself for similar reasons. Early in the story Golyadkin's German doctor advises him in faulty syntax, "You must a radical change of your entire life have, must, in a certain sense, your character break." We are told that special stress is laid on the word "break." The doctor, who means that he must break with his past seclusive way of life, thereby provides Golyadkin with the suggestion for a quite different kind of "break," one widening his split from reality and totally disintegrating his ego. Yet even though it is easy to understand that Golyadkin's double provides him with an excuse to explain his misfortune, various details of the narration seem on the surface not to have any connection, but are undeniably linked and important. Why is the doctor's role so crucial, turning up as he does in the apartments of his Excellency (the chief bureau-crat) and at the house of Berendeyev, Klara Olsufyevna's father and Mr. Golyadkin's "quondam benefactor"? What were Golyadkin's rela-tions with Karolina Ivanovna, the "German woman" at whose lodg-ings he used to board? How is it that Golyadkin reasons in this fashion concerning Anton Antonovich, the head clerk: "I'm afraid to trust him; his hair's too gray, and he's tottering with old age"?

Freud's study of Dostoevsky helps give psychological coherence to these puzzles and nonsequiturs.[25] This essay dwells on Dostoevsky's sadism and masochism; on his unconscious guilt for death wishes against his doctor father, a guilt reinforced by the seeming fulfillment of this childhood wish when Dostoevsky *père* is murdered by his serfs; on Dostoevsky's epilepsy (a disease often linked with autoscopy) as a malady combining discharge of libido in seizures and signifying in those deathlike seizures an identification with the dead parent, the disease being at the same time a punishment for death wishes directed toward the father. It considers also the bisexuality of Dostoevsky's disposition, the feminine side resulting from Dostoevsky's attempt to propitiate the father by his passivity and by winning the father's love through identifying with the mother as a love object of the father. It emphasizes the "hard, violent and cruel" superego Dostoevsky devel-oped on the basis of similar traits in the father. Freud also suggests that Dostoevsky's passive acceptance of largely undeserved punishment at the hands of "the Little Father, the Tsar" amounted to acceptance of punishment for his psychological crime against his real father. Freud sees further evidence of this in Dostoevsky's passive acceptance of an authoritarian God. Though Freud confines his discussion of Dostoev-sky's work to *The Brothers Karamazov,* his commentary proves equally revealing when applied to *The Double.*

No overt theme of parricide appears in *The Double;* on the contrary, the protagonist makes repeated declarations of loyalty and submissiveness to authoritarian figures, declarations which are often suspiciously out of context. Several times Golyadkin says that he regards his bureaucratic superiors as fathers. To Andrey Filippovich he states, "I regard my beneficent superior as a father and blindly entrust my fate to him" and to his Excellency, the chief bureaucrat, he plans to declare, "Do not destroy me, I look upon you as my father, do not abandon me . . . save my dignity, my honor, my name . . . save me from a miscreant, a vicious man." He blurts out a similarly couched appeal in his Excellency's chambers only to have Golyadkin Jr. (who by this time has won his Excellency's confidence and been given "special assignments") demand with righteous severity, "Allow me to ask you, in whose presence you are making this explanation? Before whom are you standing, in whose study are you?" The answer, in psychoanalytic terms, is The Father. Almost all of the personages in the story, with the exception of Golyadkin's double, his servant, and the women, are father surrogates. They are old men with an authoritarian manner—including even Gerasimych, the old valet of Olsufy Ivanovich who turns Golyadkin out of doors. Of Olsufy Ivanovich, Golyadkin's "benefactor" and Klara Olsufyevna's father, Golyadkin remarks that he "has, in a sense, been a father to me," so that Golyadkin's humiliating expulsion from the birthday party amounts as well to total rejection by the father. Golyadkin Jr. represents the loved and accepted son that Golyadkin wishes to be. It becomes apparent from the letter which Golyadkin imagines he receives from Klara Olsufyevna that Golyadkin's double has merged in his mind with Vladimir Semyonovich, Klara Olsufyevna's successful suitor, whose promotion to the rank of assessor Golyadkin envies, though he denies it. This promotion, in fact, may possibly precipitate Golyadkin's disorder, for he discusses it with his doctor, Krestyan Ivanovich, at the beginning of the novel. Krestyan Ivanovich, of the same profession as Dostoevsky's father, functions as a key father surrogate in the work, and it is he who condemns Golyadkin to hell or the insane-asylum (it is not clear which) at the end of the story: "Krestyan Ivanovich's answer rang out, stern and terrible as a judge's sentence: 'You will get quarters at public expense, viz. firewood, light, and service, which you don't deserve.'"

In continually protesting his submission to authority Golyadkin protests too much. His unconscious hostility becomes clear, for example, when Anton Antonovich berates him for impudence, saying, "I don't allow anyone to be impudent. I've grown gray in the government service, sir, and I don't allow anyone to be impudent to me in my old age." The charge is just, as is Anton Antonovich's annihilating accusation that Golyadkin has damaged the reputation of both "a wellborn maiden," meaning Klara Olsufyevna, and "that other maiden who, though poor, is of honorable foreign extraction," meaning the German woman. Golyadkin's ambivalence toward women, particularly as sexual objects, need not be explored directly, because it will become understandable by implication in terms of his paranoia.

Kohlberg challenges Rank's claim that *The Double* offers a classic example of the paranoid state, particularly because of the mechanism of projection used, on the grounds that the true paranoid always feels himself completely blameless and never has any awareness of a second half. His argument that Golyadkin and other doppelgänger of Dostoevsky manifest the symptoms of an obsessive-compulsive character, whose separation of selves amounts to a defensive "balancing or undoing" of a force or idea by its opposite, is accurate enough and a valuable formulation but one which does not exclude the presence of paranoid elements, obvious in Golyadkin's delusions of persecution. In fact, the complexity of the double in this work is borne out by the fact that no single nosological label of psychiatry applies to him. But recognition of the presence of elements of the paranoia syndrome helps us to comprehend that Golyadkin Jr. is largely a superego double, embodying variously faults that Golyadkin feels guilty about, punishment for that guilt in the form of persecution, and the ego-ideal elements of the good, submissive, loved son. At the same time he embodies the introjected values and characteristics of the father which come to constitute the superego and hence technically serve as a symbol of the internalized father. Since the father is viewed as an implacable tyrant, so is the double. The homosexual disposition invariably underlying paranoia appears in veiled form in *The Double,* especially in the seductive way Golyadkin Jr. behaves toward Golyadkin Sr., pinching, patting, and kissing him and calling him "darling."[26] This behavior also represents the narcissistic self-love which can be expected wherever we encounter subjective decomposition, a narcissism betrayed early in the novel in Golyadkin's case when the bald, unprepossessing man feels "satisfied" with his image in the mirror. More profound implications of the psychotic's characteristic withdrawal of object-libido into the ego can be seen in the form of Golyadkin's delusions of persecution (a man who feels the entire world to be against him cannot fail to appreciate how important he must be to warrant so much attention) and in his delusions of grandeur, symbolized among other ways in the novel by Golyadkin's aspirations for promotion, romantic love, and acceptance by high bourgeois society.

Yet in spite of the fascination which Golyadkin exerts over the reader, he can never long forget that this man who sees his double is mad, mad in a clinical sort of way which we are not aware of when we hear the wild and whirling words of a Hamlet or the tempestuous lamentations of a Lear. The reader, therefore, inevitably disengages himself to some extent from Golyadkin and his double, all of the ambiguities of the work notwithstanding, in a manner which does not occur when Dostoevsky (and other authors) employ the medium of latent decomposition.

The Secret Sharer

The elements of the psyche as they find expression in manifest and latent doubles are analogous to the state of elements in mechanical mixtures and chemical compounds. Elements merely mixed together can be separated with relative ease, whereas those in a compound can be separated only by analysis, often with considerable difficulty. The elements which form the constituent parts of the compound may bear little resemblance in their pure states to the characteristics they have when combined. To extend the analogy, if it is more difficult to analyze latent than manifest decomposition, the goal is more worthwhile because the constituent parts of the composite character have been compounded or fused within the crucible of art by the catalytic heat of creative fire. In art, at least, the compound is esthetically superior to the mixture. Such a conception of the basic difference between manifest and latent doubling corresponds closely to Coleridge's distinction between fancy and imagination, the latter characterized by a fusion of discrete parts into an imaginative whole which makes the product superior to the often striking but esthetically inferior result of fanciful thought.[1]

Interpretation of latent doubling does not prove inordinately arduous because the artist seldom covers all of his tracks. In addition to making deductions concerning the presence of latent decomposition in a work on the basis of certain characteristic patterns of the human mind, the literary analyst usually can find textual clues left by the writer, much as the psychoanalyst has the errors, dream symbols, free associations, and symptoms of his patient to guide him. Two stories which contain fairly obvious clues and therefore are intermediate between works presenting manifest doubles and those in which the decomposition is latent are Hawthorne's "Alice Doane's Appeal" and Conrad's "The Secret Sharer." The characters representing doubles in these tales have a more or less autonomous existence on the narrative level—unlike Peter Schlemihl's shadow or Golyadkin Jr., for example —and yet are patently fragments of one mind at the psychological level of meaning. These stories bridge the gap between overt doubling and the unconscious fragmentation of the soul which represents an essentially secret kinship between two or more characters.

Just such a secret kinship exists between Leonard Doane and Walter Brome in "Alice Doane's Appeal." Leonard and his sister Alice feel closely united; their affection has a "consecrated fervor" and they enjoy a "sense of lonely sufficiency to each other." When Leonard learns, or suspects he learns, of a similar "secret sympathy" between Alice and Walter, Leonard kills the man he regards as both a rival for his sister's affection and a spoiler of her sexual purity. But since Leonard recognizes his own inclinations in Walter, it becomes apparent that by killing Walter he has symbolically murdered his own intolerable incestuous impulses:

> Searching . . . into the breast of Walter Brome I at length found a cause why Alice must inevitably love him. For he was my very counterpart! I compared his mind by each individual portion, and as a whole, with mine. There was a resemblance from which I shrank with sickness and loathing and horror as if my own features had come and stared upon me in a solitary place . . . Nay! the very same thoughts would often express themselves in the same words from our lips, proving a hateful sympathy in our secret souls . . . Here was a man whom Alice might love with all the strength of sisterly affection, added to that impure passion which alone engrosses all the heart.

Hawthorne stresses the psychic rather than the physical kinship of the two men, adding that "the similarity of their dispositions made them like joint possessors of an individual nature." Complicating the theme of incest is that of parricide, for when Leonard gazes down at the face of his dead enemy, he sees a likeness of his father in Walter's physiognomy. Thus, the mechanisms of decomposition and condensation operate conjointly, Walter symbolizing both Leonard's repressed incestuous impulses and Leonard's father conceived as a sexual rival. Ironically, the wizard to whom Leonard confesses his crime is a father figure. He is implicitly linked in the story with two others, Hawthorne's own ancestor John Hathorne and Cotton Mather.[2]

There are flaws in Hawthorne's handling of decomposition in this story. The advantage of the relative latency of Walter Brome as a double figure over a simple mirror image or hallucinated double is that he has an independent existence as a character in the work. But the directness and explicitness with which Hawthorne reveals him to be a "counterpart" of Leonard Doane subtracts from the ambiguity which Hawthorne tries to establish elsewhere in the tale. The revelation near the end of the story that Walter Brome is actually Leonard's twin brother, though it perhaps intensifies the incest theme by making Alice Walter's sister as well as Leonard's, detracts from the force generated by the intimations that Walter is an alter ego figure. Here and in innumerable other works the Dioscuri theme functions as a not too subtle metaphor for the standard manifest double; while twins can be symbolic doubles, they are dynamically much closer to the lower register of the manifest double. Much more effective than the decomposition in "Alice Doane's Appeal" is Hawthorne's handling of Cloverdale and Westervelt as doubles in *The Blithdale Romance*.[3]

No story better illustrates the intermediate stage between overt and covert decomposition than Conrad's "The Secret Sharer." Thus, it not only provides a useful introduction to latent doubling but shows as well that a veritable spectrum of doubles ranging from the obvious to the well-nigh indiscernible can be found in literature. As a rule, however, most doubles are either manifest or latent.

The fact cannot escape notice at the narrative level that the admirable but criminal first mate of the *Sephora,* Leggatt, is a doppelgänger of the captain who gives him refuge. The narrator makes numerous references to Leggatt as his "double," his other self, his secret sharer, his ship's second captain, and so forth. It has even been suggested that Conrad belabors the point. Yet at the realistic level of narrative action Leggatt is presented as a flesh-and-blood creature, that is, the narrator does not in a fit of madness simply imagine the sequence of events in the way that Golyadkin does. The story therefore embodies a happy combination of the literal and the symbolic, and

Conrad exercises a superb sense of balance and timing in moving back and forth between the two levels of meaning. Proof that in doing so he sustains an enormous amount of ambiguity can be seen in the number and wide-ranging variety of interpretations which the work has excited. They extend from the adventure-story reading, which is too literal, to the archetypal journey-into-the-self reading, which is certainly justified, and include what might be termed a Rorschach reading, which sees the relationship of Leggatt and the captain as involving a cozy but physically enervating homosexual interlude.

Since Leggatt's role as the captain's double is central to the work's meaning, it must be asked what Leggatt represents to the captain or in combination with the captain. Leggatt is a criminal. Therefore the captain's rescue of him, while it does not necessarily imply complete approval of the crime, does indicate that the captain identifies himself with the guilt of Leggatt. We know that Conrad associated his own first voyage as captain of a vessel with the killing of a seaman aboard the *Cutty Sark* by one of her mates, though there are many differences between the historical event and the narrative version.[4] Examination of the narrative indicates that in various ways Leggatt and the captain reflect the contradictions which Conrad's biographers see in him, those between loyalty and rebellion, patriotism and exile, maturity and youth, order and passion, realism and idealism, and so on; as Albert Guerard puts it, Conrad "the dreamer, adventurer, audacious seaman, and innovating subjective writer was also a cool rationalist, political conservative, and withdrawn spectator."[5]

Whatever the biographical parallels, our understanding of the story will be furthered if we remember that the customs and usages of the sea declare that the captain of a ship is God on a poop deck, at once the embodiment of almost unlimited authority and the father of his crew. In any story with a psychological dimension, as can be seen so preeminently in a work like *Billy Budd,* the captain of a ship is almost certain to be associated with the psychological father. Yet Leggatt's crime against discipline aboard ship has all the earmarks of the primal crime of the son: rebellion against authority. Therefore the narrator's identification with Leggatt would seem to place the father in the role of son. Guerard's astute suggestion that in being responsible for a ladder dangling over the side the captain has symbolically summoned his double leads to the question of why, psychologically speaking, the double is summoned at this particular time in the narrator's career. It is the captain's first command and he feels insecure about his role, about his ability to be "faithful to that ideal conception of one's own personality every man sets up for himself secretly." In Eriksonian terms, the story portrays the new-made captain as undergoing an "identity crisis," an identity crisis which in Freudian terms harks back to the earlier oedipal crisis.

Overstrained by the added burden of keeping his double hidden, the captain worries at one point about "appearing an irresolute commander" to his crew. When we bear in mind that the captain of the *Sephora* is a timid, anxiety-ridden man who in time of stress proves totally inadequate to his proper role of the resolute commander, and when we remember that Leggatt's crime involves the paradox of being against the established order of discipline yet committed in the interests of maintaining order in a crew mad with fear, it becomes clear that Leggatt has, *in extremis,* usurped the role of his commander in both a maritime and a psychological sense. And the narrative makes it evident that were it not for Leggatt the *Sephora* would have gone down in the storm. While the narrator's crime of assuming the paternal role in taking command of his new ship seems on the surface no crime at all, the parallel of Leggatt's crime explains the anxiety of the narrator and accounts for the basis of his identification with Leggatt. It is also consonant with the "happy" ending of the story in which the narrator, having worked through his identity crisis and sloughed off his scapegoat double (who lowers himself into the water "to take his punishment"), then proves himself equal to the role of the competent and resolute commander by the successful avoidance of perilous reefs through skilled seamanship and supreme self-control. The captain now possesses both security in his professional role and—to complete the oedipal triangle—his feminine-maternal ship: "I was alone with her. Nothing! no one in the world should stand now between us, throwing a shadow on the way of silent knowledge and mute affection, the perfect communion of a seaman with his first command."

This interpretation helps to show that whenever we encounter decomposition in a literary work we may expect to find that the splitting depicts, in one way or another, some very elemental division in the human mind. And even so brief an analysis may indicate—however indirectly—the effectiveness of marshaling doubles in a manner calculated to enhance the ambiguity of their significance.

A still more subtle kind of decomposition, one verging on complete latency, can be seen in Conrad's use of the narrator, Marlow. The device works in much the same way as in Poe in the case of the narrator-friends of Roderick Usher and Auguste Dupin, for example.[6] One senses that the secret sympathy shared by these friends transcends the normal bounds of friendship. The same situation holds true with respect to the special sharing of Marlow and the protagonists of *The Heart of Darkness* and *Lord Jim*. Ostensibly Marlow goes to the Congo to captain a river boat, but symbolically his trip to the interior and his encounter with Kurtz involve, as Guerard says, another night journey—a plunge into the dark depths of the self which lie beyond the threshold of consciousness. The clues that imply the alter ego relationship are mostly indirect. Marlow's growing dossier of information about Kurtz appears on the surface to be the result of mere happenstance, and his growing interest in "the chief of the Inner Station" does not seem to reflect a quest. But Marlow declares at one point, "If anybody had ever struggled with a soul, I am the man," and he goes on to say, "But his soul was mad. Being alone in the wilderness, it had *looked within itself,* and, by heavens! I tell you, it had gone mad. I had —for my sins, I suppose—to go through *the ordeal of looking into myself"* (italics added). This passage is the only one in the novel which explains in direct fashion Marlow's deep emotional involvement in Kurtz's career. The story expresses the fascination of a man schooled in reason and self-discipline who looks more deeply within himself only to find a part of his soul "that knew no restraint," a mad, monomaniacal soul, but a soul which ultimately becomes so "satiated with primitive emotions" that it can exclaim on its deathbed, "The horror! The horror!"

Much the same kind of a relationship subsists between Marlow and that other admirable criminal, Lord Jim. While in this case Marlow's affinity with the guilty mate seems even more puzzling—and his efforts to aid Jim even more supererogatory—he does pose this question: "Was it for my own sake that I wished to find some shadow of an excuse for that young fellow whom I had never seen before?" And early in his telling of Jim's story Marlow remarks that his auditors will concede "that each of us has a familiar devil." Jim, in a sense, is that familiar devil, for Marlow remarks that he does not need to listen to other men speak of their "hidden plague spots" because, God knows, he has on his own side "enough confidential information about myself to harrow my own soul till the end of my appointed time." Once again

45

Marlow is really sharing his own secret guilt with his auditors in relating the heroic self-punishment and redemptive self-sacrifice of the man who came to be known as Lord Jim.

That decomposition tends to occur wherever an artist feels moved, however unconsciously, to depict Manichaean extremes of good and evil within a single personality can be seen worked out to perfection in Dostoevsky's *The Idiot*. Simon O. Lesser has shown in a series of studies devoted to the novel that "Rogozhin and Nastasya are alter egos of Myshkin—passionate opposites who act out the impulses, above all the lust and aggression, the Prince so sternly represses."[7] Lesser regards Myshkin as the victim not only of his epilepsy but of an underdeveloped sense of reality and a tyrannical superego. The large middle portion of the novel dramatizes Myshkin's attempts to learn to live in a real, even if corrupt, society; the Christ-like purity of Myshkin which makes it impossible for him to do so reflects an extreme moral masochism. Myshkin represents a purely masochistic orientation, while in Rogozhin sadism is dominant and in Nastasya masochism and sadism occur in roughly equal proportion. The secret sympathy which Myshkin and Rogozhin have for each other, symbolized by the exchange of crosses that makes them "brothers," results in part from the latent homosexual bond uniting them, a bond of tender feeling between rivals for a woman often depicted elsewhere in Dostoevsky's works. And through Nastasya, suggests Lesser, "the Prince acts out certain passive and feminine tendencies."

Some points in Lesser's analysis need qualification, and others might profit by further evidence. Nastasya Filippovna may not be on a par with Rogozhin as a portion of the composite figure, though some evidence does exist that she forms such a portion, as when—in the magnificent party scene—she allows Myshkin to decide whether or not she is to marry Ganya, implying that he can speak for her in so momentous a matter. Lesser's reading of the denouement (where Myshkin and Rogozhin lie down side by side and Myshkin tenderly strokes the hair and cheeks of the now demented Rogozhin) as signifying in a fairly direct fashion the homosexual bond seems a bit too literal. But there is ample evidence that Myshkin and Rogozhin, at least, are component parts of a psychological entity. Besides the structural considerations of their being together at the beginning and ending of the story, Myshkin admits to being plagued by "double thoughts" and "double ideas"—by which phrases the pure Myshkin confesses to guilty impulses and identifies with guilty people in much the same way that the pure Aloysha in *The Brothers Karamazov* does —and he realizes that "in his own soul there was a darkness." To Rogozhin he says, "I understand what you were feeling, that day, *as though it were myself*" (italics added). In fact, the first chapter of the novel is devoted to developing their complementarity: they are of the same age, but one is noble, the other plebian; one is gentle and passive and humble, the other is cruel and proud; one knows nothing of women, the other is a lecher. The principal sharing they do, as Lesser demonstrates, is the contrasting kind of love they have for Nastasya Filippovna and the murderous impulses they have in common: Rogozhin makes an attempt on Myshkin's life, but Myshkin's absent-minded preoccupation with the knife implies that he would like to kill Rogozhin, and of course Myshkin obviously shares Rogozhin's guilt in the slaying of Nastasya Filippovna.

While a more elaborate analysis might be sufficient to show still other occurrences of both subjective and objective decomposition in this complex novel, and to relate the psychological decomposition to other levels of meaning in the work, the point to be stressed is the esthetic superiority of Dostoevsky's treatment of doubling in *The Idiot* to that in *The Double*. Although Golyadkin succeeds in hiding his own aggressive and murderous impulses from himself by the defense mechanism of projection, it is relatively clear to the reader what is going on and the identification of reader with character is partially inhibited. In *The Idiot,* however, the reader remains largely unconscious of the impulses which the Prince represses because they are attributed to the seemingly autonomous character of Rogozhin. As Lesser suggests, in *The Idiot* Dostoevsky solved "the apparently insoluble problem of at once concealing and divulging his hero's lust and murderous habits" by displacing them on to Rogozhin and in so doing gave us a book which, like all great narrative, satisfies and balances the needs of the entire personality, that is, in terms of metapsychology it makes a coordinated appeal to the id, ego, and superego of the responding mind.[8] If we love Prince Myshkin more than any other hero in literature—if we give up our hearts to him as we cannot with such figures as the austere Oedipus or the melancholy Hamlet or even the winsome Tom Jones— it may be because in our unfettered identification with him we find him "faithful to that ideal conception of one's own personality every man sets up for himself secretly." Besides being a person of deep feeling, powerful intellect, and unlimited kindness, he is also a man who can inspire adoration in such specimens of womanhood as Nastasya and Aglaia. At the same time we sense him to be a man, like ourselves, haunted by a darkness of the soul so terrifying that it can lead to madness.

Of all the secret sharers in the world of literature perhaps the most remarkable pair are Macbeth and his Lady. Although they may seem unlikely candidates for such a dual role, they number among the earliest examples of latent decomposition noted in psychoanalytic criticism, and authority for considering them to be doubles comes from Freud himself. After explaining how Lady Macbeth conforms to the type of person who is "wrecked by success," Freud seizes upon the idea of Ludwig Jekels that "Shakespeare frequently splits up a character into two personages, each of whom then appears not altogether comprehensible until once more conjoined with the other" and suggests that the Macbeths are such a pair, this suggestion being a kind of desperation hypothesis calculated to explain what otherwise seems, in his view, "impossible to divine," namely, how in a short space of time "the hesitating, ambitious man can become an 'unbridled tyrant' while his 'steely-hearted instigator' turns into 'a sick woman gnawed by remorse.' "[9] Freud outlines the complementarity of Macbeth and Lady Macbeth by saying that

> the stirrings of fear which arise in Macbeth on the night of the murder do not develop further in him, but in the Lady. It is he who has the hallucination of the dagger before the deed, but it is she who later succumbs to mental disorder; he, after the murder, hears the cry from the house: 'Sleep no more! Macbeth does murder sleep. . . ,' and so 'Macbeth shall sleep no more' but we never hear that King Macbeth could not sleep, while we see that the Queen rises from her bed and betrays her guilt in somnambulistic wanderings. He stands helpless with bloody hands, lamenting that not great Neptune's ocean can wash them clean again while she comforts him: 'A little water clears of this deed'; but later it is she who washes her hands for a quarter of an hour and cannot get rid of the bloodstains. . .Thus is fulfilled in her what his pangs of conscience had apprehended; she is incarnate remorse after the deed, he incarnate defiance—together they exhaust the possibilities of reaction to the crime, like two disunited parts of the mind of a single individuality, and perhaps they are the divided images of a single prototype.[10]

But Freud leaves dangling the question of just what or who this "single individuality" is. He notices that the entire play is strewn with references to the relation of fathers and sons, and says that the murder of Duncan is symbolic parricide. It follows that Macbeth is a son figure but remains unclear what aspect of the son Lady Macbeth might represent, though her remark that she herself would have killed Duncan if he had not resembled her own father (II. ii) coincides with the theory that she is a double of Macbeth.[11] In view of the strongly maternal cast of some of Lady Macbeth's speeches ("Come to my woman's breasts" and later on the mystifying "I have given suck . . ."), she may represent the mother fantasied as an accomplice in the son's overthrow of the father, although this theory does not explain why she becomes conscience-stricken while Macbeth suddenly weans himself from "the milk of human kindness."

Ludwig Jekels argues that Macbeth and his wife are doubles patterned on Queen Elizabeth, an interesting but not very helpful contention.[12] More useful is Jekels' idea that Macbeth, Banquo, and Macduff are all son figures, with Macbeth switching to the role of the father when he becomes king. Thus, Duncan is a good father and Macbeth a bad, rebellious son; when Macbeth becomes king, he is a bad father who tyrannizes over his son-rivals, killing Banquo and trying to kill Macduff. Jekels also recognizes that Macbeth and Macduff are doubles, but in using the labels "good son" and "bad son" he often confuses psychoanalytic categories with moral ones. He thinks (wrongly, I believe) that Macduff is partly guilty of the death of his wife and children, and he does not seem to understand that as doubles Macbeth and Macduff form a kind of composite hero, the latter part of the drama depicting symbolic "restitution" for the crime committed in the first part. Macduff is a good son because he remains loyal to "mother Scotland" and to the legitimate heirs of Duncan, though in overthrowing the reigning monarch, Macbeth, he plays the role of the bad son. In a sense, he is the complete son in a way that Macbeth, psychologically speaking, cannot be. Once we understand Jekels' contention that Macbeth switches to the role of father in the latter part of the play we can better comprehend the personality change which Freud found so much in need of explanation.

Still requiring further illumination is the precise nature of the relationship between Macbeth and Lady Macbeth. David B. Barron accounts for it in a richer, fuller way than other commentators have. He links the influence of the witches (as evil mother figures) with that of Lady Macbeth on her husband-son, as others have done; he shows that within the context of the play the witch-mother is not only treacherous but treacherous in the feeding situation;[13] he sees that the bearded weird sisters and the "unsexed" Lady Macbeth are domineering, masculine women who instill their own "vaulting ambition" and aggressive competitiveness into the husband-son, Macbeth; he argues that Macbeth's submission to female influence "implies his identification with mother rather than father and that as a result he has great qualms over his masculinity"; and he demonstrates convincingly that after the initial crime Macbeth hopes by a series of violent actions "to break out of his confined and smother'd state and thus prove his regality and masculinity." Barron is more aware than any other commentator of the pervasiveness of the manhood theme in the play and how that theme relates to the fertility theme. But for all his understanding of the symbiotic relationship between Macbeth and his Lady, who lives as much through the activities of her husband-son as he through her, Barron goes out of his way, gratuitously it would seem, to distinguish his analysis from Freud's: "Our interpretation is, however, different. Lady Macbeth and Macbeth together do not represent a single composite personality, but they seem to do so because they have failed to differentiate from one another. There is a failure of individuation." According to Barron, Macbeth and Lady Macbeth are not to be conceived as a composite personality but as "a mother and son who have failed to achieve separate identities."

Since identification involves incorporation, it becomes a theoretical quibble to try to distinguish Macbeth as a component character in Freud's sense from a Macbeth who has not achieved "wholeness" or individuation because his better self is combined with an evil one resulting from his identification with the aggressive mother. Barron's analysis actually rounds out those of Freud and Jekels without contradicting them, as Norman N. Holland perceives in saying that Barron "is showing beneath the oedipus conflict pointed out by the first psychoanalytic writers on *Macbeth* an earlier, oral understructure that shapes the form of the phallic or oedipal conflict in development."[14]

Granting that Lady Macbeth is both a double of and mother to Macbeth gives rise once again to the old question, how many children had Lady Macbeth? The answer, according to one's point of view, must be none, one, or several—for Macbeth, Banquo, Macduff, Malcolm, and Donalbain may be numbered among her "sons." We might also ask, how many doubles had Macbeth? The answer should be several: Banquo, Macduff, Malcolm, Donalbain, Duncan (playing the good-father to Macbeth's bad-father), the original Thane of Cawdor (a bad son, obviously), and we might even include Macduff's son, so loyal to his father in spite of his mother's bitter jesting. Lady Macbeth, in turn, has her mother-doubles in Lady Macduff (the "good" mother-wife); the weird sisters, who include in their phallic brew the "finger of birth-strangled babe"; and Scotland herself, which "cannot/ Be called our mother, but our grave." Thus it seems that in the cast of *Macbeth* we have what Rank discerned was often the case in hero myths: a complex array of personages who, when reduced to their lowest common denominator, actually represent only the various relationships subsisting within the nuclear family, that is, those between the hero and his parents—not a surprising thing at all in a play which deals with patricide.

If the kinds of psychological dividedness represented by decomposition in literature are limited, the mother-son double in Macbeth being a rather unusual case, the permutations of doubling nevertheless seem almost protean in their variety once we move beyond the stereotypes of the manifest double, such as the following variation on the bad-son, good-son dichotomy will illustrate. The fragmentation symbolized by Georg and his "friend" in Kafka's "The Judgment" is so effectively veiled that it would presumably not occur to anyone unfamiliar with species and subspecies of decomposition that the friend is a psychological component of the protagonist. More than half of the narrative or manifest level of the story relates to Georg's mysterious friend in Russia, whom we know to be a once-successful merchant. He is a bachelor to whom Georg writes a letter at the beginning of the story in order to inform his friend of his impending marriage to Fräulein Frieda Brandenfeld. We are told that Georg has felt concern over his friend's bachelorhood, that he is reluctant to speak of his forthcoming marriage, and that—for no apparent reason—Georg feels impelled to inform his father that he is sending news of his engagement to the friend in St. Petersburg. The father responds by accusing Georg of doing things behind his back in the business which he began and Georg has taken over, with great success. Suddenly the father says, "Don't deceive me. Do you really have this friend in St. Petersburg?" In one of the several portentous nonsequiturs of the tale, Georg replies in great embarrassment, "Never mind my friends. A thousand friends wouldn't make up to me for my father." He then appears to be extremely solicitous of his father's health, undresses him, and carries him to bed. The father, as if to prepare for his next accusation, pulls up the blankets and asks twice, "Am I well covered up?" When Georg eventually admits that he is, the seemingly senile father springs "erect in bed" and says, "You wanted to cover me up, I know, my young sprig, but I'm far from being covered up yet [in the grave, presumably]." He then not only admits to knowing the anonymous friend but says the friend "would have been a son after my own heart." The father charges Georg with having betrayed his friend and finally declares that Georg could not succeed in betraying the friend because he (the father) has been writing to him all along. "I've been representing him here on the spot." Meanwhile the father also accuses Georg of disgracing his mother's memory and trying to get rid of his father by making up to the fiancée "because she lifted up her skirts," at which point he mimics the action by lifting up his nightshirt. At the end of the scene the father proclaims, "I sentence you now to death by drowning!" whereupon Georg rushes out of the house and throws himself off a bridge, saying, "Dear parents, I have always loved you, all the same."

Except for the revealing statement by the father that the anonymous friend in Russia would have been a son after his own heart, ambiguity obscures the relationship of the friend and the father, the friend and Georg, and the friend and the fiancée (who declares quite out of context in another of the nonsequiturs of the tale that "since your friends are like that [capable of being disturbed by the news of Georg's engagement?] you shouldn't ever have got engaged at all"). And the amount of time which the other characters devote to thinking and talking about the friend seems quite out of proportion to the main section of the story. Kafka's diary makes it evident that the author was unconscious of what the friend stood for in this story, which was written at a single sitting and which Kafka described as coming out of himself "like a real birth, covered with filth and slime."[15] In his diary Kafka notes in what amounts to a kind of secondary elaboration on the dream-like story that he will write down

> all the relationships which have become clear to me in the story as far as I now remember them. . .The friend is the link between father and son, he is their strongest bond. . .The father. . .uses the common bond of the friend to set himself up as Georg's antagonist, Georg is left with nothing; the bride, who lives in the story only in relation to the friend, that is, to what father and son have in common, is easily driven away

by the father since no marriage has yet taken place, and so she cannot penetrate the circle of blood relationship that is drawn around father and son. What they [the father and the friend] have in common is built up entirely around the father. Georg can feel it only as something foreign, something that has become independent, that he has never given enough protection.

But the entry does not reveal why the friend is the strongest common bond between the protagonist and his father, why the "bride" lives only in relation to the friend, nor just what it is that Kafka thinks the father and the friend have in common. The last part of the entry makes it clear that Georg and the fiancée represent Kafka himself and his own fiancée, Felice B.—parallels which anyone familiar with Kafka's life would recognize without the help of the diary. On the other hand, twice in the diary Kafka records astonishment that his sister should infer that the setting represented in "The Judgment" was the Kafka home because "in that case, then, Father would have to be living in the toilet." None of this information reveals the identity of the "friend," and Kafka's admission in his diary that in describing the friend he repeatedly thought of his recently engaged friend, Steuer, throws Kafka—and us—even further astray.

On August 14, 1913, Kafka wrote in his diary:

> The opposite has happened. There were three letters. The last letter I could not resist. I love her as far as I am capable of it, but the love lies buried to the point of suffocation under fear and self-reproaches.
>
> Conclusion for my case from *The Judgment*. I am indirectly in her debt for the story. But Georg goes to pieces because of his fiancée.
>
> Coitus as punishment for the happiness of being together. Live as ascetically as possible, more ascetically than a bachelor, that is the only possible way for me to endure marriage. But she?

This passage, plus a general familiarity with Kafka's life—his neurosis, his attitudes toward his father, his compulsion to break off his own engagement—indicates that "The Judgment" needs to be interpreted within an oedipal framework. Within this framework it becomes evident that the father recognizes in his son's surface concern for his health an oversolicitousness amounting to a reaction-formation. Beneath Georg's humility lurk death wishes toward his father whom he wishes to supplant, both in a business and in a psychological sense. Georg reveals his true hostility at one point by calling his father a "comedian" and at another point by thinking in a wishful fashion when his father stands up in bed, "Now he'll lean forward . . . What if he topples and smashes himself! These words went hissing through his mind." In terms of the son's oedipal rivalry and hostility, therefore, the father—here as always in Kafka, the Primal Sire—is just in condemning Georg to a judgment from which there can be no appeal.

Much less obvious is the fact that the father is fantasied as being a sexual rival of the fiancée. A series of details which at first seem unrelated to the main line of the story indicate sexually seductive behavior on the part of the father and sexual attraction on the part of the son. As the father rises when the son first enters his room, his heavy dressing gown swings open, its "skirts" fluttering, and Georg thinks, "My father is still a giant of a man." The son offers to undress his father and let him lie down in his (the son's) bed. The father accuses Georg of being a "leg-puller": "and you haven't even shrunk from pulling my leg." Immediately after this Georg is described as pulling off his father's dressing gown. Anal sexuality is suggested by the condition of the father's underwear, which is soiled [compare Kafka's notation about his father living in the toilet]. It is after he springs "erect" in bed that the father says, "You thought you'd got him [the father] down, so far down that you could set your bottom on him and sit on him and he wouldn't move, then my fine son makes up his mind to get married." The anal-erotic motif continues when, after the father's obscene mimicry of the alleged lifting up of the skirts of the fiancée, Georg shrinks into a corner, watching every movement his father makes and fearing "a pounce from behind or above," a passage reminiscent of the fantasied sodomy-rape depicted in "The Metamorphosis": "From behind his father gave him a strong push which was literally a deliverance and he flew far into the room, bleeding freely." In short, mingled with the rebellious hatred for the father of the "bad son" is the even more deeply repressed sado-masochistic love of and submission to the father by the loyal "good son" who has been unable to compete with his father or make a satisfactory identification with him.

It now follows that Georg and his friend, whom the father regards as "a son after my own heart," represent an irreconcilable division between the two possible orientations of the son to the father. While Georg is portrayed in the course of the story as sometimes alternating in his behavior between the two roles, it is in his role as the disloyal,

54

heterosexual son that he is condemned to death, the bachelor friend in Russia being a pure version of the loyal, homosexual son who will never marry because of his submission, sexual and otherwise, to the mighty sire. Georg's passive submission to his father's death sentence and his dying words reflect the relative dominance of the loyal-son orientation.

Another variation on the father-son relationship occurs in one of Kafka's most coherent and powerful stories: "In the Penal Colony."[16] There are two father figures in the tale. One is the former commandant of the colony, whose spirit of harsh "justice" lives on in his fanatical adherent, the officer, and in the mechanical apparatus which is still used to punish offenders. The other father figure is the new commandant, who is gradually allowing the execution machinery to fall into disrepair and who appears to favor more humane, merciful modes of discipline. Besides this object doubling of the father, a complex subject decomposition of the psychological son occurs in the story. This division of the son is almost completely latent; the only hint that any of the characters may be alter egos lies in the fact that at the dramatic turning point of the action the officer substitutes his own body for torture in place of the condmened man's. With this exception, the psychological sons—the explorer, the officer, and the condemned man—appear to be autonomous characters. What is unusual and instructive about the decomposition of the son is that the division conforms to the classic configuration of id/ego/superego, though the neatness of the configuration is complicated by the fact that the characters in question are not pure metapsychological types because their dominant orientations are geared to their relationships with the parents.

"It's a remarkable piece of apparatus" are the first words of the story. One remarkable feature of this remarkable apparatus is the way it symbolizes the parents. Specifically, it symbolizes their bodies in the act of intercourse. The punishment machinery consists of three parts: the Bed, or lower portion, which represents the mother; the Designer, or upper portion, which represents the father; and the Harrow, provided with needles and spikes, which represents the father's phallus. "When the man lies down on the Bed and it begins to vibrate, the Harrow is lowered onto his body. It regulates itself automatically so that the needles barely touch his skin; once contact is made the steel ribbon stiffens immediately into a rigid band." Several features of the machinery suggest that it is not so much animated as animate. The Bed and Designer are powered by an electric battery. "As soon as the man is strapped down, the Bed is set in motion. It quivers in minute, very rapid vibrations, both from side to side and up and down." The movements of the Bed and Harrow are synchronized. Moreover, once the machinery begins to operate "it works all by itself." On the surface the story deals with the theme of crime and punishment within the context of a rigid authoritarian ethos, but the sexual overtones of the machinery and the form of punishment serve to establish a psychosexual matrix for the dramatic action. Only the wildest flights of a radically masochistic imagination could have conceived of a punishment fantasy which makes the ultimate form of submission to authority effect upon the victim the ultimate ecstasy of at once joining in, obstructing (by being between mother and father), and being destroyed by parental intercourse. (The latent irony is devastating; the son is destroyed by the very act which created him.) Only when the symbolic function of the torture machine is perceived can the relationship between the three main characters of the story be understood.

Least developed of the three is the condemned man, a crude, brutish "stupid-looking wide-mouthed creature with bewildered hair and face." He looks like "a submissive dog." Neither he nor the soldier who resembles him understand the conversation of the explorer and the officer, which is conducted in French. The condemned man's crime was to disobey and subsequently threaten to kill his superior officer. As punishment the slogan "Honor Thy Superiors" will be inscribed on his naked body by the torture machine. We learn little else about the condemned man except that he and the soldier greedily devour the bowl of rice pap which is intended to slake the thirst and hunger of anyone being tortured by the machine. Despite the limited information we have about the condemned man, it can be inferred that because of his bestial, appetitive, and aggressive qualities he represents the id.

Abundant clues in the story indicate the officer to be a superego figure—or more accurately, the submissive, "castrated," homosexual son who has introjected the tyrannical superego of the father and who prostrates himself at the altar of the punitive traditions of the omnipotent former commandant. Indicative of the officer's flaccid spirit—his psychic castration—is the statement that "he looked uncommonly limp." Ostensibly the remark refers to the officer's being rather wilted in his heavy uniform by the tropical heat, and in this same connection we are told that he wears two ladies' handkerchiefs tucked into the collar of his uniform. Later, when the officer undresses before immolating himself, he rather mysteriously throws the handkerchiefs to the condemned man, saying, "Here are your handkerchiefs." To the explorer he explains, "A gift from the ladies." If the condemned man is an id figure, the ladies' gifts should indeed belong to him, but the fact that the officer tucked them into his own collar has different connotations. It reflects his effeminate personality. In any case, the officer ritualistically breaks his sword and throws the pieces into the pit, symbolizing his complete submission to the psychological father and his final renunciation of the male role. As for the officer's role as a superego figure, he declares, "My guiding principle is this: Guilt is never to be doubted." He makes this declaration as part of his explanation that the condemned man has had no trial, did not need one because "He has had no chance of putting up a defense," and does not even know that he has been sentenced. Since the story makes it clear that the officer has made himself a fanatic devotee of the old commandant's zeal for retribution, he becomes a perfect example of the psychological process of the introjection of the paternal superego.

The explorer represents both the kind of observing ego we have already encountered in narrator doubles and the ego in the structural sense. Great stress is laid on the explorer's perceptual function. Besides surveying the penal colony itself, he observes in particular the main events of the story. With certain exceptions he does not act. His judgmental function seems quite different from that of the officer. While he remains almost completely neutral in the sense that he neither allows the officer's fervent plea and desperate sacrifice to gain his sympathy, nor his revulsion with the punitive system to cause him to speak against it, he nevertheless does judge. Yet his disapproval seems to be that of a man of the world who has been many places and seen many things. He is, in short, in contact with reality, with things as they are, and perhaps in touch also with certain basic humanitarian values which he has not so much introjected as understood, rationally, to have their proper place and function in society. The explorer, whose perception of events is never warped, cannot read the elaborate script of the master copy of the condemned man's sentence, which will be placed in the Designer by way of programming the movement of the needles. His inability to read the script symbolizes the imperviousness of the ego to distortion by the irrational forces of the sado-masochistic superego which holds the officer in thrall.

To the extent that the explorer (as ego) refuses to join forces with the officer (as superego) against what the officer regards as the growing laxity of the administration of "justice" in the microcosmic penal colony—a little world of pain and punishment and abject slavery—the explorer figures as the stable, reality-oriented ego. But the aggression he manifests toward the soldier and the condemned man when they attempt to enter the boat which will take him to the steamer suggest that the story depicts the nightmarish conflict of a mind in which the ego has never become strong enough and mature enough to mediate between id and superego. The ego resorts to flight from forces which threaten to overwhelm it.

Regardless of its denouement, I think one reason for the success of "In the Penal Colony" as a work of art lies in its balanced appeal to the various components of the reader's psychic makeup. And it is precisely because the explorer, the officer, and the condemned man are secret sharers that the unsuspecting reader is left free to make the partial identifications with the various characters which allow him to experience the full force of the psychological conflict incorporated in the work. While the reader will tend to identify in a more-or-less conscious way with the explorer, he will at the same time unknowingly associate himself with criminal and judge. Only when he is unconscious of what is going on can the reader let the writer cut him to the quick in this manner, much as only an unconscious patient can allow a surgeon to perform a major operation on his body. Otherwise the pain would be too great.

The emphasis has been not so much on similarities between manifest and latent decomposition as on the way they differ. Surreptitious doubling allows for a relatively uninhibited, anxiety-free identification of the reader with the protagonist, an identification made possible by the displacement of the hero's guilt onto his secret sharer. The clandestine nature of this sharing, which corresponds to the unconsciousness of guilt resulting from the forces of repression, permits the reader to involve himself freely and deeply with the fortunes of a character like Macbeth. By the same token, it has been assumed that the lack of consciousness by an author of the significance or even existence of doubles portrayed (a lack of awareness susceptible of demonstration in the case of Kafka's "The Judgment"), enables the writer to exercise much greater freedom in dramatizing the kind of painful truths his role as seer, prophet, *vates* sometimes obliges. Prima facie evidence of the greater degree of "flexibility of repression" available to the artist depicting latent decomposition is the superior esthetic quality of the narratives discussed in this chapter. The fact that latent decomposition is a crucial element in these masterful works (excepting "Alice Doane's Appeal") makes it imperative that Tymm's assertion that "doubles are among the facile, and less reputable devices of fiction" be modified. His generalization is accurate only insofar as it applies to the manifest double.

The Opposing Self

Because decomposition always reflects psychic conflict, one would expect doubles to be portrayed as characters highly antagonistic to each other. Contrary to expectation, overt dramatic conflict between doubles proves to be the exception rather than the rule. At times, as in Poe's "William Wilson," Hogg's *Justified Sinner,* and Dostoevsky's *The Double,* opposition between doubles at the narrative level corresponds to the underlying opposition of psychic forces which the characters represent. Yet even Golyadkin tries to make friends with his double, offers to put him up for the night in his apartment, and makes several attempts to come to an amicable understanding with him. Generally speaking, doubles are on good terms with each other, as in the case of Georg Bendemann and his friend in St. Petersburg. Not much conflict develops among the explorer, the officer, and the condemned man of "In the Penal Colony." Macbeth and his wife are literally married to each other. Emblematic of the closeness between Myshkin and Rogozhin, and in contrast to the murderous impulses they feel toward each other, is the way they lie down side by side in the room which contains Nastasya Filippovna's dead body. A perdurable sympathy links Marlow and his doubles, Kurtz and Lord Jim, and the empathy is even more pronounced in the case of the captain and Leggatt in "The Secret Sharer."

The Opposing Self

Some further examples will illustrate that subject doubles are more apt to play the friendly role of secret sharers than that of bitter antagonists at the narrative level. Such a sharing occurs in *Moby Dick*, as might be expected where one of the doubles serves as narrator. A key to the special sympathy which Ishmael has for Ahab's cause can be found in Ishmael's declaration, "Ahab's quenchless feud seemed mine," an example all the more interesting in view of the fact they are never depicted as having anything directly to do with each other. They never even speak to each other. Perhaps the most inseparable companions in all literature are Don Quixote and Sancho Panza. If Sancho Panza is conceived as symbolizing the id, or appetitive nature of man, and the ego, or reality-perceiving ability of man, then Don Quixote stands for the superego in both of its principal capacities, that of censor dictating abstinence ("It is a point of honour with knights errant not to eat once a month") and the ego ideal, which imposes honorable duties and noble standards of conduct.[1] The knight and his squire may quarrel a good deal, but nothing can undo the tie that binds them, for they are as interrelated in psychological terms as they are intertwined in the memory of centuries of readers. Denis Diderot, the creator of another servant-master combination which functions as a psychological composite, says of his pair that Jacques and his master "are worth no more separated than Don Quixote without Sancho."[2] They too quarrel but are inseparable. While they seem to represent social and philosophical dualisms more than psychological ones, Jacques and his master resemble Sancho and Don Quixote in many respects, particularly in their complementary attitudes toward the opposite sex. Another narrator-double pair, in John Knowles's *A Separate Peace,* are prep school chums. While it is true that Gene injures his doppelgänger, Phineas, and ultimately causes his death, the antipathy which Gene feels for Finny is largely unconscious, and on the surface they are the best of friends. Antagonism between doubles, then, may be portrayed as outright hostility on the narrative level, or as a mixture of friendliness and antipathy ranging all the way from moderate philosophical disagreement to physical violence, or antagonism may be entirely absent as far as appearances go; but in almost all cases some feeling of closeness and sympathy will be manifested by the doubles at some point in the story.

Although amicable relations may subsist between doubles on the surface of a story, disharmony invariably exists between subject doubles at the unconscious level of the narrative. Even such soulmates as

Leggatt and the captain in "The Secret Sharer" are antithetical selves in the sense that Leggatt embodies guilt which the captain only temporarily shares but must liberate himself from if he is to assume his proper role as a resolute commander untrammelled by nagging doubts about his right to the position. Despite occasional surface appearances to the contrary, the double is always, in some basic way, an opposing self.[3]

These opposing selves may be the bad self and the guardian angel, as in "William Wilson"; the normal self and the diabolical self, as in Hogg's *Justified Sinner;* the good son and the bad son conceived as rivals, as in Dostoevsky's *The Double* and Kafka's "The Judgment." They may represent such contrasting psychosexual orientations as masochism and sadism, as in Dostoevsky's *The Idiot,* or activity and passivity, as will be seen in Henry James's "The Jolly Corner." Often the opposing selves symbolize possible alliances and divisions among the categories of id, ego, and superego. Usually the divisions are complex rather than simple, as when, for example, the evil self will turn out to have a sadistic, homosexual orientation, passive in some ways and active in others. Another typical double, according to Mark Kanzer, is that of the pursuer and the pursued, as in the case of Javert and Jean Valjean in *Les Misérables* and the police inspector and Raskolnikov in *Crime and Punishment.*[4] Still another possible decomposition is that between male and female—as distinct from heterosexual and homosexual—such as can be seen in the remarkable change of sex undergone by Virginia Woolf's hero-heroine, Orlando. A similar male-female dichotomy holds for the doubles of *Mrs. Dalloway:* the titular heroine and Septimus Smith.[5]

Some special instances of decomposition, which find their matrix in myth more than in individual psychology, occur in Attic Comedy. F. M. Cornford's exploration of the ritual patterns underlying Aristophanes' comedies demonstrates that most of the important types of character depicted reduplicate each other in a curious but meaningful fashion.[6] Cornford argues that the series of imposter scenes in the latter part of the plays which feature various boastful, swaggering characters who interrupt the sacrifice or wedding feast and claim a share of the fruits of the hero's victory, only to be subsequently mocked, beaten, and driven away, are really not discrete episodes but variations on the same theme. The consequence is that these sundry personages may all be telescoped "into a single character—the Imposter." In other words, a doubling by multiplication of the imposter (the *Alazōn*) occurs in the latter part of the comedies. Besides this doubling by multiplication of the imposter, the imposter himself appears to be a double of the antagonist in the first part of the play (specifically, in the *Agōn*). Furthermore, the hero, or agonist, has his own double in the *Agōn* in the person of the buffoon, "a subordinate character in some way attached to the hero as friend or attendant," whose function it is to play a portion of the composite role of the hero, that of ironical buffoon, during the more serious initial conflict. In this portion of the drama the hero plays the role of the ironical man (*Eiron*), but after his symbolic victory toward the middle of the work he plays a composite role, treating the *Alazōn* with a mixture of irony and buffoonery.

But far more important than these decompositions, at least in terms of the ritual origin of comedy, is the fact that the agonist and antagonist are doubles, which means that the hero and the imposter are also doubles. As Cornford puts it, "We must bear in mind the curious confusion by which the enemy of the God is also a double of the God himself. This arises from the very nature of rites which involve the ritual killing, dismemberment, and eating of the divine victim." The ritual parallels here are those of death and resurrection of the God, the supplanting of the old king by the young king, the succession of the old year by the new year, the victorious battle of summer over winter, and in general the celebration of fertility over barrenness. From a psychoanalytic point of view the victory of the hero over the antagonist in comedy constitutes a crude version of the victory of eros over thanatos, or id over superego, or of son over father. The duplications of role in Attic Comedy present still another analogy to the situation which Rank found in the myth of the birth of the hero, that of many personages being reducible in their psychological roles to a few basic types. Whenever decomposition takes place in narrative, the cast of characters is never quite so large as it would appear to be, as *Macbeth* so well exemplifies.

We may next consider why such fragmentation of the personality occurs at all. More specifically, what, in general terms, is the function of doubling? One function has already been assumed, the function of representability. Freud speaks in *The Interpretation of Dreams* of "considerations of representability," the idea being that the dream-work has the task of portraying all sorts of wishes, fears, thoughts, associations, and so on in the form, for the most part, of "visual and acoustic memory-traces." By the same token, a most natural way for art to depict endopsychic conflict is to picture it as being interpersonal conflict, the seemingly separate characters representing the psychological forces at odds.[7]

This representative function of decomposition—which in terms of literature is essentially a formal and esthetic rather than a psychological one—may be set aside at this point to inquire into the basic psychological function of decomposition, its defensive purpose. Doubling has already been linked with the defense mechanism of projection. In his analysis of Dostoevsky's doubles Kohlberg emphasizes decomposition as a form of balancing or undoing. With respect to autoscopic phenomena, Lukianowicz considers them as being "of a self-defensive character," and he cites J. Hoffmann's contentions that hallucinations of a "phantom limb" constitute a form of denial of the loss of the limb.[8] Fenichel considers some cases of a split in the personality as involving the defense mechanism of isolation.[9] Decomposition may also involve the mechanisms of displacement, repression, regression, reaction-formation, and turning against the self. Since there are, as Fenichel says, "no sharp lines of demarcation between the various forms of defense mechanisms" and since most of them are related in various ways, we can suggest that decomposition—besides ranking alongside of condensation, displacement, and symbolization as one of the fundamental mechanisms of the human mind—may be thought of as constituting a basic defense mechanism. Rank makes it quite clear that he considers it to be one: "In psychoanalysis these alterations are considered a defense mechanism by which an individual separates himself from a part of his self which he wishes to escape."[10] And Freud, who entitled one of his papers "Splitting of the Ego in the Defensive Process," relates decomposition to defensive activity.[11] The remainder of the chapter emphasizes the defensive strategies involved when an author depicts conflict between opposing selves.

Two such opposing selves can be found in Euripides' *The Bacchae,* a play so remarkable for the way it dramatizes conflict of elemental psychological forces that it is surprising the work has not elicited more comment from psychoanalysts. Dionysus personifies the id. He is an orgiastic god, associated in the play with wine, the remover of inhibition; with rapture, revel, and ecstasy, both in the sexual and crypto-sexual modes (such as dancing); and with freedom, so that Pentheus' futile attempt to incarcerate Dionysus in prison is laden with irony.

Dionysus is the god of laughter, joy, union of the soul, peace, and sanity. Since in psychological terms Dionysus stands for release of the libido, the peace he brings must be that which ensues after orgasmic or other violent discharges of excitation. Therefore, the sanity he gives is the opposite of insanity, or neurosis, which results from repression. The various totem animals which are associated with Dionysus—the goat, bull, and serpent—symbolize the phallic potency of the god. Most important, the cruelty of which Dionysus is capable is directed only toward those who deny his godhead, Pentheus, his mother Agauë, and Agauë's sisters, who spread the false rumor that Dionysus is not the son of Zeus. In other words, the retribution which Dionysus visits upon them amounts to a retaliation against repressive forces.

These repressive forces are paired off against those Dionysus stands for. Early in the play, before the *Agōn* between Dionysus and Pentheus, a comic scene occurs in which Cadmus and Teiresias prepare to join in the revels: "Where should we go to dance, and take our stand with the rest, tossing our old grey beards? You must guide me in this, Teiresias—you're nearly as old as I am, and you understand such matters. No, it won't be too much for me; I can beat time with my thyrsus night and day!" Together, hand in hand, they start to totter off. Pentheus appears, first to deliver a tirade against the sexual license encouraged by the Stranger God and then to mock—with a disrespect of his elders characteristic of the hubris of the tragic hero—the costume and intentions of the two old men, who drop their comic airs and seriously remonstrate with Pentheus about his attitudes toward Dionysus. After Pentheus exits, Teiresias declares him to be raving mad. In speaking for Dionysus at this point Cadmus and Teiresias serve as buffoon doubles of the god, doubles analogous to the buffoon double of the agonist who battles the antagonist early in the course of a comedy, the only difference being that their buffoonery itself is not directed at Pentheus but precedes the remonstrance. Furthermore, the chorus of Bacchants, which always sings Dionysus' praises, stands in the relation of a double to the god.

Cornford himself calls attention to the much more important fact that Dionysus and Pentheus are doubles.[12] After mentioning that both Pentheus and the herdsmen who separately spy on the orgiastic activities of the Bacchae in the woods function in the role of the imposter who disturbs the rites, Cornford suggests that Pentheus as antagonist fulfills the role of the imposter in the three main essentials of (1 disturbing the rites; (2 vaunting his insolent authority, the vanity of which the God will expose, and (3 being "set at nought, beaten, blinded, slain, torn to pieces, cast out, or, like the Titans, blasted to ashes." He mentions the irony with which Dionysus, as *Eiron*, treats Pentheus as *Alazōn*, and one might point also to elements of buffoonery in Dionysus' handling of Pentheus later in the play, especially the scene in which he persuades Pentheus to don the feminine garments of the Bacchant and then mocks him ("Wait—this curl of hair is out of place," he says, and "Your girdle is loose; and the folds of your gown are not hanging straight to your ankles"). Two features of the play which clinch the identification between Dionysus and Pentheus are Pentheus' role in the *sparagmos* (the dismemberment of the *Pharmakos*, the totem scapegoat which symbolizes the dying god) and the fact that prior to the *sparagmos* Dionysus places Pentheus in the top of a lofty pine tree and lets it spring upright (a mockery of Pentheus because the motion of the tree symbolizes an erection), the connection in this case being that Dionysus was worshipped as a god of trees.[13] Were this not evidence enough to establish that Dionysus and Pentheus are really parts of a whole, roughly the components of id and superego, one might point to such minor parallels and antitheses as the following: in terms of genealogy both Dionysus and Pentheus are grandsons of Cadmus; Pentheus' name means "grief," while Dionysus is the god of joy; and Pentheus ironically threatens Dionysus with symbolic castration (to behead and to hang him), whereas Dionysus symbolically castrates Pentheus by making him play the transvestite, by having the symbolic tree deracinated by the Bacchae, and of course by having him beheaded (ironically, by his mother Agauë, in the male role of hunter).[14]

A number of defense mechanisms can be discerned in *The Bacchae*. Because the Bacchic orgy is synonymous with libidinal release, it is evident that the orgy is the antithesis of the superego's defensive tendencies. More specifically, the indulgence which Dionysus stands for is the reverse of Pentheus' main line of defense, repression. In conjunction with his repression, he quite literally employs the defense of denial by refusing to accord Dionysus his due. So rigid is his behavior that it suggests the presence of a reaction-formation against what are almost overwhelming libidinal impulses, manifested not only in his ultimate eagerness to view the secret rites but more especially in the voyeuristic nature of his impulse. His desire takes the passive form of wanting to watch rather than actively participate in the orgy, which in the present context amounts to wishing to view the primal scene.[15] Pentheus' role as scapegoat, made quite explicit when Dionysus says to him, "You alone suffer for the whole city—you alone," may be thought of as involving, at least on the city's part, the defense of isolation, for a typical feature of the scapegoat ritual in primitive culture is the driving out of the guilt-laden scapegoat from the community.[16] The defense of regression may possibly be reflected in the passage where Dionysus tells the mesmerized Pentheus that he will be carried home in his mother's arms. Pentheus responds, "Why, you make a weakling of me! Yet it is what I deserve." He has regressed, as it were, to the less dangerous days of childhood.

The relationship of these instances of defensive strategy to the principal decomposition in the play, that between Dionysus and Pentheus, makes clear how the work dramatizes the dangers for mankind of repressing basic libidinal impulses and supports the contention that decomposition always involves defensive maneuvers. What appears to be the missing whole, that is, the composite of which Dionysus and Pentheus comprise the constituent elements, is in the play, even though no single character represents it. It is the mind of man.

In Melville's "Bartleby the Scrivener" the composite mind which is subject to a dramatic split can be identified with relative ease as that of the author. A number of critics agree that Bartleby's refusal to continue writing and his rejection of society seem to reflect Melville's disillusionment after the large audience for his early South Sea "romances," *Typee* and *Omoo,* spurned his writing once he began to undertake works of the complexity of *Mardi* and *Moby Dick,* both colossal flops on the market. As Richard Chase says, "The commercially successful American culture had asked Melville to go on producing palatable adventure stories, and Melville had in effect answered with the words of Bartleby: 'I would prefer not to.' "[17] But Chase extends his interpretation by remarking that "Melville-as-writer appears not only as Bartleby but also as the lawyer himself" since the lawyer, like Melville, is a "drawer-up of recondite documents of all sorts." On quite different grounds Mordecai Marcus argues that Bartleby is a "psychological double" of the lawyer-narrator. He suggests that Bartleby's role amounts to a critique of "the sterility, impersonality, and mechanical adjustments of the world which the lawyer inhabits," assumes that Bartleby's willed demise symbolizes the lawyer's "Thanatos," and concludes that the theme of the tale is that "man is hopelessly trapped by the human condition in an acquisitive society."[18] While one must agree with Marcus that Bartleby and the lawyer are latent doubles, his rejection of the idea that Melville wove the threads of a personal allegory into the tale must be disputed.

Besides the one Chase mentions, a host of details in the work hint at the writer allegory. Most of the characters are engaged in writing. The narrator (this seems to be another narrator-double composite, like that of Ishmael and Ahab) remarks that his inability to write a "satisfactory biography" of Bartleby is "an irreparable loss to literature." He praises Bartleby's "incessant industry." The work involves only writing, because Bartleby would "prefer not to" do anything else. Allusions to two authors crop up in significant contexts. With respect to Bartleby's unwillingness to proofread—a pedestrian task naturally scorned by the creative genius—the narrator says, "I cannot credit that the mettlesome poet, Byron, would have contentedly sat down with Bartleby to examine a law document of, say five hundred pages." (Law documents do not normally run that long, but Melville's novels often did.) When Bartleby first appears the lawyer associates him with another writer, Cicero: "I should have as soon thought of turning my pale plaster-of-paris bust of Cicero out of doors"; and later we are told, "He did not look at me while I spoke, but kept his glance fixed upon my bust of Cicero." The screen behind which Bartleby works folds up like "a huge folio." And at the end of the story, after telling us of his discovery that Bartleby formerly worked as a clerk in the Dead Letter Office, the narrator resignedly sighs out the last two sentences: "On errands of life, these letters speed to death. Ah, Bartleby! Ah, humanity!" This passage is reminiscent of the one in *Moby Dick* where Melville, speaking almost directly as author in the chapter called "Cetology," ruminates about his "ponderous task; no ordinary letter-sorter in the Post-Office is equal to it. To grope down into the bottom of the sea after them; to have one's hands among the unspeakable foundations, ribs, and very pelvis of the world; this is a fearful thing."

In addition to these threads of evidence, it would seem that the shenanigans of the other two "scriveners," Turkey and Nippers, constitute a comic curtain-raiser to the more serious drama about writing which ensues in the tale. They are also doubles, their moods being perfectly complementary. Nippers' "irritability" subsides at noon, whereas Turkey's "paroxysms" come on about twelve o'clock. "Their fits relieved each other, like guards," and one can always copy while the other is unfit for the task. Turkey's problem is the blots he makes on the precious documents during his fits, while Nippers' principal incapacity is his inability to adjust the height of his desk to a comfortable level.

The Nippers-Turkey farce seems to reflect the minor quirks and neurotic blocks to which the creative writer is subject, while the tragicomedy of the relationship of the narrator and Bartleby symbolizes the despondency which Melville must have felt at the rejection by the public of his masterpiece. To understand what presumably went on in his mind it will be helpful to think of Melville as having suffered a narcissistic blow at this point in his career. As a result, the libido which he had invested in his work by the process of sublimation was withdrawn to the extent that his craft seemed dead and meaningless. ("On errands of life, these letters speed to death.") This withdrawal, symbolized in the story by Bartleby's walling off of society, his refusal even to eat the food which was the fruit of his labor, ensued because sublimation as a libidinal outlet failed to be ego-syntonic, failed to give the kind of narcissistic gratification an ambitious writer feeds on. The lawyer-writer's exasperation with his idealistic other self is so great that he feels castrated: he reacts to "the mild effrontery" of his unaccountable scrivener with "sundry twinges of impotent rebellion," and says further, "Indeed, it was his wonderful mildness chiefly, which not only disarmed me but unmanned me, as it were. For I consider that one, for the time, is somehow unmanned when he tranquilly permits his hired clerk to dictate to him." The wording of this passage gives evidence of the psychosexual nature of the conflict, that is, the libido sublimated in art, once withdrawn from the ongoing task, is no longer "neutralized" or desexualized, and its subsequent damming up may be thought of as forcing the dissolution of the integrity of the self represented by the decomposition of Melville into the narrator and Bartleby. Since the lawyer describes himself as an unambitious, methodical, prudent man who likes to do a "snug" business, and since he is obviously well oriented to what we call everyday reality, he represents the ego, perhaps in conjunction with the id. The aescetic bachelor Bartleby, who survives on cheese, ginger nuts, and lofty idealism, would seem to represent the ego ideal.[19] While Bartleby maintains the integrity of his principles, his defenses—the gradual withdrawal, his "restriction of the ego," and the regression symbolized by his assumption of the fetal position on the cold stones of the womb-tomb (the jail is called the Tombs)—lead only to a defiant self-extinction in which the lacerated portion of the self seems to be proclaiming to the world, "If you do not love me and appreciate my work I will leave you forever."

It has been said that Shakespeare was not Hamlet but that Hamlet was the man Shakespeare would have been if he had not written a play called *Hamlet*. Similarly, Bartleby may be regarded as the man Melville might have been had he not written a story called "Bartleby." If we bear in mind that Melville had some sober Dutch blood in his veins, and that "Bartleby the Scrivener" is, among other things, a piece of sublimation through fantasy, it is understandable that Melville's fate was not Bartleby's. He ended his tale on a quizzical note. And he continued to write.

To conjecture that writing "Bartleby" served Melville's defensive needs is only to apply a concept which has wide currency in psychoanalytic criticism to a particular case. Henry James's "The Jolly Corner" may be treated in a similar manner. When James speaks of this story as a psychological "adventure-story" more thrilling than a tale dealing in detectives, pirates, or "other splendid desperadoes," he explains that it is full of adventure for him because "the spirit engaged with the forces of violence interests me most when I can think of it as engaged most deeply, most finely and most 'subtly' (precious term!). For then it is that, as with the longest and firmest prongs of consciousness, I grasp and hold the throbbing subject."[20] The extraordinary metaphor employed suggests an aggressive, predatory animal exercising the full force of its potency as it seizes its passive, trembling victim. For James, as an artist, penetrating consciousness is a kind of virility, even when that consciousness has as its subject the theme of the impotence of the unlived life, as in "The Jolly Corner," so it may not be amiss to stress once again that libidinal components have been transmuted into art by the process of sublimation, as in "Bartleby." Both the composing of the story and the doubling of its protagonist serve defensive purposes.

It is a strange tale. Spencer Brydon, who is fifty-six years old and who has spent most of his life abroad, returns to New York to view some inherited property, which consists of a house "on the jolly corner" and property where once stood another "not quite so 'good' " house, now the site of a skyscraper under construction. The act of supervising this construction excites Brydon, makes him wonder what sort of a man he might have been had he stayed in America and lived a different sort of life. He discusses this idea with his friend, Alice Staverton, and she admits having seen this man, Brydon's alter ego, in a dream. Brydon becomes obsessed with the urge to encounter his alter ego, and most of the story shows him wandering through the jolly corner house (the house where he spent his childhood) in search of this figure, which he thinks of as active, forceful, moneymaking, yet terrible and beast-like. As he prowls about the house by candlelight Brydon is thrilled, nervous, excited; he is obsessed by the fear of what may happen to him by going through doorways. When he does meet his "other self," he notes "a special verity that surpassed every other," namely that one of the hands which at first covers the face of the alter ego has two fingers missing. As the figure advances "as for aggression," Brydon backs off and then faints. Upon reviving he finds himself in the lap of Alice Staverton, to whom he says, "I can only have died. You brought me literally to life." They then discuss the encounter.

I have discussed the implications of this encounter from a psychoanalytic viewpoint at greater length elsewhere.[21] Following the lead of Saul Rosenzweig, who concludes that James reacted to his feeling of being unable to compete with his father and his gifted older brother in the oedipus context by a profound repression of his aggressive and sexual instincts, and relying on Leon Edel's insight that the germinal basis for the story was what James recorded as being "the most appalling yet most admirable nightmare of my life," I construed the alter ego as an id figure associated with both Henry James Sr. and William James.[22] The house on the jolly corner was seen as an elaborate symbolic representation of the mother's body, the womb in particular, the fear of going through doorways stemming from the inhibition of heterosexually oriented libido. When James recalled the short story in his notebook in 1914, Edel remarks, he gave a version of the dream, not of the story, for in the story Brydon only intends to outface his antagonist—and fails to do so. Alice Staverton, like May Bartram and similar characters in James, is a mother figure, so that Brydon speaks the psychological truth when he says that Alice brings him "literally to life." The strange detail of the alter ego's missing fingers, as Rosenzweig perceives, represents Brydon's sense of being castrated projected onto the beast-like alter ego for defensive reasons.

In terms of its defensive strategies, "The Jolly Corner" is another attempt to rationalize the same fault James pictures John Marcher as being guilty of in "The Beast in the Jungle," the failure to live life to the full, which always means in James's works the failure to participate in the erotic side of life. Spencer Brydon's principal defense, that of sexual repression, may be considered as falling asunder due to the combined stimuli of his return to the scene of his childhood, his attraction to Alice Staverton, and his dabbling in the process of the construction of a rather phallic skyscraper. He falls back on the more specific defense of projection, imputing to the hallucinated alter ego the kind of virility he both wishes for and finds himself appalled by because of the angst it provokes. By projecting this libido he compartmentalizes or isolates it, which amounts to an attempt to gain control over it while at the same time repudiating it. At that point in the story where Brydon cannot bring himself to open the door behind which he feels certain the bestial alter ego lurks, ready to pounce, he declares to himself, "I retire, I renounce." His candle is symbolically burned at this moment "well-nigh to the socket." Renunciation, a recurrent leitmotif in James's work, usually refers in his plots to the rejection of marriage and always refers, psychologically, to the repudiation of the normal male role. Another defense employed by Brydon is fainting.[23] But even more characteristic of Brydon's personality is the defense which sounds the keynote of the entire third part of the story: regression. When he awakes from his swoon Brydon has regressed to a level of childish dependence on the mother, and he is conscious as Alice holds him "of tenderness of support" and that she "had made her lap an ample and perfect cushion for him." When repression fails him as a defense, Brydon turns to projection in the form of an anxiety-provoking game of hide-and-seek with his alter ego. When that fails, he resorts to regression.

Further examples of the relationship of decomposition to defense occur in *Measure for Measure* and *Othello,* two dramas in which doubling is crucial. In analyzing these works the suggestion by Norman N. Holland that the success and failure of the defensive strategies portrayed in Shakespeare's plays correlate with the genres of comedy and tragedy will prove a helpful guideline. Holland contends that "it is a necessary condition for tragedy that the defense it embodies fail, leading to punishment for an impulse toward pleasure; it is a necessary condition for comedy that it build up a defense, leading to gratification without punishment of an impulse toward pleasure."[24]

One might begin by insisting that *Measure for Measure* is a comedy and not a tragedy manquée. While in many ways an unusual and highly original comedy, it should no longer be viewed as a "dark" one, a botched one, or even as a "problem comedy." Coleridge may have called its comic elements "disgusting" and its tragic elements "horrible," but the mid-twentieth-century mind can safely ignore nine-teenth-century critics' aversion to the bawdiness in the play, which Hanns Sachs points out did not trouble readers when it occurred in other works, and the passages of high seriousness ("Be absolute for death . . ." and so forth)—if the play is a comedy—can be seen, in all their poetic force, to mobilize anxiety the same way a joke does, the better to generate a sense of relief at the punchline. On the other hand, let us not endeavor to justify the artistry of the play by assuming it to be about such topics as "government" (in the political and moral senses of the word), "philosophy," and "poetry-of-the-theater" as one contem-porary critic does.[25] Above all, let us not conjure up problems where none exist by reading *Measure for Measure* simply as a morality play devoted to the thesis that the Old Testament justice of talion law should be tempered by the New Testament spirit of mercy. This theme threads its way throughout the play, and the theme of "Judge not that ye be not judged," together with the verbal motif of "measure for measure," comes straight out of the Sermon on the Mount. Yet the problems which critics have read into—not out of—the drama arise because its theme is really more circumscribed than they think it to be.

These problems disappear if the play be read as a comic exorcism of sexual guilt. All the crimes, foibles, and jokes represented in the play are either sexual or related to sexuality with the exception of the drunkenness of Barnadine.[26] The licentious jokes begin in the second scene with allusions to venereal disease, and the parody of the judg-ment theme starts when Madam Mitigation (Mistress Overdone) ap-pears and Lucio says, "I have purchased as many diseases under her roof as come to—

2nd GENTLEMAN: To what, I pray?
        LUCIO: Judge.
2nd GENTLEMAN: To three thousand dolors a year.

The "crime" for which Claudio is to be beheaded, getting his fiancée pregnant, is parodied when Lucio is forced to marry Kate Keepdown and mocked in a broader way when the ingratiating pimp, Pompey, and his bawd, Mistress Overdone, are hauled off to prison for the same general offense, illegal sexuality. Even the good Duke, the "old fantastical Duke of dark corners" as Lucio calls him, seems to relish sexual innuendo when he says to Friar Thomas,

> Believe not that the dribbling dart of love
> Can pierce a complete bosom; why I desire thee
> To give me secret harbor hath a purpose
> More grave and wrinkled than the aims and ends
> Of burning youth. (I.iii)

In short, if the play is as well stoked with libidinal fire as it appears to be, it would seem that the theme of judgment must be restricted to the context of passing judgment on sexual activity. Awareness of the way in which decomposition operates in the drama leads on to a decision about who may be considered as passing sexual judgments on whom.

The substitution motif in the play points to the presence of doubles. Escalus and Angelo substitute for the Duke during his supposed absence. Disguised as a friar, the Duke substitutes for himself, so to speak, by his incognito presence in the city. Mariana substitutes her body for Isabella's during the assignation. Barnadine's head is to be substituted for Claudio's as evidence of the execution, but the head of the already dead Ragozine ("A man of Claudio's years, his beard and head") is in turn substituted. At a somewhat further remove, Angelo's crime duplicates Claudio's, just as the sexual crimes against law and order of the pimps and the punks duplicate Claudio's offense. Another motif in the play, that of "authority," dictates a classification of the doubles implied by all of these duplications as threefold: fathers, sons, and mistresses.

As chief of state the Duke stands as a patriarch to his people. He even casts himself in the role of the "fond father" who has spared the rod and spoiled the child by letting sexual license develop in Vienna (I.iii.23ff.). He vests his authority in Angelo, saying, "Be thou at full ourself" and "Your scope is as mine own," alleging that he hopes Angelo will "strike home" in the "ambush of my name." If Angelo is a substitute father, then his sexual crime imputes sexual lawlessness to the father, who is depicted as pretending to sexual purity while being, in reality, full of lust. Claudio, however, would appear to be a son figure who arrogates the sexual preogatives of the licentious father (even though we are told by Escalus, who seems himself to represent the benevolent, asexual, merciful side of the father, that Claudio "had a most noble father"). Despite Lucio's repeated assertions that the Duke

74

is a lecher, the Duke's bearing and his claim to be "A man of stricture and firm abstinence" appears to establish his sexual probity; yet the Duke's ambiguous "Twice treble shame on Angelo,/ To weed my vice and let his grow" (while "my vice" might refer to the vice prevalent in the dukedom) looks rather suspicious when coupled with his remark in Act V apropos of excusing Angelo his faults, "I find an apt remission in myself." All things considered, the Duke would seem to be the whole father, of which Escalus and Angelo and the Duke-as-Friar are but fragments. When the Duke resumes his proper role as father to the state in Act V, he is benevolent, countenances a fair measure of sexual activity in forgiving the various criminals, promotes sexuality within the framework of marriage, and also figures as the fantasied omniscient parent who discovers all of his children's evil deeds in the passage where the repentant Angelo says,

> O my dread lord,
> I should be guiltier than my guiltiness
> To think I can be undiscernible,
> When I perceive your grace, like power divine,
> Hath looked upon my passes.

But if Claudio is a son figure, then Angelo must be one as well because Angelo's crime duplicates Claudio's. Isabella's words underscore this duplication when she reminds Angelo that

> If he had been as you, and you as he,
> You would have slipped like him; but he, like you,
> Would not have been so stern.

Further emphasis on the special relationship between Angelo and Claudio turns up a few lines later when the deputy of the Duke declares, "Were he my kinsman, brother, or my son, / It should be thus with him." If Angelo represents both the father and the son in various ways, then one of the things the play seems to be saying from the son's point of view is, "It is unjust to punish or restrict my sexual impulses, father, because you are just as guilty of such impulses as I am." Another symbolic father-son conflict, that between the Duke and Lucio, bears out this interpretation. Lucio, a comic scapegoat figure, suffers at the end of the play the appropriate punishment of being forced to marry the whore he got with child because "slandering a prince deserves it," that is, Lucio's principal crime is making rebellious accusations against the psycological father. At the same time, he alone is punished—though in fair measure—for the sexual transgressions which the other sons are forgiven because his scapegoat function requires that he suffer for the deeds of others.

Indicative of the fact that the main conflict in the play lies between father and son is the symbolic nature of the punishment to be meted out for sexual indulgence, beheading. Decapitation—together with hanging, which is symbolically interchangeable in the play with be-heading—represents the one punishment truly appropriate for sexual transgression, namely, castration. We have already seen the psychological appropriateness of that punishment in *Macbeth* and *The Bacchae*. The attribution of this significance to beheading in *Measure for Measure* cannot be considered arbitrary because several of the playful variations on the motif occur within a manifest sexual context. Lucio says to Claudio, "Thy head stands so tickle on thy shoulders that a milkmaid, if she be in love, may sigh it off." A much more involved conceit on this theme occurs when the Provost asks Pompey to help Abhorson, the executioner, saying, "Can you cut off a man's head?" Pompey replies with astute psychosexual logic, "If the man be a bachelor, sir, I can; but if he be a married man, he's his wife's head, and I can never cut off a woman's head." To construe the passage as meaning that a husband should rule over his wife in marriage takes it out of the context of the play, which has nothing to do with marital relations in that sense. But a wife's maidenhead cannot be removed because she has already lost it; a woman cannot be castrated because there is nothing there to remove; and above all, it would be a gross injustice to castrate a married man because his penis, properly speaking, belongs to his mate. While only Claudio and Angelo are threatened with beheading, Lucio senses that his marriage to a prostitute amounts to castration of a sort: "Marrying a punk, my lord, is pressing to death, whipping, and hanging."

Far from asserting, in the words of sonnet 129, that "The expense of spirit in a waste of shame / Is lust in action" as many have thought, the drama strikes a proper balance between extremes of gratification and repression. In one sense "measure" means due sexual restraint or moderation. Even without pressing into service the biographical parallel of Shakespeare's premarital relations with Anne Hathaway, it is clear that several characters in the play pass a consensus judgment against undue sexual restraint. When Lucio asks Claudio, "Whence comes this restraint?" (Claudio's arrest) Claudio replies, "From too much liberty. . . . Our natures do pursue, / Like rats that ravin down their proper bane, / A thirsty evil, and when we drink we die." But Lucio asks in wonderment, "Is lechery so looked after?" He thinks it a shame that Claudio should lose his head over "a game of tick-tack" (played on a board, with pegs fitted into holes) and says later to Isabella,

> . . .if myself might be his judge,
> He should receive his punishment in thanks.
> He hath got his friend with child.

Pompey echoes Lucio's judgment when he asks Escalus, "Does your worship mean to geld and splay all the youth of the city?" and adds, "If you head and hang all that offend that way but for ten year together, you'll be glad to give out a commission for more heads." These opinions, which might be questioned for coming from a lecher and a pimp, are backed up by the dignified and responsible figures of Escalus, who says, "It grieves me for the death of Claudio," and the Provost, who says of Claudio,

> He hath but as offended in a dream.
> All sects, all ages smack of this vice—and he
> To die for't!

And the Duke, who looks askance at unbridled lechery, nevertheless passes the definitive judgment on sexual activity at the end of the play by extending a charitable mercy to all of the guilty parties and by promoting Eros within the framework of matrimony. Mercy becomes equated with sexual latitude.

Rather than asserting that lust in action is an expense of spirit in a waste of shame, the play seems to emphasize the other side of the paradox stated in sonnet 129, that "till action, lust/Is perjured, murderous, bloody, full of blame," as the result of Angelo's defensive repression of instincts so well illustrates. The Duke remarks early in the play that Angelo "scarce confesses / That his blood flows, or that his appetite / Is more to bread than stone." Lucio puts the same idea in a more spritely way: "They say this Angelo was not made by man and woman after this downright way of creation. . . . Some report a sea-maid spawned him; some that he was begot between two stock-fishes [dried cod]. But it is certain that when he makes water his urine is congealed ice." And later he says, "Sparrows must not build in his house eaves because they are lecherous."

Not only does Angelo's individual repression break down, but the combined repressive forces represented in the play by the successive judgments against sexual activity are nullified in the culminating scene when we learn that Angelo will marry Mariana, Claudio will marry Juliet, Lucio will marry Kate Keepdown, the Duke will presumably marry Isabella, Constable Elbow will continue in marriage with his wife, who "was respected with him before he married with her" as Pompey joshingly puts it, and—who knows?—Mistress Overdone might even find a tenth husband. Thus, *Measure for Measure* conforms to Holland's dictum that "it is a necessary condition for comedy that it build up a defense leading to gratification without punishment of an impulse toward pleasure." The play as a whole, and its denouement in particular, constitute a victory for Eros which dissolves the kind of fragmentation represented by the division of roles into those such as the kind father, the castrating father, the obedient son, the guilty son, the pure woman, and the bawd. Marriage will cement these fragments together.

In contrast to *Measure for Measure*, *Othello* treats similar material in almost the opposite fashion. Eros goes down to defeat. Marriage precipitates a division of the soul of Othello instead of leading to a harmony of its components. And the various defensive maneuvers employed by Othello fail, resulting in the "punishment for an impulse toward pleasure" which Holland leads us to believe will always hold true for tragedy.

The theme of sexual frailty in women so common in Shakespeare's works, stated so memorably in Hamlet's "Frailty, thy name is woman" and echoed in Angelo's "Women are frail too," becomes the focus of *Othello*. Unlike *Measure for Measure*, which deals in broad terms with the degree of sexual activity which both men and women may freely enjoy, *Othello* confines itself with rigor to the much more limited subject of male attitudes toward the sexual behavior of women. Shakespeare adheres to this subject even more strictly than we might expect in a play in which the plot hinges on the question of marital fidelity, so much so that almost every scene of the drama calls woman's sexual nature into question except for the peripheral business relating to the war with the Turks. While the Temptation Scene and the Brothel Scene highlight possible male attitudes toward women, lesser scenes like that at the beginning of Act II when Cassio parades his gallantry and Iago his misogyny serve to enlarge upon the theme, which crops up in the very first lines of the play when Iago speaks the puzzling line which has become a textual crux: "A fellow almost damned in a fair wife" (meaning Cassio).

There are four basic opinions a man may hold about the sexual nature of women. He may regard womankind as pure, as lecherous, as castrating, or as normal, that is, neither pure nor lecherous but a mixture of the two. A variation of the first two views occurs when women are conceived as falling into two groups instead of one: nubile maidens who are objects of worship or affection more than lust and sluts who are not particularly worthy of one's esteem but are good to go to bed with, a view known as the sexual double standard. All of these different attitudes toward woman's sexual nature permeate *Othello,* provide the conditions of its drama, and correlate with the various fragmentations of Othello's soul which make the play so mysterious and yet so satisfying.[27]

With respect to decomposition in the play, the first to realize that the conflict between Othello and Iago is essentially an endopsychic rather than an interpersonal one was James Joyce, who has Stephen Dedalus say of Shakespeare, "In *Othello* he is bawd and cuckold . . . His unremitting intellect is the hornmad Iago ceaselessly willing that the moor in him shall suffer."[28] F. R. Leavis comments: "Iago's power, in fact, in the temptation scene is that he represents something that is in Othello . . . *The essential traitor is within the gates*"[29] (italics added). Numerous other critics regard Iago as a double of Othello, though most of them see this splitting of the self in broad moral terms, treating Iago as Evil and Othello as Good without inquiring precisely how doubling relates to the particulars of the play. But since so many see these characters as doubles, let consensus substitute for demonstration while we explore the as yet unmentioned possibility that Cassio represents still another fragment of Othello's soul.

That Cassio reflects a "side" of Othello can be seen in terms of the way in which Cassio adheres to the sexual double standard in its classic form. A worshipful, nonerotic attitude toward women characterizes the handsome cavalier's speeches to the "divine Desdemona" in Act II, as when Cassio tells Montano that Othello has married

Most fortunately. He hath achieved a maid
That paragons description and wild fame;
One that excels the quirks of blazoning pens,
And in th' essential vesture of creation
Does tire the ingener.

Shakespeare allows Cassio a hyperbolic, overelaborate verbiage in speaking of Desdemona which Cassio does not customarily use elsewhere in the play, one distinctly artificial as compared to Othello's sublime yet controlled passages about Desdemona. The style of this and other passages reveals the exaggerated nature of Cassio's respect for Desdemona, though the well-bred courtier would presumably treat any lady of Desdemona's station to similar speeches; he even extends his "bold show of courtesy" to the lower-caste Emilia by kissing her hand. Cassio gives further evidence of his idealization of women during Iago's futile attempts at the beginning of Act II, Scene iii, to arouse in Cassio an erotic interest in Desdemona: to Iago's suggestive "man-talk" speculations about how voluptuous Desdemona may be in bed, Cassio —the perfect gentleman—responds primly with polite compliments about the "exquisite lady." Yet Cassio has his whore, and he shows no reluctance to indulge in persiflage with respect to his mistress in the scene where Iago pretends to Othello that he and Cassio speak of Desdemona. Cassio laughs about Bianca's passion for him, and when Iago mentions marriage Cassio responds, "I marry her? What, a customer? Prithee bear some charity to my wit; do not think it so unwholesome." Thus Cassio behaves as though all women fall into two distinct groups: sexual saints and sexual sinners. In view of the sexual double standard that Cassio entertains, the suggestion that he functions as a psychological double of Othello acquires special point. That this relationship obtains seems at least tentatively indicated on the grounds that Cassio was present at Othello's wooing of Desdemona; that he stands as Othello's "second" or lieutenant; that he takes Othello's place as governor of Cyprus; that he takes Othello's sexual welfare to heart, hoping he will survive the storm to make "love's quick pants in Desdemona's arms"; that he shares Othello's idealization of women; and that just before Othello dismisses Cassio from his position he declares, "He that is approved in this offense,/ *Though he had twinned* with me, both at a birth,/ Shall lose me" (II.iii.211–12; italics added). In a sense what happens is that just after Othello cashiers Cassio he jettisons—by calling into doubt—the worshipful attitude toward women he has in common with Cassio, his psychic twin in many respects.

The trouble with the plaster-cast conception of Desdemona which Othello shares with Cassio is that it is so friable. Othello's conscious worship of his "cunning'st pattern of excelling nature"—however noble and admirable—betokens an unrealistic and therefore precarious assessment of womankind. The audience knows that the beautiful, honorable, devoted Desdemona is only human and hence fallible, as we see when she proves evasive if not mendacious about the handkerchief when straightforwardness might have saved her. Leo Kirschbaum remarks in calling Othello a romantic idealist who overvalues Desdemona, "He loves not Desdemona but his image of her."[30] Perhaps it should be said that he loves both but cannot distinguish between the two. More accurately, we have to do with only one Desdemona but with at least three psychic dispositions of Othello toward her. One is that of the romantic idealist. Another is that of the normal, sensual, integrated Othello, who is able under ordinary conditions to combine the currents of affection and eroticism, who can say to Desdemona without any romantic claptrap, "The purchase made, the fruits are to ensue;/ That profit's yet to come 'tween me and you" (II.iii), and who reveals that "the young affects" in him are not entirely defunct when he cries with anguish in the brothel scene, "O thou weed,/Who art so lovely fair and smell'st so sweet,/ That the sense aches at thee." The third disposition is that of the Othello whose jealousy doth mock the mind it feeds on, the Othello who considers Desdemona a whore.

If Cassio represents that side of Othello which views women as sexual saints or sinners, what side does Iago represent? Wived or not, Iago hates women. His antipathy reveals itself when he says in apparent jest in a passage which is nothing if not critical,

> You are pictures out of doors,
> Bells in your parlors, wildcats in your kitchens,
> Saints in your injuries, devils being offended,
> Players in your housewifery, and housewives in your beds.

The best thing he can say—in answer to Desdemona's playful challenge—in his series of witty paradoxes on the theme of the infidelity of women is that the most worthy of women is fit only "to suckle fools and chronicle small beer." This "most lame and impotent conclusion," which seems on the surface to reflect only one strain of the cynicism which permeates Iago's views, may be taken at a deeper level as correlative with his unconscious homosexuality. Throughout the play Iago's behavior reflects that of a paranoid personality whose repressed homosexual tendencies have erupted under stress in the form of delusions of grandeur, persecution, and jealousy, as Martin Wangh's sound analysis of his character explains.[31] With the paranoid's marvelous ingenuity he converts his delusional system into a plan of revenge. That this plan singles out Cassio as the cuckolder of Othello is overdetermined. Consciously Iago wants revenge on Cassio because of the promotion. Unconsciously he wants revenge because of the characteristic envy of Cassio he experiences: "He hath a daily beauty in his life / That makes me ugly" and "The knave is handsome, young, and hath all those requisites in him that folly and green minds look after." This hatred of Cassio amounts in turn to a reaction-formation against the sexual desire he feels for Cassio, a desire he uncovers without intending to in the lie he fabricates to the effect that Cassio mistakes him for Desdemona one night as they sleep side by side:

> And then, sir, would he gripe and wring my hand,
> Cry, "O sweet creature!" and then kiss me hard,
> As if he plucked up kisses by the roots
> That grew upon my lips; then laid his leg
> Over my thigh, and sighed, and kissed, and then
> Cried "Cursed fate that gave thee to the Moor!" (III.iii)

Iago's delusional jealousy (he fears both Othello and Cassio with his "nightcap") masks his repressed homoerotic inclinations. As he unwittingly admits, the kisses which Cassio is said to pluck *grow* upon his own lips.

There remains the formidable task of explaining how Iago's character relates to that of Othello and to the action of the drama as a whole. As an aid to comprehension, let it be granted that Othello is a composite character in the play. The composite may be designated the Normal Othello, a man more gifted than the average, but normal and healthy psychologically in that he possesses control ("Keep up your bright swords, for the dew will rust them"), awareness of reality, and self-respect. This is the "noble Moor whom our full Senate / Call all in all sufficient," the man "whom passion could not shake." He is good and trusting, "of a free and open nature / That thinks men honest that but seem to be so." He is a manly, masculine man, the man called to mind by G. Wilson Knight's description of him as "a symbol of human —especially masculine—'purpose, courage, and valour.'" This is the Othello described earlier as the integrated, sensual man who is able under ordinary circumstances to combine the currents of affection and lust. But under great emotional stress of a particular kind the Normal Othello begins to disintegrate into the Romantic Othello and the Psychotic Othello. The Romantic Othello is more refined, sensitive, idealistic. His impulses in these respects are seen in exaggerated form in Cassio, especially in the matter of the sexual double standard for women. Certain ontogenetic features in Othello's life which underlie his disposition can be discerned in the fact that prior to his marriage Othello's arms have found "their dearest action in the tented field" and his bed has been "the flinty and steel couch of war"; he is a man who if he knew women at all before his marriage must have known them either politely and remotely or else in passing dalliance, as Cassio has. So great is the stress, however, that the division of women into Saints and Sluts leads to the development of another dissociated personality: the Psychotic Othello, personified by Iago, who can experience neither affection nor lust except in perverted form.

Two events occur immediately prior to the present action of the play: Othello's marriage and Cassio's promotion. While the latter event seems to precipitate Iago's plotting, the former must in actuality be the decisive factor. More important still, marriage precipitates the division in Othello's soul. The psychosexual stresses on Othello which are mobilized by the marriage can be understood within an oedipal framework. Conflict with the father resulting from the prohibited marriage is dramatized as conflict with the father-in-law, Brabantio. Before the marriage, Othello tells us, "Her father loved me." Brabantio invited Othello into his home repeatedly and presumably treated Othello with all the pride of a father whose son has returned from the wars. If Desdemona be regarded in part as a mother surrogate, as several critics have, then the second principal anxiety mobilized by marriage must be that of the incest taboo. The natural flood of libidinal excitation aroused in Othello by the prospect of the "fruits" of matrimony, as Othello refers to them, further pressures him. When we concentrate our attention on Iago it is not difficult to understand the defensive strategies he employs in terms of those characteristic of paranoia; but only when we look at the play as a whole, and Othello as a "whole," can we see that Iago, as a fragment of Othello's soul, represents in terms of his words and deeds a deep-seated but futile effort to defend against the anxiety which signals the conflict in Othello's mind over the combined crimes of violating the incest taboo and displacing the father in the affections of the mother. The latter crime seems shadowed forth in these words of Desdemona to her father:

> And so much duty as my mother showed
> To you, preferring you before her father,
> So much I challenge that I may profess
> Due to the Moor my lord.

The crime of violating the incest taboo dictates that Othello must kill Desdemona rather than enjoy her.

In brief, Othello's premarital defenses of sublimation-through-war-fare, asceticism (the "flinty and steel couch of war"), and the technique of isolating or compartmentalizing his mutually exclusive views of women as sexually pure or tainted fail him when he marries. Dissociation of his personality only makes things worse. As for the measure of tragic insight Othello attains, it may be argued that at the end he comprehends that he loved too well and that this adoration was unwise but not why it was unwise. His talk of "one not easily jealous" and his choice of metaphor in saying, "threw a pearl away," suggest that he has not yet grasped how his idealization of Desdemona betrayed him into the strategy of employing all his troops in conducting an external defense against an imaginary danger instead of attacking the real, internal enemy—the one within the gates, as Leavis puts it.

While amicable relations may often subsist between the opposing selves of the latent double on the surface of the narrative, some form of psychological dichotomy always prevails beneath the surface which serves defensive purposes. The pain defended against stems from conflict over impulses or orientations. Projection involving isolation constitutes the most typical version of the defense. These defenses usually fail, though in cases where the work ends on a "happy" or positive note the defensive process of decomposition may be thought of as having a useful purpose. Conrad's "The Secret Sharer" and Shake-speare's *Measure for Measure* would be examples of successful defense against anxiety, since the decomposition inherent in these two works terminates at the end of the story, suggesting that doubles may be thought of as unstable psychological entities analogous to certain chemical elements which are not found in nature except in combination with other elements. Still more indicative of the instability of these psychic components is the disaster the division between them precipitates in the more common case of the tragic or negative ending, as we see, for example, in *The Bacchae* and *Othello*. While decomposition as a defense normally leads to disaster within the framework of the narrative, the author of such stories may be thought of as having served his defensive needs in a salubrious way, particular instances of this operation being Melville's "Bartleby" and James's "The Jolly Corner." The observations in this chapter about decomposition as a defensive process will hold true for Dostoevsky's *The Idiot*, Kafka's "The Judgment," and other works previously discussed.

Fragmentation of the Mind

If the mind of man has always seemed something of a puzzle, one reason is that the hypothetical unity we call the mind appears to be composed of many pieces. Many vernacular idioms reinforce this idea. In speaking of psychological crises we use such phrases as "having a breakdown," "cracking up," "going to pieces," "falling apart." Like the title of this chapter, and like the popular psychiatry term "split-personality" (usually confused with schizophrenia), these terms are mere metaphors, descriptive but somewhat misleading.

Assuming that a mind can become fragmented, just how many pieces of the stuff of the mind can we profitably distinguish? Thus far the analysis has focused on dualities, though certain exceptions, as in *Macbeth* and *Othello,* have been considered. In some case histories more than two personalities appear. At times the multiplicity of personality patterns approaches the kind of complexity seen in the theme of role playing which figures so largely in the novels of John Barth. Jacob Horner, for example, is "owl, peacock, chameleon, donkey, and popinjay, fugitive from a medieval bestiary." In *The Sot-Weed Factor* Henry Burlingame III appears in an almost endless series of guises and disguises. And Harold Bray in *Giles Goat-Boy* not only functions as an imposter double of the hero but in a bewildering variety of other poses —avant garde poet, psychotherapist, entomologist, explorer, and messiah. " 'Sometimes I think he's a species instead of one man,' Eierkopf declared. 'At least he must be quintuplets.' " Perhaps the wittiest comment on multifarious behavior in a single man is Dryden's satirical portrait of Zimri as "A man so various, that he seemed to be/Not one, but all mankind's epitome." Yet despite the permutations to which personality patterns are subject in a case like that of Miss Beauchamp, basic roles rarely exceed four.

We can begin with an example of dual rather than multiple personality—that of Bernard Hart's "one-fifth man."[1] The patient was admitted to an asylum after he began to wander aimlessly about during fugue periods. Sometimes during these periods he sent threatening telegrams to various people. The forgotten events of the fugues were restored after hypnosis. A more or less spontaneous development of the secondary personality occurred when the physician began to question the man about his violent aversion to an uncle. "The patient's demeanour, hitherto always very courteous, rapidly began to change. Finally he burst into a rage, and when I mentioned events which he had himself told me on former occasions, vowed that . . . he had certainly never told me anything of the sort." At this point the man declared that he had seen his physician only once, though some twenty long interviews had taken place, and he knew neither where he was nor how he got there. Subsequently this secondary personality, dubbed the one-fifth man, underwent further development. He could remember the events of earlier appearances but knew nothing of the former except what he was told. Since the one-fifth man's hostility toward the physician increased, a technique for making him "disappear" had to be developed through the use of the posthypnotic suggestion that the four-fifths man would reappear when a certain metal object was exposed. When enough repressed material had been uncovered during the course of treatment, the one-fifth man ultimately disappeared for good—though not before he nearly succeeded in stealing the metal object!

The two features of this case of particular interest at the moment are that the one-fifth man was diagnosed as embodying a crystallization of the patient's resistances to treatment and that since the "birth" of the one-fifth man resulted entirely from the psychological investigation he can be regarded as a kind of psychological or therapeutic artifact.

Two artifact personalities develop in the celebrated case described by Thigpen and Cleckley.[2] The "original" personality, called Eve White, is the one referred for treatment and the one known to most friends, to her parents, and to her husband. She is a quiet, demure, prim, neat, conservative, responsible, industrious person who is uncritical of others. She is afflicted with severe headaches. Eve Black, the antithesis of Eve White, is a lively, spontaneous person much given to joking. A sexy provocativeness is her most striking behavior pattern. Though likeable and attractive, Eve Black is mendacious and irresponsible. A typical example of her behavior is to go on a fling and purchase expensive dresses which her husband cannot afford and which Eve White not only does not know were purchased but cannot wear because they do not suit her personality. Eve Black's idea is to get the most fun out of life, by which she means mostly dancing, dressing extravagantly, and flirting. Flirting does not lead her to sexual intercourse, however. Something of a tease, she is nevertheless capable of retreating from a sexually threatening situation by letting Eve White suddenly take her place, leaving the aroused male angry and mystified. Eve Black is extremely narcissistic as compared to Eve White's superego orientation to life. She dislikes her husband and cares nothing about her little girl. With certain reservations, she can be said to play id to Eve White's superego.

Eve Black had made some "appearances" before therapy began. After therapy (including hypnosis) commences another secondary personality, "Jane," makes her appearance. Jane is a therapeutic artifact. Although the authors are unwilling to commit themselves specifically about the relationship of Jane to the other two, Jane seems a compromise between the two Eves. She retains many of Eve White's values, especially social values, and at the same time has a better developed ego; she has Eve Black's warmth but not her irresponsibility. Rather like Hart's one-fifth man, Jane is a *tabula rasa* type. She is "born" knowing nothing of the other two personalities, and except from her ability to speak and think, her mind and memory are almost total blanks. One sign of her stronger ego is that she has dignity and poise which the two Eves lack. Another sign is that when she learns about the two Eves she can evaluate them with detachment and objectivity. Yet Jane is only a fragment and not a whole personality. Eve Black continues to put in her unwanted appearances, and Jane is subject to headaches and nightmares (she dreams that her limbs turn into serpents). After an abreaction of a forgotten early experience of being forced by her mother to touch her dead grandmother's face, Jane and the other personalities disappear in that they seem to coalesce. In any case, they are replaced by a new, integrated personality combining the other three but perhaps resembling Jane most of all. This personality, called Evelyn Lancaster, remains stable and normal.

The most famous example of dissociation is the Beauchamp case, encountered by Morton Prince at the turn of the century and described in sometimes bewildering detail in a volume of more than 500 pages.[3] While various secondary personalities are dealt with, only four basic ones need concern us. They are designated, in order of occurrence, as BI, BII, BIII, and BIV. BI, the "original" personality, is christened "Miss Beauchamp." Her complaints are essentially neurasthenic, and at the beginning Prince has no suspicion that other personalities will develop. He describes Miss Beauchamp as reticent, reserved, conscientious, truthful, refined, and very nervous. As a child she was given to daydreaming and now as a young woman she has a literary bent. She suffers from severe headaches, nightmares, insomnia, fatigue, and aboulia (paralysis of the will), and she sometimes goes into trances. She is a rather formal person with a great sense of personal dignity. BII has no name, initially at least; she is simply Miss Beauchamp in hypnotic trance, and she reflects the usual trance behavior. Although Miss Beauchamp's complaints are relieved temporarily as a result of hypnotic suggestion, they soon return. After a while BIII, initially called "Chris" and later on known as "Sally," puts in her appearance during a therapeutic session. Sally knows all about Miss Beauchamp, whom she despises, but Miss Beauchamp knows nothing about her, although Sally claims to have had independent existence since early childhood and states that she continues to exist when BI is "on stage." Almost a mirror opposite of Miss Beauchamp, Sally is lively, vivacious, bold, saucy, gay, reckless, willful, irresponsible, and given to playing all sorts of pranks on Miss Beauchamp, such as causing her to tell fibs. Miss Beauchamp knows French, but Sally cannot read a word of it. In her behavior Sally is naughty rather than wicked, and Prince stresses her child-like qualities. Although Sally originally "appears" only during hypnosis, she later tricks Miss Beauchamp into rubbing her eyes (Prince did not allow the hypnotized patient to open them) and thereby "gets out." After this point Sally becomes an alternating personality capable of appearing outside of the therapeutic session until she is squeezed out of existence by the integration of personality which eventually takes place.

BIV, the last basic personality to develop, is given no other designation. A *tabula rasa* type, like Jane and the one-fifth man, she appears like "one who had dropped from the planet Mars," and though she proves clever at feigning knowledge she does not have, she does not even recognize Dr. Prince. Miss Beauchamp knows nothing about BIV until she is told, but Sally—curiously—knows about everything that BIV does yet remains unaware of BIV's thoughts. BIV differs from Miss Beauchamp in being basically healthy in both mind and body and having more self-control and courage and less reserve. Prince draws up a long list of the temperamental differences between BI and BIV. For example, BI eats things she supposes to be good for her, rarely drinks wine, never smokes, cannot stand oysters, hates tight clothing, is fond of church services, and never reads the newspapers; BIV not only eats what she likes but likes wine, cigarettes, oysters, tight clothing, and keeping up with what is going on in the world. She cannot stand church services. Yet BIV is not the "real" Miss Beauchamp either. In time another personality begins to make occasional appearances. The new personality amounts to a fusion of BI and BIV, a normal healthy person whom Sally conspires against because she feels pressured out of existence when this "synthetic" personage is present. Eventually it turns out, according to Prince, that this synthetic type corresponds to BII, who is the "real" Miss Beauchamp with her eyes shut, so to speak, and the integrated personality becomes relatively stabilized.

The main personalities of the Eve and Beauchamp cases resemble each other strongly. If we make allowance for such factors as difference in age, marital status, education, social change, and so forth, Eve White seems almost a replica of Miss Beauchamp. The hysterical symptoms and the character traits are nearly identical. Eve Black resembles Sally except that Eve Black's behavior reflects an older personality, late teens or early twenties, whereas Sally's behavior, though it covers a considerable range, belongs closer to the age of puberty. The apparent age of various personalities exhibited in true instances of dissociation may differ radically, however, as in the case history reported by C. C. Wholey of a Mrs. X, who experienced three secondary states of personality: one of a coquette, one of a male, and one of a baby with the mental age of about one year.[4] An even closer correspondence holds for

Jane and BIV. Both are *tabula rasa* artifact personalities who still experience emotional difficulties but who reflect greater maturity and balance. Evelyn Lancaster and the "real" Miss Beauchamp represent the final integration of the other conflicting personality orientations. When the two cases are regarded in psychoanalytic terms, there is in each a personality correlative with the superego, id, and ego, respectively, together with a concluding personality representing a synthesis of the three components—an integrated personality which reflects no serious imbalance of the total mind.

Bernard Hart remarks that "the whole history of psychology consists in the enumeration of successive attempts to carve discrete parts out of that continuum which we call mind."[5] From Plato's man-lion-monster triad to Janet's conscious-subconscious and on to Freud's topographical system of the conscious-preconscious-unconscious the task has proved a vexing one, as is further indicated by Freud's dissatisfaction with, and partial abandonment of, the topographical system for the partly structural, partly functional concept of the id-ego-superego.[6] What the case histories just described show is that in some sense the mind or soul or psyche of man is susceptible to fragmentation. Yet as Hart recognizes in his important paper on dissociation (1926)—in which he tries to reconcile the theories of Janet and Freud—all attempts to speak of the mind in material terms, as an entity capable of being broken up into hunks or pieces, invariably end by being rather crude formulations. Prince states in *The Dissociation of a Personality* that "the mind may be disintegrated in all sorts of ways. It may be divided, subdivided, and still further subdivided. The lines of cleavage may run in all sorts of directions, producing various sorts of combinations of systems of consciousness."[7] Yet Prince, whose phrase "systems of consciousness" reveals the extent to which his therapy was oriented to conscious psychology, manages to grasp in the first decade of the century the crucial distinction that "the disintegration resulting in multiple personality is only a *functional* dissociation of that complete organization which constitutes a normal self."[8] Hart, writing in 1926 with the benefit of having read Freud's formulations on the ego and the id, makes this distinction even more clear:

> Dissociation does not separate the mind into pieces, it only produces more or less independently acting functional units, each such unit comprising material which may be peculiar to itself, but which may just as well form a part of any number of other functional units. The dis-

tinguishing character does not lie in the material of which it is composed, but in the set or pattern. Instead of regarding dissociation as the splitting of conscious material into separate masses, it must be regarded as an affair of gearing, the various elements of mental machinery being organized into different functional systems by the throwing in of the appropriate gears.[9]

Freud himself, in one of his few references to multiple personality (a phenomenon never of much interest to psychoanalysts because they abandoned hypnosis, which tends to weaken the ego, and focused all their therapeutic efforts on strengthening the ego), also treats dissociation from a functional point of view, suggesting that it may occur when the ego's various object-identifications come into severe conflict with each other.[10] Dynamically considered, the appearance of an alternating personality can be understood in terms of the drives which have been repressed and impulses which are defended against. It should therefore be remembered, as I indicated at the beginning of this chapter, that when phrases like "fragmentation of the mind" are used, they are only roughly accurate metaphors which unfortunately tend to reify mental functions (as even metaphors like "defense" and "drive" tend to do, of course).

What gets left out of summaries of case histories of multiple personality, inevitably, is the almost uncanny quality of seeming autonomy which the alternating personalities possess. Each appears to live a life of his own, and mere mention of such details as the fact that Miss Beauchamp can read French while Sally cannot fails to convey a sense of the distinctiveness which each of these "characters" possesses. Their sundry modes of dress, speech, and manner furnish them with an aura of a special "personality." One investigator remarks that he instinctively spoke to one of the disparate personalities of a case he was treating in a manner quite different from the way he spoke to another one of the personalities.[11] One of these girls, "Louise," even seemed prettier than the other one, "Norma."

The obvious literary counterpart of these apparently distinct personages is the component character in fiction. Centuries of literary criticism and simplistic modes of reading have habituated us to think of a story as a story and a character as a character; instead we should remember that such Aristotelian elements as plot, character, and setting are but parts of a larger gestalt, parts not in themselves independent of their larger whole. As should be clear, some literary characters, like

Othello, have no more real psychological autonomy than do personality fragments, like Sally Beauchamp. At the same time, the necessary illusion of independence in the literary character at the surface of the "story" always obtains, except perhaps when we are confronted with manifest doubles like William Wilson and Golyadkin. All of the innumerable things which a literary character may be shown to be and to do—say, a Negro general who falls in love with a beautiful Venetian, marries her, becomes jealous of her, murders her, and then commits suicide—all such qualities and activities are part of the subtle magic which causes us willingly to suspend our disbelief that the character lives a life of his own.

The value of discussing multiple personality in connection with multiple decomposition in literature is largely analogical. There do not seem to be many literary works which exhibit a precise correspondence to the phenomenon of true dissociation. One example mentioned by Ralph Tymms is Heinrich von Kleist's *Penthesilea*.[12] In this work, in which the Amazonian queen displays personality orientations of maidenly modesty, masculine aggressiveness, and extreme eroticism in the form of masochism, the key features resembling multiple personality are the trance states which occur, the radical alternation of personality in the same literary character, and the fact that in her "normal" state of mind Penthesilea has no recollection of what actions she has performed in other states. By way of comparison, Othello suffers from trance states (they seem to be epileptic fits rather than fugue periods), but there is no amnesia and the component parts of the composite character are represented by other characters. The literary work usually cited in connection with multiple personality is Stevenson's *Dr. Jekyll and Mr. Hyde,* but even this work does not strictly correspond with multiple personality because Jekyll's transformation of himself into Mr. Hyde is deliberate and depends—initially, at least—on the drugs which Jekyll has concocted.

Discussions of this novella rarely mention the relationship of Mr. Utterson, the lawyer who draws up Jekyll's will, to the personality split reflected in Jekyll and Hyde. The story is told from a limited third person point of view, the person in question being Mr. Utterson. This means that while Utterson is not technically the narrator, the story is told almost as though he were. In effect, he functions like the narrator doubles whom we have already met, such as Conrad's Marlow. A kindly and very staid, balanced, responsible sort of man, Mr. Utterson nevertheless finds his imagination "engaged, or rather enslaved" by the strange behavior of Jekyll's beneficiary, and he experiences "an inordinate curiosity to behold the features of the real Mr. Hyde." Since Hyde is a criminal, Utterson is not only a narrator double but a "pursuer double" as well, as Stevenson hints at in the rather quaint joke of Mr. Utterson: "If he be Mr. Hyde, I shall be Mr. Seek."

Psychologically, Mr. Utterson represents a third component of the Utterson-Jekyll-Hyde composite. Jekyll declares in the written statement he leaves before he kills himself that "man is not truly one, but truly two. I say two, because the state of my own knowledge does not pass beyond that point," and he adds, "I learned to recognize the thorough and primitive duality of man." Although the statement gives us no specific account of Hyde's behavior, he seems to represent the body. We are told that the "pleasures" he seeks are "undignified" and later "monstrous." "His every act and thought centered on self; drinking pleasure with bestial avidity from any degree of torture to another." In short, libido finds its outlet in sadism, as the episode of running down the small child indicates. Jekyll, the rich and prominent physician, personifies the ego ideal portion of the superego. He is proud and is driven to accomplish great feats: "It was thus rather the exacting nature of my aspirations than any particular degradation in my faults that made me what I was." Both Jekyll and Hyde exhibit a Faustian rebelliousness, Jekyll in his chemical experiments and Hyde in scrawling blasphemies in the margins of pious books and in destroying the letters and portrait of Jekyll's father. The destruction of the portrait seems to tie in with what looks like a patricide motif in the otherwise unexplained murder of Carew by Hyde, Carew being described as "an aged and beautiful gentleman with white hair." Compared to Jekyll and Hyde, Mr. Utterson would seem to correspond roughly with the functions and values associated with the ego. He somewhat resembles Melville's lawyer-narrator in "Bartleby." As for the transformational drug which Jekyll takes, we are told that its effect is merely catalytic: "It was neither diabolical nor divine; it but shook the doors of the prisonhouse of my disposition." Aside from the device of the transformational drug, then, the story approximates the phenomenon of multiple personality with respect to Jekyll and Hyde, though there is no special reason for distinguishing "multiple personality" in this story from "multiple decomposition" in the works discussed below.

Herman Hesse's *Steppenwolf,* difficult to categorize, is a "novel" larded with extended portions of didactic, discursive commentary which spells out in explicit fashion the theme of the multiple self much more successfully, I think, than the concrete portions of the novel embody that theme. Introducing the reader to Harry Haller, whose anti-social self is symbolized as a wolf of the Steppes, is the nephew of the bourgeois landlady who rents Harry Haller a room for a time. The nephew serves as a narrator double of Haller. Although the narrator states that he intends to leave his own personality in the background as he tells us about this "genius" whom he has encountered, he does relate enough about himself to make it clear that he represents exactly the kind of stuffy, unimaginative, abstemious, middle-class man whom Harry Haller at once despises and yet envies. Rather like Mr. Utterson's interest in Mr. Hyde, the nephew's involvement in Haller's life is more than casual, as his frequent dreams about Steppenwolf betray.

Steppenwolf's ambivalent feelings about bourgeois life comprise a major element in the book. Early in the memoirs that he leaves behind at the rooming house, which constitute the bulk of the novel, he speaks of the bourgeois' "quiet, flabby and slightly muzzy half-and-half god of contentment." Such contentment fills him with nausea and makes him long for wild emotions and keen sensations: "What I always hated and detested and cursed above all things was this contentment, this healthiness and comfort, this carefully preserved optimism of the middle classes, this fat and prosperous brood of mediocrity." Yet Haller, himself of bourgeois origin, admits that "I, the homeless Steppenwolf, the solitary, the hater of life's petty conventions, always take up my quarters in just such houses as this." He enjoys the contrast of it to his "lonely, loveless, hunted, thoroughly disordered existence." A potted araucaria placed in a spotless vestibule of this abode where neatness and cleanliness are household gods is emblematic of the ordered life which Haller sporadically yearns for, the araucaria evoking a hunger for the past in much the same way that the chance taste of the "petite madeleine" stirs a deep nostalgia in the narrator of *Rememberance of Things Past*. At this point in the story Haller lives a divided life: physically he resides on the little island of disorder of his room surrounded on all sides by the sea of bourgeois stability. Spiritually he lives a life of the mind, a life of lofty intellectualism interrupted at rare intervals by forays against the bourgeois life in the form of anti-militarism articles in journals.

Harry Haller begins to understand himself better when he reads the "Treatise on the Steppenwolf" which he obtains from the anonymous peddlar in so mysterious a fashion. The Treatise informs him of some things which he more or less already knows: that he has two natures, "a human and a wolfish one"; that the man and the wolf live together in continual enmity, alternating in dominance; that artists are like this, with two souls, a God and a devil; and that the bourgeois seeks to be neither profligate nor martyr but to have the best of both worlds. The bourgeois man achieves a kind of balance or harmony only through compromise "at the cost of that intensity of life and feeling which an extreme life affords." What the Treatise tells him is that his idea of himself as a Steppenwolf is "a fiction." When he feels himself a werewolf and a twofold being, he avails himself "of a mythological simplification," the reason being that no one is so conveniently simple "that his being can be explained as the sum of two or three principal elements." While acting like a savage who can only count to two, he does in fact consist of "a hundred or a thousand selves." Men have an inborn need to regard the self as a unit.

> And if ever the suspicion of their manifold being dawns upon men of unusual powers and of unusually delicate perceptions, so that, as all genius must, they break through the illusion of the unity of the personality and perceive that the self is made up of a bundle of selves, they have only to say so and at once the majority puts them under lock and key, calls science to aid, establishes schizomania and protects humanity from the necessity of hearing the cry of truth from the lips of these unfortunate persons.

In literature even Goethe errs when he has Faust declare that two souls inhabit his breast; Faust "has forgotten Mephisto and a whole crowd of other souls that he has in his breast likewise." The Treatise reveals what Peer Gynt discovers, that "man is an onion made up of a hundred integuments."

Having learned this much from "books," Harry Haller has yet to glean from actual experience how to give free rein to his various selves. As yet he is too inhibited and he suffers from various conflicts, as is indicated by his ambivalence toward jazz ("hot and raw as the steam of raw flesh"). He detests it, but it holds a secret charm for him. His un-Vergilean guide to the polymorphous world of pleasure is the incomparable Hermine, a prostitute. Hermine, too, is a double of Haller—his "opposite" in sex and other matters. Matching his intellect is her sensuality. Besides being a kind of double, she functions as pimp (in introducing him to Maria), mother ("she was like a mother to me"), sister, and of course dancing instructor. She teaches Haller, for one thing, to enjoy frivolity, or what he has regarded as frivolity in the past. She also introduces him to the extraordinary Pablo, a jazz musician constituting another un-Vergilean guide who exposes him to the wonderworld of drugs and the underworld of pleasures ranging from unbridled aggression, to Don Juanism ("All Girls Are Yours"), to homosexuality, to polymorphous-perverse sexuality (at one point, before the magic theater episode, Pablo proposes a love orgy *à trois*). The culminating portions of the action take place, after the Dionysian preliminaries of the Masked Ball, in the Magic Theatre. This theater ("For Madmen Only—Price of Admittance Your Mind") is presumably the mind of Harry Haller freed of all restraint. The climax of the action occurs when Haller stabs Hermine as she lies naked on a rug alongside of Pablo in the sleep of exhaustion after "love's play." This episode combines a medley of themes: primal-scene voyeurism, symbolic incest, homosexuality, and raw aggression. Pablo, as impressario of the Magic Theatre, shows Haller that the pieces of his various selves can be rearranged at will like chess pieces in the game of life, the ability to manipulate the pieces freely being what Pablo calls "the art of life."

Steppenwolf leads us back to the question, how many pieces of the mind, or selves of the personality, can we profitably distinguish from each other? Hesse's emphasis on the multiplicity of the soul seems to correspond to Morton Prince's contention that the mind may be divided, subdivided, and still further subdivided. Carried to its logical conclusion, such a position implies that—if anger is brief madness—even a sudden shift of mood amounts to a kind of microdissociation of the personality, just as, in Barth's *End of the Road,* Jacob Horner's personality changes with his mood, changes which are compared with the fluctuations of the weather. While such an extension of the concept of personality makes a strange sort of sense within the context of Barth's novel, Hesse's splintering of the mind of man in *Steppenwolf* passes the point of diminishing returns long before we arrive at the "hundred" and "thousand" selves of which the Treatise so glibly speaks. For all the baroque ingenuity of Hesse's multiplication of the self (such as we see when Harry Haller perceives a multitudinous host of Harrys in the gigantic mirror at the Magic Theatre), no discernible

97

differences can be recognized where so many entities are involved. Personality is dual in the majority of the seventy-six case histories listed in the Taylor and Martin survey of multiple personality.[13] Almost all of the rest of the cases listed involve only three to seven distinct personalities. These data establish beyond doubt that in real life only a handful of separate personalities can be generated within a given "individual."

Hesse's idea that the fully developed man ought to be able to rearrange or manipulate the pieces of the self at will recalls Bernard Hart's gearshift analogy. Hart emphasizes that the mind does not so much dissociate into pieces as produce "more or less independently acting functional units." Hesse's implied claim that the initiated man can satisfy—presumably in a continuum of time—all of his various selves is at odds with the basic nature of mental dynamics. Any kind of harmony or balance among various components of the self, such as Plato advocates, Hesse sees as a bourgeois compromise. Freud's balance-of-power theory of the mind accepts without any romantic regrets the necessity of robbing Peter to pay Paul, even though such a civilizing of the mind gives rise to innumerable discontents. Harmony is a desideratum. As for conflict, it should be minimal, yet not totally absent, for out of sublimated psychic conflict such things as art are born. By comparison, Hesse—"the last of the romantics"—resembles in his mystical bent and in his implied ideal of the conflict-free soul that neo-Romantic of psychologists, Norman O. Brown, who proclaims the utopian ideal of a return to polymorphous perversity in *Life Against Death* and later announces the dissolution of all mind-body conflict in *Love's Body*. For Brown, "souls, personalities, and egos are masks, spectres, concealing our unity as body."[14] In contrast to Hesse, psychoanalysis values ego integrity; in contrast to Brown, psychoanalysis recognizes the inevitability of body-mind dynamics.

On the other hand, Hesse's emphasis on the radical multiplication of the self holds true insofar as it applies to fantasy life in general, notably that of writers and actors. If the case histories of multiple personality seem to indicate that basic constellations of personality are few in actual life for any given individual, this limitation does not necessarily obtain where the artist's powers of fantasy are free to explore various permutations of role playing. Richard Ellmann suggests, for example, that the members of the family in *Finnegan's Wake* are all symbolic of "aspects of Joyce's imaginative life."[15] Of the main

characters in *The Scarlet Letter* Richard Chase remarks: "Chillingworth, Dimmesdale, and Pearl can be conceived as projections of
different faculties of the novelist's mind—Chillingworth, the probing
intellect, Dimmesdale the moral sensibility; Pearl the unconscious or
demonic poetic faculty."[16] A bizarre yet illustrative example in painting
can be seen in some of the work of a schizophrenic patient who
represents himself several times in the same drawing.[17] When the
physician, with the patient's time-space system in mind, points out that
Mr. A. cannot be in the same landscape eight times at a given moment,
Mr. A. argues that he can. Discussing another of his paintings, the
patient not only declares that he is all of the human figures in it but the
tree as well, saying, "You can be all these things. You eat yeast, which
comes from the tree, so you become a tree. I am a tree and I am all the
people in the world." Similar inferences of the "plasticity" of the artist's
personality can be drawn from Ernst Kris's fascinating study of a series
of busts sculpted by Franz Xaver Messerschmidt, who habitually
glanced into a mirror every minute to make with his own face exactly
the grimace he wished to reproduce in the bust at hand.[18] We have, in
short, the artist as Proteus, able at will to transform himself, or aspects
of himself, by identifying, unconsciously, with the characters he projects.

Indications of a protean guile in the feat of multiple fragmentation
can be discerned in Henry James's *The Portrait of a Lady,* a far more
subtle, realized, and concrete instance of the phenomenon than the
narrative portions of *Steppenwolf* provide.

James's "The Jolly Corner" presents an overt doubling of the artist
in the person of Spencer Brydon and his alter ego, a split which reflects
active and passive male roles. Related to this splitting is the overt
doubling in James's unfinished *The Sense of the Past,* in which the
alter ego of the hero is one of his ancestors, for James records in his
notebooks his apprehension of repeating himself, of being "a little
handicapped if I chose to think so by the fact of my having made use
of a scrap of that fantasy in The Jolly Corner." It should be noted, in
passing, that *The Sense of the Past* begins with the rejection of the
historian protagonist by a young woman "because her heart is set all on
a man of action and adventure, some sort of a type like that, and not
on a sedentary student or whatever, my young man."[19] Another occasion on which James presents manifest doubles—lest there be any
doubt concerning his interest in the motif—is a tale called "The Private

Life," which James variously refers to as "rank fantasy" and "small game." While Leon Edel remarks that the two principal characters assuredly reflect aspects of James's own personality, they are based at a more conscious level on two men James actually knew: Robert Browning and an unidentified "F. L." Of Browning, whose literary genius seemed to Henry James disproportionate to the poor figure he cut in society, James says in the Prefaces, "our delightful inconceivable celebrity was *double,* constructed in two quite distinct and 'water-tight' compartments—one of these figured by the gentleman who sat at a table all alone, silent and unseen, and wrote admirably deep and brave and intricate things; while the gentleman who regularly came forth to sit at a quite different table and substantially and promiscuously and multitudinously dine stood for its companion." As the narrator says in the story itself, after discovering that Clare Vawdrey [Browning] writes in his room at the same time that his other self circulates in public: "One goes out, the other stays at home. One's the genius, the other's the bourgeois, and it's only the bourgeois whom we personally know." By way of contrast to this pair, James creates another character called Lord Mellifont, who is a dazzling public performer of "high shining elegance": "So far from there being here a question of an *alter ego,* a double personality, there seemed scarce a question of a real and single one, scarce foothold or margin for any private and domestic *ego* at all." Part of the fun of James's *jeu d'esprit* is that Lady Mellifont is always hunting for her husband and perpetually worrying "that he'll never come back." And part of the fun for us is to know that Henry James managed to shine both within his study and on the stage of polite society.

One other tale, entitled "Benvolio," ought to be mentioned before considering *The Portrait of a Lady.* The handsome young hero "with clustering locks" is a poet of shifting moods who falls in love with two women, one a charming, worldly young widow known only as the Countess, the other a lovely but pale and retiring woman called Scholastica, the daughter of a learned professor of neo-Platonic philosophy. Over a period of time Benvolio devotes his gallant attentions for months on end first to the Countess ("You represent the world and everything the world can give.") and then to Scholastica, who symbolizes the attractions of the study. We are told of Benvolio that "It was as if the souls of two very different men had been placed together to make the voyage of life in the same boat, and had agreed for convenience'

100

sake to take the helm in alternation." Eventually, after the jealous Countess has managed to beguile her rival into taking a trip to the Antipodes, Benvolio tells the Countess that he has loved her only by contrast to Scholastica and that in killing the contrast "you killed everything else. For a constancy I prefer *this!*" and he taps his "poetic brow." Like Henry James, Benvolio throws over all other women to marry his muse.

The question of marriage—in the work of James it is always a question—constitutes one of the foci of the action of *The Portrait of a Lady*. And here, as elsewhere in his work, there seems to be no such thing as a good marriage. There are also some secret marriages in this novel in that several of the characters enjoy the clandestine relationship of being latent doubles, or parts of a composite Henry James. As Leon Edel notes in his perceptive biography, "There is a kind of continuous endowment of the characters with aspects of their author and the questions arising in his life even as he was writing the book—as if he were putting on different hats and different neckties and looking at himself in a series of mirrors."[20] Any number of superficial points of resemblance between the author and his characters can be advanced. What will be Isabel's great adventure? Why, to go to Europe, as James did. And how will she amuse herself? She will do so, as Lord Warburton says, not by occupying herself with trifles. She will "select great materials; the foibles, the afflictions of human nature, the peculiarities of nations," like the creator of the international novel. And of course she hails from Albany. Little Ned Rosier, also a native of New York State, represents in his worship of the proprieties and his passion for delicate objects that side of James which might be termed "the precious." As for national identity, all of the major characters in the novel are Americans with the exception of Lord Warburton. The most nationalistic of them, Henrietta Stackpole, though she seems to be more of an "observed" than a "felt" character, resembles James superficially when at the end of the novel she decides to marry into England, as it were: "She was at last about to grapple in earnest with England," as James did. Of the many other minor biographical parallels which might be proposed, one more may serve as representative. The advice of Touchett Sr. to Ralph that he marry seems to correspond indirectly to a passage of a letter to James from his mother: "You know Father used to say to you, that if you would only fall in love it would be the making of you" (*James*, I, 47).

By themselves these minor biographical parallels prove little; they are of a kind to be found in the work of almost any novelist. And in seeming contradiction to the assertion that Isabel represents James is the author's avowal that the character of Isabel is based on his cousin, Minny Temple. Edel explains the correspondences at length (*James,* I, 426). Like Isabel, Minny has a "splendid shifting sensibility," "a serious mind," and she is "afraid of nothing." She was courted, or at least admired, by many men, including a future novelist (James), a future philosopher (William James), and a future Supreme Court Justice (Oliver Wendell Holmes). What Henry James seems to have admired most of all were her aspirations and her "noble flights" of mind, a metaphor which applies to another heroine commemorating Minny: Milly Theale (of *The Wings of the Dove*). But as Edel makes abundantly clear, Henry seems to have felt insufficiently masculine by comparison to Minny Temple's other admirers (as is borne out in the tale called "Poor Richard," which is also based on Henry's relationship with Minny). He did not seriously compete with the other males, preferring to worship Minny from a discreet distance until after she died of tuberculosis, at which time he could safely admit his great "love" for her—in much the same way that Stransom could love the dead better than the living in "Altar of the Dead."

Nevertheless, James *is* Isabel Archer, the passionate pilgrim to Europe. What James has done is to identify with certain qualities of mind and sensibility which he perceived in Minny Temple, including her femininity. That Isabel represents Henry James more than Minny Temple can be seen best in terms of the puritan strain in Isabel. When we are told early in the novel of the mysterious second door of the house in Albany, a "condemned" door which opens onto "the vulgar street" and which is secured "by bolts which a particularly slender little girl found it impossible to slide," the sexually symbolic language suggests that we have to do not with an inhibited Minny Temple but with essentially the same kind of person as Spencer Brydon in "The Jolly Corner." When Isabel experiences a deep sense of "dread" at the marriage proposal of Gilbert Osmond, the underlying significance of the metaphor she uses is unmistakable: the sharpness of the pain she feels suggests to her "the slipping of a fine bolt—backward, forward, she couldn't have said which." Nothing we know about Minny Temple leads us to believe that she felt with Isabel that "it was perfectly possible to be happy without the society of a more or less coarse-minded person of another sex." This is not Minny Temple but one side of Henry James speaking. Who else but James, in fact, might be capable of the imperturbable irony of the phrase "another sex"? How many sexes are there anyway?

To invoke the biological fact that there are only two sexes oversimplifies the veritable spectrum of psychosexual orientations represented in *Portrait*. Caspar Goodwood figures as James's conception of the masculine-masculine male. He presses Isabel. He is "plated and steeled, armed essentially for aggression." He is as "straight, strong and hard" as his name implies. Lord Warburton has more class but is hardly less masculine. Then there are masculine-feminine males like Ralph and Rosier and Osmond. The masculine-feminine females are represented by Henrietta Stackpole, Madame Merle, and Isabel Archer—all three possessing significant surnames. Pansy, whose name is also significant, might be said to round out the feminine-feminine extreme of the psychosexual spectrum, though she is child-like and not a mature woman.

Further consideration of the sexual orientations of some of these characters may be postponed in order to dwell on the mystery of Isabel's marriage and refusals of marriage. Her refusals of the truly acceptable men are little short of perverse and her reasons but rationalizations. At the time he first proposes, Goodwood is "the finest young man she had ever seen," and the fact that Isabel wishes to see more of life before making any marital commitment does not adequately account for the way she treats Goodwood, especially at the end of the novel. Her refusal of Warburton seems even more perverse, for he has advantages Goodwood lacks. When she tells Warburton that marrying him would amount to escaping "her fate," he quite reasonably asks, "Why should not *that* be your fate as well as anything else?" And Isabel gives a sigh of relief "at the thought that Mr. Touchett was one of those admirers who couldn't propose to marry her." There is more than dramatic irony at stake when Isabel decides to wed the man with "a genius for upholstery," as she later describes him; "a sterile dillettante," as Ralph calls him; an esthete who in spite of his putative amours says of himself in all innocence, "I myself am as rusty as a key that has no lock to fit it." Only James's great narrative skill makes this marriage even remotely plausible. His narrative skill includes the wisdom of saying as little as possible about the intimate, personal matters associated with marriage. Beneath the surface it makes sense, however. The dramatic rightness of the marriage lies in the fact that by marrying the New World (Isabel's innocence) to the Old World (Osmond's decadence) James exposes his heroine to grave risks of a kind which are quite different from the implied dangers of erotic love —the dangers she would have faced with more masculine men.

A better understanding of what these risks are and how they transcend the superb comedy of manners which *Portrait* displays can be gained by the realization that some of the major characters are not so much doubles of Henry James as they are doubles of each other which, taken together, added up to something like a composite psychological "portrait" of Henry James.

Two characters who overlap Osmond are Rosier and Madame Merle. The Countess Gemini (another symbolic name?) says to Madame Merle, "You're capable of anything, you and Osmond. I don't mean Osmond by himself, and I don't mean you by yourself. But together you're dangerous—like some chemical combination." And James leaves no doubt that without Madame Merle's arranging, Osmond would never have married Isabel. Of the two, Madame Merle is far the more active personality. Rosier can be described as an innocent Osmond. While he shares Osmond's passion for esthetic objects, his esteem for a dowry, and his concern for the proprieties (Osmond tells Isabel, "No, I'm not conventional; I'm convention itself"), Rosier lacks Osmond's cruelty and paranoid tendencies. Similarly, Isabel might be said to overlap Madame Merle in some ways. She becomes almost her protégée and takes Madame Merle as a model. What is said of Madame Merle, that "her will was mistress of her life," might also be said of Isabel. And Isabel perceives "a kind of maternal strain" in her feeling for Osmond early in their marriage that can be likened to the maternal concern which Madame Merle has for Osmond's welfare.

These overlappings are but minor clues to the extraordinary psychological interrelationships of the novel's cast. On the major scale there are three characters who form an important composite: Ralph, Isabel, and Osmond. When Ralph says of Isabel's decision to marry a man like Osmond, "It hurts me as if I had fallen myself!" he reveals the extent to which he not only hangs onto life long enough to see what will happen to *his* protégée but the extent to which he lives vicariously through Isabel. A passage which reveals the complementary attitudes of Isabel and Osmond occurs when she taunts him with wanting to make sure of Warburton as a husband for Pansy: she realizes that her words "made a comparison between Osmond and herself, recalled the fact that she had once held this coveted treasure [Warburton] in her hand and felt herself rich enough to let it fall." A fuller understanding of how these three characters relate to each other can be obtained by considering them together in the light of three themes: renunciation, narcissism, and what may be called "the spectator motif."

Renunciation is a pervasive theme in the works of Henry James. As a rule the act pertains to renunciation of sexual or aggressive behavior and often takes the specific form of renouncing marriage or revenge. It is never simply a negative act but one always replete with secondary gains. While Ralph Touchett's tuberculosis is ostensibly one of the données of the story (Minny Temple's illness has been displaced from Isabel onto Ralph), it serves him psychologically in much the same way that Henry James's psychosomatic "obscure hurt" served to reduce him to a mere observer of the battle of the sexes. In terms of defense, Ralph exhibits a self-imposed restriction of the ego: "A secret hoard of indifference—like a thick cake a fond old nurse might have slipped into his first school outfit—came to his aid and helped to reconcile him to sacrifice. . . . As he said to himself, there was really nothing he had wanted to do." The novel clothes Ralph's renunciation of the possibility of wooing Isabel in the vestiments of a quiet heroism. Of Isabel we are told near the end of the novel when she wishes to escape from her marriage but decides she must remain committed to it, "Deep in her soul—deeper than any appetite for renunciation—was the sense that life would be her business for a long time to come." Besides renouncing her freedom, she also gives up her powerful impulse to wreak revenge on Madame Merle in the scene at the convent. And enough has already been said about her rejection of virile suitors to indicate her renunciation of sexual passion, especially "white lightning" kisses from the potent Goodwood. Rather like Ralph, Osmond says that his life has been "as quiet as possible . . . Not to worry—not to strive nor struggle. To resign myself. To be content with little," and he speaks a few lines later of his "indifference" and of "my studied, my wilful renunciation." All three main characters—Ralph, Isabel, and Osmond—share a common inclination to renounce the ordinary fruits of life.

With respect to the theme of narcissism Ralph seems not to qualify. The only deed he performs which might betray any narcissism, apart from his vicarious self-glorification in boosting Isabel toward her high destiny, is the fact that in elevating her to wealth he obeys not so much the dictates of a generous heart as the unbridled impulse of a curious mind. Isabel's galloping narcissism is apparent enough. We soon learn that she is "liable to the sin of self-esteem," that she treats herself "to occasions of homage." Ralph twits her about thinking no suitor in the world too perfect for her, and James himself, as author, remarks with pungent humor after she has savored a bit of praise, "Her desire to think well of herself had at least the element of humility that it always needed to be supported by proof." But Isabel's egoism must be considered almost normal as compared to the delusions of grandeur which Osmond manifests. He believes himself to be simply "the most fastidious man alive," and his sister lets Isabel know that Osmond "has always appeared to believe that he's descended from the gods." Short of playing god, he would be the Pope, if he could—for the consideration he enjoys. Osmond's intense narcissism can be linked with his paranoid personality. He is incapable of loving anyone but himself. He is envious. He reveals his suspiciousness when he accuses Isabel of having intercepted Warburton's letter (proposing marriage to Pansy) and regards Isabel's intention of going to her cousin on his deathbed as nothing short of an adulterous affair with another man. While a full-fledged persecution complex cannot be descried, Osmond seems to believe that fortune has never dealt him all the good cards he deserves. When coupled with these aspects of his personality, Osmond's fastidiousness appears to reflect those tendencies to be associated with the repressed homosexuality underlying paranoia. In any case, Edel regards Isabel and Osmond as doubles on the grounds of their shared egotism: "Isabel and Osmond are then, for all their differences, two sides of the same coin, two studies in egotism—and a kind of egotism which belonged to their author." He says further:

> Strange as it may seem Osmond clearly expresses one side of Henry James—the hidden side—not as malignant as that of his creation but nevertheless that of the individual who abjures power by clothing it in meekness and deceptive docility. In this sense, Henry is the "original" of his villain. . . .Henry put into him his highest ambition and drive to power—the grandiose way in which he confronted his own destiny— while at the same time recognizing in his villain the dangers to which such inner absolutism might expose him. In the hands of a limited being, like Osmond, the drive to power ended in dilletantism and petty rages. In Henry's hands the same drive had given him unbounded creativity. (*James*, II, 426)

Fragmentation of the Mind

Even stronger than the common bonds of renunciation and narcissism which link these three characters is their shared preference for seeing rather than doing—the spectator motif. As a spectator of the human scene, Osmond does not compare with Isabel and Ralph, his impulse to look being limited almost entirely either to objets d'art which challenge his supersubtle sensibility or to seeing himself reflected in others. His only interest in others has a narcissistic basis, which the following contemplation of Isabel's suitability as a wife reveals: "What could be a happier gift in a companion than a quick, fanciful mind which saved one repetitions and reflected one's thought on a polished, elegant surface?" Isabel, in contrast, is possessed by a consuming interest in the human scene. She has "an immense curiosity about life" and is "constantly staring and wondering." She worries about "her possible grossness of perception" and hopes her experience of Europe will refine her vision of life. When Ralph remarks on how much she wants to "see life" and drain "the cup of experience," Isabel answers that she is afraid the cup may be poisoned and remarks, "I only want to see for myself." To this answer Ralph acutely replies, "You want to see, but not to feel." Isabel rejoins, "I don't think that if one's a sentient being one can make the distinction" and thereupon declares her intention—like Henrietta—not to marry "till I've seen Europe." Henry James tended to make no distinction between seeing and feeling, either. For him, as Edel says, "to look was to feel." Edel argues that James "is concerned above all with things his eyes can rest upon" (*James*, II, 54-55). And only James, as Max Beerbohm implies in the funniest parody ever written, only James could rest the full weight of his observant eyes so heavily upon "the mote in the middle-distance."

The chief spectator of the novel is Ralph Touchett. It is "this sweet-tasting property of the observed thing in itself," we are told, that initially stirs Ralph's interest in Isabel. Later on he reminds Isabel that being her cousin gives him privileges: "What's the use of adoring you without hope of a reward if I can't have a few compensations? What's the use of being ill and disabled and restricted to mere spectatorship at the game of life if I really can't see the show when I've paid so much for my ticket?" He will content himself, he informs her, "with watching you—with the deepest interest." The substitution of passive watching for active loving is pointed up when Ralph tells his dying father that he would like to put "a little wind in her sails" by giving Isabel money so that he may "see her going before the breeze." Touchett Sr. sighs, "Young men are very different from what I was. When I cared

for a girl—when I was young—I wanted to do more than look at her."
Looking at Isabel continues to be Ralph's main reason for being:
"What kept Ralph alive was simply the fact that he had not yet seen
enough of the person in the world in whom he was most interested: he
was not yet satisfied. There was more to come: he couldn't make up his
mind to lose that. He wanted to see what she would make of her
husband. . . . This was only the first act of the drama, and he was
determined to sit out the performance." Like Ralph, Henry James is
the spectator par excellence, almost the novelist as voyeur, as his
famous critical conceit of the "house of fiction" in the preface to
Portrait reveals if the sexual implications of its metaphors are borne in
mind:

> The house of fiction has in short not one window, but a million—a
> number of possible windows not to be reckoned, rather; every one of
> which has been pierced, or is still pierceable, in its vast front, by the
> need of the individual vision and by the pressure of the individual will.
> These apertures, of dissimilar shape and size, hang so, all together, over
> the human scene that we might have expected of them a greater same-
> ness of report than we find. They are but windows at the best, mere
> holes in a dead wall, disconnected, perched aloft; they are not hinged
> doors opening straight upon life. But they have this mark of their own
> that at each of them stands a figure with a pair of eyes, or at least with
> a field-glass, which forms, again and again, for observation, a unique
> instrument, insuring to the person making use of it an impression dis-
> tinct from every other. . . . The spreading field, the human scene, is the
> "choice of subject"; the pierced aperture, either broad or balconied or
> slit-like and low-browed, is the "literary form"; but they are, singly or
> together, as nothing without the posted presence of the watcher—
> without, in other words, the consciousness of the artist.

Small wonder it is that James became famous for his contributions to
the handling of point of view.

Enough of the threads connecting the various characters in *The
Portrait of a Lady* to each other and to James have been unravelled to
demonstrate that there are many separate figures in the carpet of the
novel which, taken together, form a special configuration, a psychological self-portrait of the artist—or a portrait, at least, of orientations at
war within him. The kind of fragmentation of the mind in this work
is representative of many other works of James. Thus, while decomposition more often takes dual forms, it may also be multiple, as in
Macbeth, and *Othello.*

CHAPTER VI

The Paths of Ambivalence

An individual suffering from internal conflict often attempts to deal with contradictory impulses by developing separate personality constellations, fairly well defined ones in the case of autoscopic vision and multiple personality. In literature these separate constellations take the form of characters representing manifest or latent doubles. Our attention has focused thus far on subject doubles, where the decomposition reflects a division of the self. As common in literature is object doubling, the division—or "split-vision"—in these instances being of other individuals. While the dynamics of object doubling are always ultimately subjective in origin (the split symbolizing conflicting attitudes on the part of the perceiver rather than significant dualities in the object), it is useful to label this kind of decomposition as objective to distinguish it from the other basic type.

Doubling by division of objects occurs without exception as a result of the perceiver's ambivalence toward the object, though this rule does not hold true for the doubling by multiplication of objects. The composite person who is perceived as component persons is always a love object in the usual sense of that phrase in psychoanalysis. More accurately, he is a love-hate object, the object of conflicting emotions so powerful that the unstable perceiver cannot tolerate the resultant anxiety. The perceiver attempts to dispel this anxiety by the magical gesture

109

of separating the seemingly untidy whole into tidy compartments. Actuality is denied, a good-bad father becoming in the sublogic of the primary process the good, loved father and the bad, hated father. F. Scott Fitzgerald once remarked that it is a sign of a first-rate intelligence to be able to entertain two opposed ideas in one's mind at the same time and yet maintain an ability to function. Correspondingly, it is a sign of a healthy, mature mind to be able to tolerate the opposed emotions of love and hate toward a single individual at the same time, or over a period of time, without suffering an incapacitating conflict as a result. Children, neurotics, psychotics—and all of us to some extent—find it difficult to follow a single path in our relations with love objects, and in emotional confusion we allow our feelings to diverge into separate paths.

Any person regarded with ambivalent feelings might, in theory, be decomposed. In practice, only original incestuous object-choices are decomposed: mother, father, siblings (normally of the opposite sex), or surrogates of these figures. Object doubling of siblings of the same sex is rare. The brother doubles of Farquhar's *The Twin-Rivals,* for example, fall into the category of subject rather than object doubles, much as in the case of the brother doubles in Hogg's *Justified Sinner* and the twins in "Alice Doane's Appeal." There is a simple reason why most object doubles are parent figures. Just as psychoanalysis is essentially a child psychology in the sense that it regards most basic conflicts, values, and attitudes of adult life as having their origin in childhood, so in the psychology of literature we discover that the protagonist is almost invariably a son or a daughter figure. Whatever the point of view used in telling the story, in the formal sense, the psychological point of view is usually that of the child, regardless of the protagonist's chronological age. *King Lear* provides a striking example of the validity of this generalization, for psychoanalytic studies show that the play about the old man who made mothers of his daughters deals more in the psychology of the child than that of geriatrics, its seeming emphasis on the sharp serpent's tooth of filial ingratitude notwithstanding.

While object doubles are usually restricted to parent figures, there is no reason to accept Stanley M. Coleman's assertion that only women perceive object doubles. He states in his discussion of the earlier work of Capgras: "It has been established that in an unbalanced mental state, subjective decomposition is liable to occur in men with the postulation of a double of the self. In women, on the contrary, under psychic stress decomposition of the object is the more likely mechanism."[1] Coleman's argument is unwarranted because subject decomposition occurs in female multiple personality, as we have seen in the Eve and Beauchamp cases. The same holds true for autoscopic vision. The fiction of such authors as Virginia Woolf and Emily Brönte indicates that subject decomposition takes place in literature told from a female point of view.[2] And there are many instances of object doubling in literature where male authors and characters are concerned.

When doubling by division of the subject takes place, the component figures usually number no more than three or four, as is true in the phenomenon of multiple personality. When doubling by multiplication of the object occurs, the number of component figures may often exceed four, as the proliferation of paternal figures in *Billy Budd* illustrates (Chapter 8). An extreme and comical instance of the enumeration of father figures which the human mind can imagine appears in Freud's study of Dr. Schreber, a paranoid personality who believed himself to be God's wife and thought that his mission to redeem the world and restore its lost state of bliss could take place if he were first transformed from a man into a woman.[3] God, no simple entity, can be divided into "upper" and "lower" God, according to Dr. Schreber's delusional system; similarly, the soul of Dr. Flechsig, one of the patient's physicians, is divided into "upper Flechsig," "middle Flechsig," and "lower Flechsig." These categories reflect doubling by division. But reflecting doubling by multiplication and illustrating the extreme is the delusional assumption that as many as "forty to sixty sub-divisions of the Flechsig soul" were in existence! We learn, happily, that when God came to appreciate Dr. Schreber better "a raid was made upon the souls, which had become multiplied into a nuisance. As a result of this, the Flechsig soul survived in only one or two shapes." Such a doubling by multiplication of objects probably stems from wish fulfillment rather than ambivalence. If so, doubling by multiplication may be a "doubling from anxiety" in a manner analogous to the common symbolization of castration anxiety by a series of phallic objects, in which loss, or feared loss, is represented by its opposite.

Ridiculous as Dr. Schreber's host of Flechsig souls may sound to the normal person, the example nevertheless reveals with great clarity an aspect of the way the human mind works at times. Fairy tales are also revealing in this respect.

111

The moral of the cautionary tale called "Little Red Riding Hood" warns young girls not to stray from the straight and narrow path in order to pick symbolic flowers in a symbolic forest lest they be attacked by a symbolic wolf. Red Riding Hood, though of indeterminate years, must be about the age of puberty. Thus, the sexual moral of the tale lies not very far below the surface of the ethical moral: the mother's warning that straying from the path may cause her daughter to fall and break the wine bottle signifies the mother's concern about her daughter's possible defloration (compare the breaking of a glass by the bridegroom at a Jewish wedding ceremony). Why, then, does the hungry wolf fail to ravish Red Riding Hood on the spot when he first meets her in the forest and afterwards go on to gobble up the grandmother instead of going to all the trouble of impersonating the grandmother in order to beguile Little Red Riding Hood into his clutches in the bedroom? The answer lies in the presence of more primitive sexual ideas in the story. If allowance be made for a considerable amount of distorting displacement in the story and if certain erroneous conceptions of the child about the nature of sexuality in general and birth in particular be kept in mind, then the full meaning of the bedroom and rescue scenes becomes clear. When the mother tells Red Riding Hood not to peer into the corners of her grandmother's bedroom, she is warning her away from the primal scene. Intercourse is represented by eating, or incorporation. Fathers may be mothers, and birth is from the viscera rather than the womb. The huntsman's operation on the sleeping wolf's belly is really an obstetrical one, and the stones which are used to replace the rescued grandmother and girl have the same symbolic value as stones in the Ducalion myth (compare the similar meaning of the operation on the wolf in "The Wolf and the Seven Kids"). As for doubling, the father has been decomposed in this fairy tale into the sexual bad father, the wolf, and the desexualized good father, the huntsman, while the grandmother is a double by multiplication of the mother. Understanding the function of object decomposition helps us to grasp the way in which this familiar cautionary tale deals below the surface with parental intercourse and fantasied incest.[4]

A revealing examination of doubling by division of the mother can be found in Marie Bonaparte's commentary on Poe's horror story, "The Black Cat."[5] Readers of this grisly tale will recall that the narrator confesses to several sadistic crimes, which include the cutting out of an eye of his pet cat, Pluto, later hanging it from a tree limb, and eventually murdering his wife in a fit of rage as she tries to prevent his destruction of a second pet cat. At the end of the story the second cat betrays the hiding place of the wife's body, immurred in the cellar, by screeching while the police inspect the premises. According to Bonaparte, we find the mother in "The Black Cat" split into three "characters": the slayer's wife, Pluto, and the second cat. Bonaparte adds:

> Each of these mothers has her own characteristics, as well as others common to all three. Though all three are symbolically castrated, either genitally, or by the loss of an eye, thus declaring themselves all mothers, there was a time when Pluto had perfect eyes, a time of more virility than the second cat ever knew, though likewise a male. Thus, the three forms of the mother, in the tale, paint the mother from different angles. Pluto is first the phallic mother, at the time the small boy really believed in his mother's penis. But once Pluto has been symbolically castrated by the man, once the mother has been punished for introducing castration into the world, as witnessed by her body, the second cat appears with the large white splotch on its chest. This second cat represents the nursing mother pleading for pardon by her milk, by her life-giving breasts in lieu of the penis. Finally, in the murderer's wife, we see the mother's original human form emerge from under its totemic cat-disguise, in the same way that, with the ancient gods, the original form of the father reappears under their primitive totemic guises. And the double murder, that of the wife after Pluto, clearly reveals who, in the first place, in cat form, was slain.

The measure of authority with which Marie Bonaparte speaks can only be taken by those who have read her entire volume on Poe. What concerns us at the moment, assuming the validity of her analysis, is the way in which the decomposition by Poe of his mother in this story reflects the enduring ambivalence he felt toward the mother for whom he continued to yearn and whom he continued to hate because of her "abandonment" of him at the tender age of three, when she died of tuberculosis. Of interest, too, is the way in which the attitudes toward the mother find expression in distinct versions of her, namely, the bad, hated, phallic mother; the good, loved, nursing mother; and the wife surrogate-mother.

A recent study of James's *The Ambassadors* reveals Mrs. Newsome, Maria Gostrey, and Mme. de Vionnet to be a subtly modulated series of mother surrogates for Lambert Strether.[6] The imposing, domineering Mrs. Newsome can be viewed as a repressing, threatening mother who will deprive Strether of the remnants of his manhood if he marries her. Even her nurturing function has been corrupted insofar as the nurture must be monetary. When Strether encounters Maria Gostrey and Mme. de Vionnet in the course of his ambassadorial journey, which is also a flight from the awful arms of Mrs. Newsome, he responds to a mixture of the pre-oedipal and oedipal mother in them in the sense that both offer sustenance with an erotic flavor, the nurturing function being more apparent in Maria and the erotic one in Mme. de Vionnet. As the novel progresses Strether moves away from the incapacitating forces of repression in the direction of autonomy, stability, and sublimation of drives through the fine though passive art of "spectatorship." Thus, Strether's journey proves to be psychosexual as well as geographical. He can never achieve full growth or arrive at the community where body and mind live together in true harmony, however, because his ambivalence toward women can never be fully overcome in a manner which will allow him to reconcile the more deeply needed nurturing attributes of the mother with her more frightening erotic potentialities. As Freud said, the incest taboo must be overcome through marriage.

Heinz Kohut devotes crucial portions of his analysis of Thomas Mann's *Death in Venice* to explaining decomposition of the father in the work.[7] He suggests that the loathing which Aschenbach feels for the four men he encounters, the apparition in the cemetery, the aged freak on the boat, the gondolier, and the street singer, reflects the child's hostile attitude toward his father combined with a secondary fear of retaliation from the stronger figure (another example, incidentally, of an elderly protagonist whose story actually reflects the psychology of the child). Kohut speaks of Mann's ambivalent attitudes toward the father and father surrogates and argues that father conflict is the central theme underlying *Death in Venice*. He concludes this part of his discussion by saying that

> the father theme is dealt with in *Death in Venice* by splitting the ambivalently revered and despised figure and by isolating the opposed feelings that were originally directed to the same object—a typical compulsive mechanism. The bad, threatening, sexually active father is embodied in the four men Aschenbach encounters. With the good one, who foregoes threats and punishment and heterosexual love—with the father, that is, who loves only the son—Aschenbach identifies himself, portraying in his love for Tadzio what he wished he had received from his father.

This love, as Kohut points out and as the story reveals, is homosexual in mode. Lest there be any confusion, it should be noted that in this work the doubling by multiplication of similar bad fathers does stem from ambivalence even though not all doubling by multiplication has such a cause, and except for the rather special circumstances of the protagonist himself playing a father role by identifying with him, the good father as an independent character is, strictly speaking, missing. While it is useful for purposes of illustration to select literary works which present contrasting halves of the good-bad father, decomposition can be said to occur in a narrative representing only one-half of the decomposed parent figure.[8]

Few novels can rival *David Copperfield* when it comes to sheer enumeration of object doubles. The book contains a veritable galaxy of father, mother, and wife figures, according to Leonard F. Manheim.[9] Mr. Murdstone, Wilkins Micawber, Esq., Mr. Creakle, Dr. Strong, Mr. Quinion, Mick Walker, Mr. Richard Babley, Mr. Wickfield, and Daniel Peggotty all serve, in one way or another, as father figures. Manheim regards Daniel Peggotty as "no attempt at analysis of the father-figure, no attack upon the father as enemy, but the final idealization of what a father ought to be, uncontaminated by social position, unhampered by poverty or indolence, untrammeled by introversion, unhindered by anything which would prevent his being the kind of passionately loving and all-wise father for which the adolescent soul of the author yearned unceasingly." Among the mother figures are Mrs. Crupp, Mrs. Crewler, the mother of Uriah Heep, Clara Peggotty, and Betsey Trotwood. As for wife figures, "even apart from Dora, the novel is replete with child-wives. What is worse, they are constantly in the habit of growing up, losing their innocence in one way or another, and joining the despised class of 'the other sort of woman.' "[10] Though only object doubles are at issue at the moment, Manheim points to a host of son figures which would fall into our category of subject doubles. David himself seems a curiously "empty" hero, says Manheim, because Dickens has broken up his protagonist into too many pieces, into a number of "hero-caricatures instead of one complete hero. . . . If we examine Uriah Heep we find that he is everything that David is not, with one single exception—he too reaches adolescence and maturity without the assistance of a father. Uriah has committed the fatal error of rejecting the 'good' father substitute, Mr. Wickfield, modeling himself exactly on his own 'bad' father." Other fragments of the hero are James Steerforth, Tommy Traddles, and Ham Peggotty.

Manifest subject doubling in Oscar Wilde's *Dorian Gray* was considered earlier. Latent object doubling in his *Salomé* offers an example of father decomposition from the viewpoint of a female protagonist.[11] In addition to Salomé's "real" father, strangled by his brother, Herod, so that Herod might assume the throne of the kingdom of Judea, two other father figures appear as a result of Salomé's lust and hatred: King Herod himself and the prophet Jokanaan. While Salomé scorns the scarcely veiled sexual advances of her stepfather (and uncle) because of the incest taboo, she chooses to lust after the old prophet rather than bestow her affection on a man of her own age, such as the Syrian captain of royal blood who adores her. She exhibits no modesty in her advances to the prophet, saying, "I am amorous of thy body, Jokanaan." What she does repress is the incestuous nature of her impulse, for Jokanaan represents a paternal type to her. The incest taboo involved is symbolized by the taboo which Herod has established in forbidding anyone to speak to the prophet. Besides being a father figure for Salomé, Jokanaan stands, in his purity and piety, as a representative of the superego which Salomé has introjected from her father, and in his superego role Jokanaan condemns the adulterous and incestuous behavior of Herodias, Herod's wife and Salomé's mother. When Salomé dances with naked feet for King Herod by way of symbolically fulfilling his erotic desires in return for the decapitated head of Jokanaan, she achieves symbolic incest with Herod, acquires the male penis which Jokanaan's head represents, and gains revenge on Jokanaan for thwarting her incestuous desire (not to mention revenge on her mother by coming into total possession of the father) by symbolically castrating him. Thus the decomposition of the father into Herod and Jokanaan allows for the possibility of dramatizing both the fairly overt denial of, and covert satisfaction of, an incest taboo, which is bad logic but good theater and good psychology.

As Frederick Crews observes in his book on Hawthorne, the protagonist of "My Kinsman, Major Molineux" finds himself virtually bombarded with paternal types as he searches the city for his mysterious kinsman.[12] This brilliant story, now widely recognized as one of Hawthorne's best, might be called a miniature classic with respect to its portrayal of the young man's ambivalent attitudes toward the father. The first indication of hostility toward the psychological father comes in the initial paragraph of the story where Hawthorne treats the reader to a brief history of the rebellions of the Massachusetts colonists against their governors. Major Molineux himself, who has offered to act as a substitute father for Robin by setting him up in life, is just such a governor, against whom the populace rebels by tar-and-feathering the old man. Robin joins the rebellion against this authority figure by participating in the mockery at the climax of the tale. While he is on the surface a polite and respectful lad, Robin's unconscious oedipal aggression can be discerned in his impulses to cudgel the series of father figures he meets who are rude to him when he inquires after his kinsman. Among these figures are the old man with the cane, the watchman with the spiked staff, and the mysterious double-faced devil figure who leads the dream pageant near the end of the story. All of them are bad or at least hostile fathers. Two characters symbolize the good, kind father: first, Robin's actual clergyman father whose household he symbolically leaves in order to make his way in the world and, second, the kindly gentleman of an "open, intelligent, cheerful, and altogether prepossessing countenance" whom Robin meets by the church and who offers to help the young man. The nature of Major Molineux' unnamed crimes can be inferred from the important scene in which the attractive prostitute who tempts Robin claims to be the Major's housekeeper; in the eyes of the son the father's crimes are sexual and—as the hostility of some of the other fathers in the story indicates—aggressive. Symbolic of Robin's ambivalence toward his father is the divided face, half red and half black, of the devil figure and the soft reminder of the kindly gentleman that a man may have several voices "as well as two complexions," a remark which would seem to apply also to Major Molineux. It is no exaggeration to say that were it not for the presence of object decomposition, there would be hardly any substance or drama at all to this story, which as it stands is masterful.

Just as Robin's repeated encounters with the father in this tale represent, in terms of the narrative present, the love and hatred of the father which dates back to the oedipal period of childhood, there being no necessary correlation between the time setting of a fictional work and the psychological time setting, so in perhaps the greatest of all dramas concerning father-son conflict the present action of the play is really a symbolic action recapitulating the crime against the father—which the play depicts as having occurred in the chronological past. I refer to *Oedipus Rex*. James Schroeter points out that the four *agons* of the drama, those which Oedipus has with Teiresias, Creon, the Messen-

117

ger, and the Herdsman, symbolize Oedipus' aggression against Laius by virtue of the fact that these four characters all function as symbolic father figures.[13] There are two main clues which indicate that they perform this function. The first is their age. All of them are of Laius' generation or older: Creon is Oedipus' uncle (and we know the uncle to be a common substitute for the psychological father) and the other three characters, especially Teiresias, are repeatedly referred to as being "old." The second clue to the common function of the four adversaries lies in the activity they perform in Oedipus' behalf: "Besides being old, they function in some conserving or protecting capacity towards him that can be referred to, at least metaphorically, as 'life-giving.'" In the case of the Messenger, who gave the baby to Polybus and Merope, and the Herdsman, who saved the child instead of exposing him as directed, this function seems obvious. Creon's role in this respect is more indirect; it is that of the avuncular counselor who gives Oedipus good, sound, practical advice and helps him rule the realm. Teiresias' conserving role consists of his having allowed Oedipus to assume and enjoy his position as king and husband by maintaining silence about Oedipus' origin. The threats of violence which Oedipus makes to these men (except for the Messenger) stem from his unconscious antagonism and are part and parcel of his hubris, for old men were always to be treated respectfully in the culture represented. Besides, Teiresias himself is a direct representative of a god.

Not only does Schroeter's analysis of the symbolic action of the drama correlate with the anthropological view of the play, which regards the *agons* as enacting the ritual contest between the young king and the old king as part of a fertility ritual, it also enhances the standard psychological assumption that the play depicts fantasied wishes and fears rather than actual deeds. The unravelling of the crime resembles the struggle in psychoanalytic therapy of the act of recovering the past, and it resembles the transference situation in which the patient acts out his infantile conflicts in relation to the therapist. In the present context the play represents object doubling by division with Polybus and Merope standing as surrogates of the actual parents and object doubling by multiplication in portraying Teiresias, Creon, the Messenger, and the Herdsman as a series of bad fathers threatened by the protagonist. Once Schroeter has called attention to this aspect of the symbolic action in the dramatic present of the play it seems so obvious that one wonders how critics could have ignored it for so long. The importance of Schroeter's commentary makes it of particular interest that he was led to his insights after considering Ernest Jones's discussion of decomposition in *Hamlet*.

The same kind of representation in the dramatic present of "past" psychological conflict that appears in the works just discussed, which is not exceptional but common, of course, can be seen worked out in great complexity in Shakespeare's Henry IV and V plays. Similarly, the symbolic action takes place between decomposed father and son figures. Ernst Kris analyzes these splittings in considerable detail.[14] He perceives that Henry IV and Falstaff are complementary father figures, while Prince Hal and Hotspur constitute complementary sons. Rebellion in the realm, with Hotspur at the head of it, signifies Prince Hal's unconscious patricidal impulse, though in defending the King and saving his life the Prince ostensibly figures as the loyal, obedient son. When the Prince kills Henry Percy in battle, he kills his alter ego, as the lines the Prince speaks just before they fight bear out:

> Two stars keep not their motion in one sphere,
> Nor can one England brook a double reign
> Of Harry Percy and the Prince of Wales.

An explicit dramatization of the Prince's patricidal impulse can be discerned in the crucial deathbed scene. Henry IV lies on his deathbed, and the Prince, assuming him already dead, addresses his apostrophe to the crown before removing it to the next room. When the King awakes, he demands to know why his son took the crown and says to his other children, "See, Sons, what things you are!" Questioned, Prince Hal replies, "I never thought to hear you speak again." "Thy wish was father, Harry, to that thought," the King answers, and accuses his son of hiding "a thousand daggers" in his thoughts. According to Kris, "Falstaff is closer to the Prince's heart than the King; he satisfies the libidinal demands in the father-son relation through his warmth and freedom." Yet the Prince triumphs over both fathers, says Kris, proving "superior" to Falstaff in wit and revelling as well as superior to the King in royal dignity when he ascends the throne. Besides these decomposed figures, Kris points out that Henry IV himself is a son figure who wrests the throne from his symbolic father, Richard II, by rebellion and regicide, a burden of guilt for which Henry V later tries to make restitution (see *Henry V*, IV. i).

Kris's analysis may be supplemented in various ways. To begin with, Prince John is not only a literal son of Henry IV but another alter ego of Prince Hal, as we see when Falstaff makes invidious comparisons between the "sober-blooded boy" who does not love him and drinks no wine (Prince John) and the "hot and valiant" Prince Harry, concluding, "If I had a thousand sons, the first humane principle I would teach them should be to foreswear thin potations, and to addict themselves to sack" (*II Henry IV,* IV.iv.). Another father surrogate is the Chief Justice, who sends the naughty Prince Hal to prison for his misdeeds. When the Prince becomes king, he commends the Chief Justice for his impartial resolution, recognizes that he was but an instrument of the King, and declares to the old man, "There is my hand. /You shall be as a father to my youth" (II *Henry IV,* V.ii.). Thus when the Chief Justice twits Falstaff about his pretended youth ("Is not your voice broken? Your wind short? Your chin double? Your wit single? And every part about you blasted with antiquity?"), we have a good father, emblematic of justice, order, and restraint, condeming a bad, Saturnalian father, a Lord of Misrule. There is one scene which cannot be ignored in any discussion of decomposition in these plays, the one in which the Prince and Falstaff "play" at father and son, exchanging roles midway. "Do thou stand for my father and examine me upon the particulars of my life," says the Prince. And Falstaff says,

> That thou art my son, I have partly thy mother's
> word, partly my own opinion, but chiefly a
> villainous trick of thine eye, and a foolish
> hanging of thy nether lip, that doth warrant me.
> If then thou be son to me, here lies the point;
> why, being son to me, art thou so pointed at?
> Shall the blessed sun of heaven prove a micher
> [truant] and eat blackberries? A question not
> to be asked. Shall the son of England prove a
> thief and take purses? A question to be asked.
> There is a thing, Harry, which thou hast often
> heard of, and it is known to many in our land
> by the name of pitch. This pitch, as ancient
> writers do report, doth defile; so doth the
> company thou keepest. (I *Henry IV*. II.iv.)

Then, in a section sprinkled with father and son references, the Prince plays his own father—thereby "deposing" the king—while Falstaff, pretending to be Prince Hal, is treated to a series of taunts which he more than deserves and which are ultimately directed toward the father imagined to be cowardly, corrupt, and licentious.

The duplicitous Falstaff not only has a double chin but he at once denies and affirms that he is "a double man." This passage occurs just after Falstaff has counterfeited death in battle and then pretended that he himself killed Hotspur. "Thou art not what thou seem'st," says the Prince, and Falstaff replies:

> No, that's certain, I am not a double man. But if I
> be not Jack Falstaff, then I am a Jack. There is
> Percy. If your father will do me any honor, so; if
> not, let him kill the next Percy himself. I look
> to be either earl or duke, I can assure you.

A Jack, as Falstaff knows, is "a knave" and "a Jacques," or privy, in Elizabethan slang (compare with the contemporary "john"). But the point to be stressed here is that the complexity of decomposition in this play is such that Falstaff cannot be regarded simply as "a depreciated father figure," as Kris recognizes. Such a view of him would be superficial and inaccurate because he is both good and bad, both looked up to and looked down at, to be pitied and condemned, to be loved and mocked. In some ways, in fact, he is a better man than the Prince's actual father. Even Falstaff's sexual status is ambiguous, as his name implies, for he is both a fallen, impotent, fustian bag of guts and a robust lecher whose eating, drinking, and farting are but the oral and anal analogs of his alleged genital prowess with Mistress Quickly and Doll Tearsheet. Exactly the same kind of ambiguity obtains with respect to Prince Hal as a good son/ bad son. His roistering is healthy, yet bad form for a Prince, and he is both the loyal son and the rebel. He is, ultimately, the complete son, the psychologically well developed young man when considered in all of his aspects, especially as a mature man in *Henry V*: valiant in battle, wise in council, and persuasive when he woos Katherine.

With the exception of *Salomé* and *Oedipus Rex* the libidinal determinants of object doubling have received little attention. On the surface, most of the works considered have little to do with overt sexuality, the libidinal elements finding expression less in plot than in such apparent "trimmings" as metaphor. In the Henry IV plays, for example, the psychological mother does not appear in any important

121

character, and the libidinal rivalry between Falstaff and Prince Hal is dramatized in an indirect fashion, such as in the series of derogatory (and symbolically castrating) phallic epithets which fat old Sir John addresses at one point to the Prince: " 'Sblood, you starveling, you elf skin, you dried neat's tongue, you bull's pizzle, you stockfish! Oh, for breath to utter what is like thee! You tailor's yard, you sheath, you bow case, you vile standing tuck [a rapier stuck in the ground]" (I *Henry IV,* II.iv.). Therefore this section on object doubling concludes with an analysis of decomposition in a play which depicts the oedipal situation with relative completeness—even to the point of emphasizing parental sexual activity.

Ambivalence toward parents as sexual actors and objects in Aeschylus' version of the Orestes myth accounts for their being split up into four figures, the classic constellation of good and bad fathers and good and bad mothers. As in *Hamlet,* the father whose death and sexual betrayal by Clytemnestra must be revenged represents the good, desexualized father.[15] Again as in *Hamlet,* the man who betrays the King sexually and assumes his throne constitutes the bad, lustful father; in fact Aegisthus' main dramatic and psychological function in the play is to serve as stud for the lecherous Clytemnestra. That Clytemnestra represents the bad, sexual mother—comparable to Gertrude—need hardly be labored. She also represents the pre-oedipal phallic mother, as we shall see. The good, kind, pure, nourishing, loving mother, for whom there would appear to be no counterpart in *Hamlet,* is symbolized by a minor character known simply as the Nurse. Her lament when she supposes Orestes to be dead reveals her mothering functions with perfect clarity:

> But my Orestes!. . .Bless his heart, he wore me out,
> I reared him, took him new-born from his mother's arms.
> And oh! the times he shouted at me in the night,
> Made me get up, and bothered me with this and that—
> And all my hopes for nothing! Why, you understand,
> A baby knows no better; you must nurse it, then,
> Like a dumb animal, whatever way seems best.
> A child in the cradle can't explain what troubles it;
> Whether it wants to eat, to drink, or to make water,
> A baby's inside takes no orders; it's too young.
> Well, often I could tell; and often, too, I know,
> I guessed it wrong; and then I'd have to wash his things,
> For nurse and laundress both were the same pair of hands.

> So I did double duty; yes, and I brought up
> Orestes for his father. And now, to hear of this,
> Orestes dead!

It might be noted that the Nurse's psychological importance as a mother double far outweighs her relatively minor dramatic value as a foil to Clytemnestra.

The psychological relationship between Orestes and Clytemnestra can be understood in terms of the queen's dream of giving birth to a snake, a dream which disturbs her so much she causes libations to be poured upon her husband's grave. The chorus of the Choephori tells Orestes about the dream. After the birth of the snake, "she wrapped it in shawls and lulled it to rest like a little child." Orestes asks, "Surely this new-born monster needed food—what food?" The chorus replies, "She herself, in her dream, gave it her breast to suck." Then Orestes says, "Her nipple surely was wounded by its loathsome fang?" And the chorus replies, "Yes; with her milk the creature drew forth clots of blood." At this point Orestes endeavors to interpret the dream:

> First, if this snake came forth from the same place as I,
> And, as though human, was then wrapped in infant-clothes,
> Its gaping mouth clutching the breast that once fed me;
> If it then mingled the sweet milk with curds of blood,
> And made her shriek with terror—why, it means that she
> Who nursed this obscene beast must die by violence;
> I must transmute my nature, be viperous in heart and act!
> The dream commands it: I am her destined murderer.

While Orestes' interpretation is accurate enough, it analyzes the dream the way he wants it analyzed. His interpretation is by no means complete. If we keep in mind the phallic symbolism of the dream snake, the anatomical point from which it issues forth, the relevance of the equation body equals phallus, and the assumption that one direction of the movement of the snake is represented by movement in the opposite direction, then the sword with which Orestes stabs his mother at exactly the same anatomical point that the dream snake bites Clytemnestra must necessarily be phallic as well. The oral-sadistic implications of the dream are undisguised, but the phallic significance of it is considerably distorted by displacement. Hamlet but speaks "daggers" to his mother in the bedroom scene; Orestes stabs his mother. And the stabbing symbolizes incest as well as aggression.

123

Without reference to Clytemnestra's dream and on the basis of a quite different set of data, including both an examination of other versions of the Orestes myth and case histories of actual matricide, Henry A. Bunker arrives at the same conclusion: matricide symbolizes incest, particularly in the Orestes story.[16]

Thus both the dream and the crime, in condensed form, embody the ambivalence—the lust and hate—which Orestes feels toward his mother. The dream also depicts one of his conceptions of the mother, namely that she possesses a phallus. For Clytemnestra, too, the dream has that meaning. Throughout the play great stress is laid on her masculine personality traits and behavior. She knows "how to dip hot steel." Clytemnestra, "in whose woman's heart / A man's will nurses hope," demonstrates her superior will when she makes her husband walk on the purple carpet against his wishes. She claims to use "a woman's words," but the Chorus says, "Madam, your words are like a man's." And Cassandra asks, "What? will cow gore bull?" These examples of Clytemnestra's aggressiveness, which could be multiplied, add up to the inference that unlike her very feminine sister, Helen, Clytemnestra has a masculine personality, one rather like that of the "unsexed" Lady Macbeth. At issue here, from the son's point of view, is the role confusion generated by the mother's aggressive sexual behavior combined with the pre-oedipal fear of the threatening, castrating, phallic mother. It is significant that, with reference to her use of a hunter's net to snare her husband before the kill, Clytemnestra is repeatedly compared to a spider (a common dream symbol of the phallic mother), and Orestes himself likens her to

> a sting ray or an adder,
> Her sole touch, without fangs, would have gangrened some victim
> In virtue of mere savagery and natural venom.

The Furies function as doubles of the phallic mother. Born as a result of the castration of Uranus by Cronus and called upon to punish the crimes of parricide and perjury, they appear to Orestes "like Gorgons, with grey cloaks, / And snakes coiled swarming round their bodies." They symbolize not only superego projections of Orestes' guilt for symbolic incest and patricide, plus actual matricide; they also depict the mother as castrator, as the comparison of them to Gorgons indicates. Freud analyzes this motif of the Gorgons as castrating mothers in "Medusa's Head."[17] To decapitate means to castrate. Perseus per-

124

forms the task of undoing castration anxiety by castrating the castrator. In the process he must use his shield as a mirror in order not to look at Medusa directly, for to do so would mean death. "The terror of Medusa is thus a terror of castration that is linked to the sight of something," the sight by a boy of the female genitals surrounded by hair. Medusa's snaky hair derives from the castration complex, the snakes serving paradoxically "as a mitigation of the horror, for they replace the penis, the absence of which is the cause of the horror." Since the sight of Medusa's head turns the spectator to stone, another defense against anxiety is embodied in the myth: the spectator "is still in possession of a penis, and the stiffening reassures him of the fact." In view of the help which Orestes receives from Pallas Athena when he is being judged for his crime, it is interesting to note that Freud calls attention to the emblem of Medusa's head which Athena wears pinned to her dress ("and rightly so, for thus she becomes a woman who is unapproachable and repels all sexual desires—since she displays the terrifying genitals of the Mother"). Decomposition of the mother may be thought of as having occurred in the play once again insofar as Pallas Athena enacts the role of the kind, sustaining mother in opposition to the vengeful Eumenides.

In sum, object doubling of parental figures occurs whenever ambivalence toward them becomes intolerable. We shall look next at a special form of object decomposition, that of the mother surrogate.

Fair Maid and Femme Fatale

Worried by the reappearance of his father, Huckleberry Finn goes to Miss Watson's Jim to have his fortune told with the hairball from the stomach of an ox. Jim first informs Huck that two angels hover around Pap: "One uv 'em is white en shiny en 'tother one is black." These are the conventional guardian and devil angels, projections of the superego and the id. As Jim continues to tell Huck's fortune he speaks, among other things, of two quite different angels: "Dey's two gals flyin' 'bout you in yo' life. One uv 'em's light en 'tother one is dark. One is rich en 'tother is po'. You's gwyne to marry de po' one fust en de rich one by-en-by." While we never learn if Jim's prophesy holds true for Huck, we do know that another major literary hero of the nineteenth century does marry . . . or pretend to marry . . . or at least becomes affianced to the same two angels. They are mentioned when Isabel informs Pierre of her dream vision of the blue-eyed, fair-haired Lucy Tartan: "Methought she was then more than thy cousin;—methought she was that good angel, which some say, hovers over every human soul; and methought—oh, methought that I was thy other,—thy other angel, Pierre. Look: see these eyes,—this hair—nay, this cheek;—all dark, dark, dark."

We know who these angels are, though they go by many names. The blue-eyed, fair-haired, light-complexioned one is the Fair Maiden, alias the Persecuted Maiden, the Virgin, the Saint, the Pale Lady, the Good Woman, the Nice Girl, the Marriageable Young Lady. Sometimes she is known simply as Wife. Her darker counterpart is the Femme Fatale, alias the Temptress, the Vamp, the Sinner, the Dark Lady, the Bad Woman, the Naughty Girl, the Trollop. Sometimes she is called Mistress or Prostitute or Eve or Whore of Babylon, depending on the circumstances.

These two sets of angels have been with us for a long time. How long is hard to say. We meet them in *Proverbs* in the "virtuous woman" whose price is "far above rubies" and the "strange woman" whose lips "drop as an honeycomb"—her mouth is "smoother than oil: But her end is bitter as wormwood, sharp as a twoedged sword. Her feet go down to death; her steps take hold on hell." The Judaeo-Christian tradition gives us both the convention of the female as temptress in Eve and the symbol of perfect female purity in the Virgin Mary. In the Middle Ages, with the rise of Mariolatry and the premium placed on physical virginity in woman, there develops a wide abyss between the actual behavior of women and man's ideal of what that behavior ought to be. During the fourteenth century women wore low-necked dresses and laced their breasts so high, it was said, that a candle could be balanced on them, while men wore short coats "revealing their private parts, which were clearly outlined by a glove-like container known as a braguette, compared with which the codpiece was a modest object of attire."[1] Yet a comparatively short time earlier the courtly love tradition began to celebrate the concept of pure love—*fin amor*—and ladies of the nobility began to be idealized within the framework of the chivalric code. It was inevitable that once man commenced to idealize woman he would end by dichotomizing her.

The *Tristan* of Gottfried and Thomas, which is within the ambience of the courtly love tradition and yet shows in its departures from the tradition how fluid and ambiguous the code was, presents the fair maid and femme fatale in the form of prototypes which have not yet become stereotypes. Isolde the Fair, "Tristan's life and death, his living death," corresponds in spite of her name to the dark, fatal temptress whose embrace eventually leads to death. Isolde of the White Hands, though her vengefulness is the immediate cause of Tristan's death, corresponds to the virginal maid who would normally be the object of a young man's ardor. While the estranged lover offers various rationalizations for marrying Isolde of the White Hands, Thomas is explicit

about the true nature of Tristan's motivation: "In such acts of venge-
ance [Tristan writhes, during this portion of the romance, at the
thought of Isolde in the arms of King Mark] I see both love and anger.
This is neither love nor hatred, but anger mingled with love, and love
mingled with anger." In modern parlance, Tristan's feelings are
ambivalent.

Consideration of only a few of the oedipal elements reflected in the
romance indicates that both Isoldes are surrogates of the mother toward whom the ambivalence was originally directed. For one thing,
the mother of Isolde the Fair is also named Isolde. It is through her
healing (and maternal) arts that Tristan is cured of his poisonous
wound and becomes "a man newborn," though it is of her daughter
that Tristan sings, "Isot ma drue, Isot mamie,/ en vus ma mort, en
vus ma vie!" King Mark completes the oedipal triangle. Along with a
host of father surrogates, such as Morold, the dragon, and various
ogres, King Mark represents the psychological father as well as being
Tristan's father in the eyes of feudal law. If Mark's wife be the
psychological mother, then Isolde the Fair and Isolde of the White
Hands may be said to be object doubles resulting from the son's
ambivalence toward the mother he unconsciously regards as both
irresistible sexual object and uncontaminated, untouchable virgin.[2]

Whether or not Tristan's Isoldes can be claimed as prototypes for
myriad good angel/bad angel women in literature down through the
centuries, and however difficult it may be to trace out the series in
cause-and-effect terms, there can be no question of the motif's longevity
and importance. Still lacking the firm delineation of the stereotype but
reflecting—and mocking—the division between the Ideal and the Real
in man's attitude toward women is the early seventeenth-century example of Dulcinea del Toboso, whom Don Quixote thinks deserves to be
"mistress of all the world," and Aldonza Lorenzo, the peasant's daughter, whom Sancho Panza admires for her muscle. By the eighteenth
century the light lady/dark lady types (whether we call them stereotypes or archetypes depends on the subtlety with which the given artist
portrays them) become more clearcut, as in the case of Sophia Western
and Molly Seagrim in *Tom Jones,* or more clearly still, in Cooper's
Alice and Cora in *The Last of the Mohicans.* Of the latter pair Leslie
Fiedler remarks in *Love and Death in the American Novel,* "Cora and
Alice (the names themselves are almost mythical), the passionate
brunette and the sinless blonde, make once and for all the pattern of

female Dark and Light that is to become the standard form in which American writers project their ambivalence toward women."[3]

Fiedler, whose book is the best source of information on these types in literature, shows that the sentimental love religion—beginning with Richardson's *Clarissa*—combines the chivalric conception of man's love for woman as "the fountainhead of virtue" with the mainly Protestant, Anglo Saxon, bourgeois postulation of marriage as salvation. Thus women, good or bad, acquire the theological epithet, "angel," and the battle of the sexes takes on some of the trappings of religious moral didacticism. In any case, after the development of the sentimental love religion the persecuted maiden type, such as Clarissa, begins to multiply, as does her counterpart (in other works), the seductive temptress. Nineteenth-century fiction is full of them. Poe's Lady Rowena of Tremaine (a blue-eyed, fair-haired Anglo Saxon) and the raven-haired Ligeia provide an interesting example because of the implied theme of sexual fidelity to the mother.[4] Hawthorne's proclivity for portraying Light Woman/Dark Woman types finds its culmination in the dove-maiden, Hilda—one of Hawthorne's "snow-maidens" —as compared to the dark, seductive Miriam in *The Marble Faun.* Even in comic, anti-sentimental novels like Harold Frederic's *The Damnation of Theron Ware* the reader encounters a fairly typical wife-mistress pair in Alice Ware and Celia Madden. And the turn of the century finds Henry James continuing to produce various puritan/-provocatress pairs, such as Mamie Pocock and Mme. de Vionnet in *The Ambassadors,* Maggie Verver and Charlotte Stance in *The Golden Bowl,* and—most notably—Milly Theale and Kate Croy in *The Wings of the Dove.*[5] Complete, normal, natural as some of these individual characters may seem to be at first glance, their psychological incompleteness and dependence on a contrasting counterpart can be discerned when they are compared to some of the more realistic, full-blown heroines in fiction, such as Becky Sharpe, Hester Prynne, Mme. de Rênal, Madame Bovary, Anna Karenina, and Lady Chatterly. Even prostitute heroines like Dostoevsky's Sonia Marmeladov and Crane's Maggie combine the attributes of morality and sexuality in a way quite foreign to the dichotomous good angel/bad angel pairs.

As might be expected, the wane of this archetype begins in the twentieth century—after Freud. By mid-century, in moviedom, the vamp is no longer a brunette, and the reigning queen is Marilyn Monroe. But she is only queen of the vamps. The ideal woman in movies is not Marilyn Monroe, but Doris Day, who proves that the girl (or wife) next door can be clean and yet sexy, desirable and yet not dangerous. While sentimental stereotypes persist in popular literature, as Fiedler shows in discussing Marjorie Morningstar as the persecuted maiden, the fair lady/dark lady pair seldom make an appearance in serious contemporary literature except when authors treat them with comic irony. Bernard Malamud's *The Natural* offers an illustration of such treatment. The dark lady, sexy but fatal, can be seen in Harriet Bird ("certainly a snappy goddess," thinks Roy Hobbs), who shoots the hero with a silver bullet—witch that she is—in the first part of the book. Her revenant in the second part is Memo Paris—she of the sick breast. Iris Lemon is the light lady, in this case a woman who is erotic but does not seem so because she isn't neurotic. Her flowery first name proclaims her a good-girl type, and her last name provides the necessary comic twist. Except when treated ironically, women in the twentieth century have become whole again, and if Popeye's corncob rape of Temple Drake (a deliberately androgynous name, it would seem) in Faulkner's *Sanctuary* did not demolish the melodramatic stereotype of persecuted maiden and lecherous villain, we can be certain that John Barth has parodied the virginal maiden/temptress prostitute dichotomy out of existence in the characters of Anna Cooke and Joan Toast in *The Sot-Weed Factor*. Perhaps for the first time since Eve picked the apple, man's attitudes toward women are reaching maturity.

This historical excursus suggests that man's changing views of women offer a crude parallel to the developmental history of the male child's attitudes toward his mother and ultimately toward all women he can love. Initially the child does not even know who his mother is. Then she becomes identified as a source of food, comfort, and tenderness. In time she becomes the object of phallic impulses. By the stage at which the child really begins to understand how he came into the world, he has repressed all awareness of his libidinal impulses toward his mother and set her up on a pedestal as a sexually pure creature. Then, as Freud says, "when he cannot any longer maintain the doubt that claims exception for his own parents from the ugly sexual behavior of the rest of the world, he says to himself with cynical logic that the difference between his mother and a whore is after all not so very great, since at bottom they both do the same thing."[6] Normally he represses this idea, too. At this point he is likely to begin to entertain a dual view of all women as sexual saints or sinners, the one type representing the good, nourishing, sexually pure mother and the other the erotic mother. Ideally, he dissolves this dualism when he marries. But before then, and even after marriage, some men are attracted to either one type or the other, or torn between the two. When this false dualism is entertained on a broad social scale, we have the sexual double standard, which means that a different code applies for men than for women but also means, as a corollary, that all women are either good girls, whom one marries, or bad girls, who provide the fun. In the Victorian period this code was doctrine. The standard treatise, by William Acton, made it clear that the Victorian wife did not have any sexual desires whatever.[7] Only mistresses and prostitutes enjoyed and were enjoyable.[8]

Some attention has been given to Shakespeare's handling of the sexual double standard. Cassio treats gentlewomen like Desdemona with elaborate courtesy and infinite respect, as we saw, and yet he has his whore, whom he would not dream of marrying. He sees women as either sexual saints or sinners. In *Measure for Measure,* Lucio sees women the same way. He tells Isabella that "though 'tis my familiar sin / With maids to seem the lapwing, and to jest, / Tongue far from heart," he holds Isabella herself

> . . . as a thing enskied and sainted,
> By your renouncement, an immortal spirit,
> And to be talked with in sincerity,
> As with a saint. (I.iv.31ff.)

Lucio does seem to be sincere at this point, yet like Cassio he has his whore, the only difference being that Lucio is forced to marry the prostitute he got with child, a cruel and comic punishment for an idealist who indulges in cynicism. Another Shakespearean example of a man in the grips of the sexual double standard can be found in *All's Well that Ends Well,* a play written within a couple of years of *Measure for Measure* and *Othello.* Parolles' words of advice to young Bertram depict the supposed drawbacks and imagined perils of connubial sex:

> He wears his honor in a box unseen
> That hugs his kicky-wicky here at home,
> Spending his manly morrow in her arms,
> Which should sustain the bound and high curvet
> Of Mar's fiery steed. (II.iv.296–300)

Bertram leaves his marriage unconsummated and his wife behind (or so he thinks). That his frantic flight from Hymen to Mars reflects a dualistic attitude toward women deriving from unconscious incest prohibition seems apparent when we consider that Bertram entertains no inhibitions about enjoying the favors, as he supposes, of Diana (whom he regards as no better than a prostitute) and when we remember that his physician wife, Helena, can almost be said to be his sister.[9] Of all the passages in Shakespeare which deal with a split in the attitude of men toward women, the most eloquently bitter one is spoken by Posthumus Leonatus after he has been led by the deceitful Iachimo to believe that Imogen has been unfaithful:

> We are all bastards,
> And that most venerable man which I
> Did call my father was I know not where
> When I was stamped. Some coiner with his tools
> Made me a counterfeit. Yet my mother seemed
> The Dian of that time: so doth my wife
> The nonpareil of this. (*Cymbeline,* III.i.1–8)

With these examples of ambivalence toward women in mind, let us return for a moment to *Tristan* in order to stress the principal psychosexual factors underlying the phenomenon of the fair maid and femme fatale. First of all, these types are always representatives of the mother, as were the two Isoldes. The taint of incest, usually only in symbolic disguise, invariably attaches itself to the dark lady, which is "psychological" rather than logical because the fair lady represents the one side of the mother as much as her counterpart does. One of the main indications of the presence of the incest motif in a work are symbols of castration, the talion punishment for incest. Tristan's death has this symbolic value, though the poisoned wounds in the loins which he suffers in combatting father figures constitute a more specific indication. Because incest is involved, love of the dark lady usually leads to death. Hence the fatal woman, the woman—in the words of Solomon—whose "end is bitter as wormwood," whose feet "go down to death." While the real danger (castration) comes from the anticipated revenge of the psychological father, in practice this danger is displaced onto the dark lady with the result that she is often described as a Gorgon figure, though not in *Tristan*. Finally, the decomposition of the mother into fair maid and femme fatale takes place as a result of the hero's ambivalence toward his mother, which was said to be dramatized in *Tristan* in the form of the hero's mixed feelings about marrying Isolde of the White Hands.

Some six and a half centuries after the portrayal of the fair maid and femme fatale in *Tristan,* Melville presents in *Pierre* the most rich, elaborate, and psychologically valid treatment of the theme in literature. As Fiedler says, "Besides Melville's lucid self-consciousness, other writers seem almost inadvertent in their uses of Dark and Fair Ladies."[10]

Early in the novel Mrs. Glendinning is referred to as Pierre's "pedestalled mother." He thinks of her as "his lovely, immaculate mother," and as "a beautiful saint before whom to offer up his daily orisons." On the surface the relationship of mother and son is gay, debonair, and without conflict. But their manners are ambiguous. They playfully call each other "brother" and "sister," thus implicitly denying the age difference between them and doubly denying the presence of the father, already dead. Pierre carries his customary gallantries toward his widowed mother to the point of offering, as he helps her finish dressing by putting a ribbon around her neck, to pin it together with a kiss. We are told that "a reverential and devoted son seemed lover enough" for the widowed mother. Harmless enough on the surface, the sickly sweet relationship of mother and son hints at seduction on her part and fixation on his. A sign of Pierre's fixation can be seen when he vows in "playful malice" that any man who should dare propose to his mother would mysteriously disappear from earth "by some peremptory unrevealed agency." Melville foreshadows the trouble to come by saying that at this stage "the fair river [of Pierre's life, presumably] had not borne its waves to those sideways repelling rocks, where it was thenceforth destined to be forever divided into two unmixing streams." The rocks signify—among other things—the shoals of Pierre's conflict with his mother, whose adamantine qualities are reflected in what Melville refers to as "the proud, double-arches of the bright breastplate" of her bosom and who, when Pierre disobeys her, turns into the threatening, dangerous, phallic, and ultimately castrating mother. After she drives Pierre from home, she mutters to herself, "Oh viper! had I thee now in me, I would be a suicide and a murderer with one blow!"

If the rocks are Mrs. Glendinning, the "fair river" is more particularly Pierre's libido and the "two unmixing streams" into which it flows are Lucy Tartan, his beautiful, blue-eyed, golden-haired, virginal fiancée, and Isabel Banford, his voluptuous, dark-eyed, dark-haired, bastard half-sister. Their names are significant, as critics have repeatedly pointed out, "Lucy" being associated with light, day, purity, radiance, sight, space, Promethean fire, and so forth, while "Isabel" is associated with darkness, night, impurity, obscurity, sound, time, and libidinal fire (the symbolic shape of a bell; the link with the Biblical Jezebel and Babylon).[11] Since Melville reiterates name and color symbolism again and again, the fundamental identification of Lucy with sexual purity (in general, the ego and superego values of society) and Isabel with id-attracting seductiveness need not be dwelt upon.

What does require elaboration is the extent to which Lucy and Isabel as "the two unmixing streams" find their origin at that point in Pierre's lifestream where it encounters the rocks of Mrs. Glendinning. Stated without metaphor, Lucy and Isabel are surrogates of the mother, each representing one of the two aspects of her which become dissociated because of the son's ambivalence. Melville links both Lucy and Isabel with either Pierre's mother in particular or maternal qualities in general. That this fact holds true for Lucy can be seen in Mrs. Glendinning's thoughts about her as a bride for her son: "His little wife, that is to be, will not estrange him from me. . . . How glad am I that Pierre loves her so, and not some dark-eyed haughtiness." She later makes an explicit comparison between herself and Lucy, saying, "Yes, she's a very pretty little pint-decanter of a girl: a very pretty little Pale Sherry pint-decanter of a girl; and I—I'm a quart decanter of—of—Port —potent Port!" And near the end of the novel, Lucy is still "in her own virgin heart. . .transparently immaculate, without shadow of flaw or vein," that is, she represents the quality of immaculateness Pierre originally attributed to his mother.

The maternal qualities of Isabel are emphasized more. After his first view of it, her face "haunted him as some imploring, and beauteous, impassioned, ideal Madonna's haunts the morbidly longing and enthusiastic, but ever-baffled artist." From the very beginning, then, Isabel figures as a passionate mother. In one of the most revealing passages in the entire novel Melville goes on at some length to the effect that the human soul is so "strange and complicate" that the wisest man would be rash to assign "the precise and incipient origination of his final thoughts and acts"; he then stresses Pierre's association of Isabel with his mother:

> This preamble seems not entirely unnecessary as usher of the strange conceit, that possibly the latent germ of Pierre's proposed extraordinary mode of executing his proposed extraordinary resolve—namely, the nominal conversion of a sister into a wife—might have been found in the previous conversational conversion of a mother into a sister.

When Pierre decides to renounce Lucy and pretend to marry Isabel in order to bestow on her the familial love and tenderness she has never experienced—while protecting his father's name and his mother's feelings—he but rationalizes his unconscious incestuous impulses, as scenes such as the following make clear: "He imprinted repeated burning kisses upon her . . . would not let go her sweet and awful passiveness. Then they changed; they coiled together, and entangledly stood mute." The themes of incest and parricide are mentioned explicitly in connection with the portrait of Beatrice Cenci (Hawthorne was to use the same portrait for the same purposes later on in *The Marble Faun*), and incest comes up in the dream vision of Enceladus, who is "both the son and grandson of an incest" and with whom Pierre identifies. Although the incest motif in *Pierre* might be supposed to refer solely to that with a sister, some facts contradict such an assumption. For one thing, Pierre feels himself "driven out an infant Ishmael into the desert, with no maternal Hagar to accompany and comfort him." Not only is Pierre portrayed as a son figure, here and elsewhere, but the repeated connections made between Isabel and milk establish her as a mother figure even more than a sister figure. At the farmhouse where Pierre first speaks to Isabel we have a scene of "pans of milk, and the snow-white Dutch cheeses in a row, and the moulds of golden butter, and the jars of lily cream." When Isabel asks, "Do I blast where I look? is my face Gorgon's?" Pierre answers, "Nay, sweet Isabel; but it hath a more sovereign power; that turned to stone; thine might turn white marble into mother's milk." As they enter New York City (Babylon, to which Isabel "leads" Pierre and with which she is associated, as opposed to Lucy's connection with the country), Isabel asks if people are hardhearted there. "Ask yonder pavements, Isabel," says Pierre. "Milk dropped from the milkman's can in December, freezes not more quickly on those stones, than does snow-white innocence, if in poverty it chance to fall in these streets." And at the catastrophic but not very plausible climax of the action, just after Lucy expires upon learning that Isabel is Pierre's sister, not his wife, Pierre snatches the vial of poison providentially "nestling" in Isabel's bosom and drinks it, declaring, "In thy breasts, life for infants lodgeth not, but deathmilk for thee and me!" The irony with which Melville referred to the novel—in a letter to Mrs. Hawthorne—as a "rural bowl of milk" might almost be said to have been curdled.

Be that as it may, Isabel's death-dealing breasts and the other passages singled out above indicate she is not only the fatal woman but also the castrating woman. Contrary to what Pierre says, her face *is* Gorgon's, and like Medusa her look turns Pierre to stone (the pun on the French for "stone" is inescapable, as critics have often pointed out). There are, in fact, a number of Gorgon allusions in the novel. As Pierre mediates about his first view of Isabel's face (just after the Madonna passage), he tries to convince himself that "the terrors of the face" are not "those of Gorgon"; he thinks they do not smite him by their repelling hideousness but allure him by their nameless beauty. Yet the face which seems to call upon him to champion "Truth, Love, Pity, Conscience" almost "unmans" him in its awful wonderfulness. When Pierre decides to challenge fate, he speaks like Ahab: "Thou Black Knight, that with visor down, thus confrontest me, and mockest at me; lo! I strike through thy helm, and will see thy face, be it Gorgon!"[12] There is a "deathlike beauty" in Isabel's face which leads him to tempt fate by crawling under the precariously balanced Terror Stone and lie there "as dead" in mimicry of what is to come. As he leaves home for the last time the butler, Dates, asks if he is sick. "To death," replies the hero. Like Orestes, Pierre feels himself pursued by the Furies, symbolized at one point by hackmen with their whips, and thus associates himself, though all unconsciously, with Orestes' crime of symbolic incest, the Eumenides being castrating figures. In the dream vision of Enceladus the castration imagery can hardly be missed when we are told that "Nature, more truthful, performed an amputation, and left the impotent Titan without one serviceable ball-and-socket above the thigh," again reminding us of Ahab. Melville leaves no doubt about the effect of both Lucy and Isabel when he has Pierre exclaim as they enter his jail cell, "Away!—Good Angel and Bad Angel both!—For Pierre is neuter now!" While the power of castration seems vested in Isabel, marriage with Lucy, immaculate and "nun-like" as she is, would be virtually as castrating as marriage with Isabel. It would amount to marriage with a degenitalized woman and would have left Pierre in his mother's power.

Lucy and Isabel as fair maid and femme fatale are object doubles representing the pure and sexual aspects of the psychological mother which have suffered decomposition as a result of the protagonist's insuperable ambivalence. That this decomposition does result from Pierre's ambivalence toward his mother must remain a theoretical assumption more than a demonstrable fact, though it is worth noting that Pierre feels unadulterated love for his mother early in the story yet experiences no grief when he learns of her death later on—as if Lucy and Isabel had taken her place as the objects of all his love for his mother after the decomposition takes place. The way in which Lucy and Isabel stand for the mother, together with the inference that Mrs. Glendinning's observable love and hatred for her son reflects his hatred and love for her, leave little question of the ambivalence which underlies the decomposition of mother into fair maid and femme fatale. Other instances of decomposition in the novel can also be discerned, though the scope of the present chapter rules out any detailed discussion of them. Charlie Millthorpe appears to be one of those "colorless" doubles of the protagonist (here a self-caricature of Melville—and Pierre—as a metaphysician) such as Ernest Jones finds Horatio to be of Hamlet. There are the two portraits of Pierre's father which are tantamount to portrait-doubles of the sexual and asexual father. Plotinus Plinlimmon and the Reverend Falsgrave can also be regarded as father figures. The pregnant Delly Ulver whom Pierre protects would seem to duplicate Isabel, or at least to represent the criminal and physiological effects of fornication. And Glendinning Stanly, Pierre's quondam friend and sometime rival, functions as a double of the protagonist, as Richard Chase points out.[13]

The way in which Lucy and Isabel—along with the Alices and Coras, the Hildas and Miriams of literature—function as mistress doubles has been the subject of this chapter. The mistress doubles are really a special case of the decomposition of the composite mother. When the "fair river" of Pierre's life encounters the rocks and shoals of conflict with his mother, it divides forever into the "two unmixing streams" of his love for Lucy and Isabel in precisely the same way that the libidinal stream of so many men has separated into love for fair maidens and femmes fatales.

Psychomachia: The Soul Battle

An almost ineluctable dualism would seem to haunt our categories of the double in literature. Masochist and Sadist, Loyal Son and Rebellious Son, Loved Father and Hated Father, Pure Mother and Mother-as-Whore, Fair Maid and Femme Fatale—they sound so polarized that skeptics might accuse the psychoanalytic critic of perpetrating a hideous and intolerable system of allegory instead of doing his job with at least a semblance of scientific rigor. Except for the tendentiousness of the phrasing, such a charge would not be quite so wide of the mark as might be supposed. The labels are allegorical. Lucy and Isabel, as Good Angel and Bad, are not really such a far cry from Chastity and Lust as they battle for the possession of Mansoul in Prudentius' *Psychomachia*. To be sure, Melville portrays little direct conflict between Lucy and Isabel; the main struggle takes place in Pierre's mind. Other than that, however, the novel presents Virtue and Vice Embattled in a manner entirely characteristic of allegory. Such a statement precipitates the question which this chapter undertakes to answer. What are the allegorical dimensions of works which dramatize psychological conflict through the medium of decomposition?

Many suppose that allegory, like God, is dead, and those who think so seldom mourn. Even in the academy no more than lip-service has been paid to allegory for some time, this despite the reputation of a

138

work like C. S. Lewis' *The Allegory of Love*. Except for medievalists, who have no choice but to take allegory seriously, the prevailing antagonism toward the allegorical mode has led Edwin Honig to approach the subject in *Dark Conceit* with almost a crusading spirit.[1] While allegory is mistrusted, he notes, studies in symbolism "abound as never before," the idea being that "in a scientific age allegory suggests something obvious and old-fashioned, like Sunday-school religion, but symbolism suggests something esoteric and up-to-date, like higher mathematics." A book that will surely be instrumental in turning back this tide of prejudice is Angus Fletcher's *Allegory: The Theory of a Symbolic Mode,* which demonstrates the vigor and flexibility of a genre long thought weak in appeal and rigid in construction.

According to Fletcher, "the allegorical hero is not so much a real person as he is a generator of other secondary personalities, which are partial aspects of himself." A major character generates a number of other figures "who react against or with him in a syllogistic manner.

> I say "generate," because the heroes in Dante and Spenser and Bunyan seem to create the worlds about them. They are like those people in real life who "project," ascribing fictitious personalities to those whom they meet and live with. By analyzing the projections, we determine what is going on in the mind of the highly imaginative projector. By the same token, if the reader wants a sketch of the character of Redcrosse in Spenser, he lists the series of adventures and tests undergone by Redcrosse, not so much for the pleasure of seeing *how* Redcrosse reacts in each case, as to see, literally, what aspects of the hero have been displayed by the poet. Redcrosse imagines Sansfoi and his brothers; Sir Guyon imagines Mammon and his cave; Sir Calidore imagines the Blatant Beast—in this sense the subcharacters, the most numerous agents of allegory, may be generated by the main protagonists, and the finest hero will then be the one who most naturally seems to generate subcharacters—aspects of himself—who become the means by which he is revealed, facet by facet.[2]

Fletcher accounts for the four basic types of doubling (of subject and object by multiplication and division), though he does not use this terminology. Thus Una helps Redcrosse (they are doubles) against Archimago (who is helped by Duessa—his double) while at the same time Redcrosse and Archimago are doubles of each other. It is Fletcher's position that fragmentation of the allegorical hero enables the writer to deal with a highly complex moral world by creating a protagonist who is by no means so restricted as he might at first seem. "Are Dante's self-image, his Virgil, his Beatrice, single in meaning? Is any main protagonist of *The Faerie Queene* restricted to a single virtue? Is Bunyan's Christian one-sided in character?" On the contrary, considered as a composite the allegorical hero can possess a very human range of weakness and strength. Fletcher even goes so far as to suggest that "Dante's journey is on one level a refraction of himself as Everyman, while Swift's Gulliver meets not one, but a hundred alter egos."

Since the allegorical hero "is either a personified abstraction or a representative type" whose characteristic way of acting is extremely limited in variety, Fletcher likens him to a man possessed by a demon. If we were to meet an allegorical agent in real life, he says, we would say that he was obsessed by a single idea, or had a one-track mind, or was a monomaniac, and we would regard a character of such rigid behavior patterns as a man compelled by a hidden, foreign force which controlled his destiny. From roughly ancient to modern times such forces were personified as demons. These demons could represent the forces of good or evil, or be intermediaries between man and the gods, good or bad. Etymologically, the word demon is derived from the Greek word meaning "to distribute or to divide. The demon is a distributor, usually of destinies."[3] Hence the demon serves to "compartmentalize function." Socrates' *daimon,* like a guardian angel [and like some autoscopic selves or like some paranoid projections], is a voice which speaks to him, which he may not disobey, enforcing him to virtue. The compartmentalized function of this *daimon,* we might say, is restricted to the role attributed by psychoanalysis to the superego. In Roman religion the division of labor attributed to demons was carried about as far as could be: "When a daemon has charge of one's eyes, one's hair, one's knife, one's hat, one's book, one's mirror, the proliferation has reached an extreme"—the uttermost end of the extreme being Dea Cloacina, the Goddess of Elimination.

In psychoanalytic literature compelling support for Fletcher's comparison of demonic possession and allegorical agency can be found in Freud's "A Neurosis of Demoniacal Possession in the Seventeenth Century," a study of the documents pertaining to the case of a painter by the name of Christoph Haitzmann.[4] The painter, it seems, made a pact with the devil after he became despondent over the death of his father. Before the note came due (nine years), he went to the religious authorities for help. Freud infers from the evidence at hand that the devil is a surrogate for the parents, both father and mother (on one occasion the devil appears naked, malformed, with two pairs of breasts; another time he has in addition to breasts a large penis "extended as a serpent"). In his introduction to this study Freud notes wryly, "Despite the somatic ideology of the era of 'exact' science, the demonological theory of these dark ages has in the long run justified itself. Cases of demoniacal possession correspond to the neuroses of the present day. . . . What in those days were thought to be evil spirits to us are base and evil wishes, the derivatives of impulses which have been rejected and repressed." Devil, demon, allegorical agent, psychological projection—they are all one.

Ralph Tymms inclines to invidious comparisons between allegorical and psychological doubles, preferring the "realism" of the latter; but he ends by saying that "no rigid distinction can be drawn between the allegorical and the realistic pictures of inward dualism."[5] Fletcher, who cites Tymms but overlooks this qualification, argues that the psychological double is allegorical.[6] Yet he implies—and would agree, I'm sure—that the verbal equation may often be reversed, that many allegorical agents may be considered psychological doubles. Not all are, any more than all allegorical figures are moral agents in a strict sense. Some allowance must be made for figures which have no psychological dimensions, such as those in George Orwell's *Animal Farm*. Here the fabric is that of purely political allegory, the activity of the men, pigs, chickens, and other animals being dictated by ideological rather than psychological motives.

The formulation that the allegorical hero "generates" subcharacters which are facets of himself suits Fletcher's purposes admirably. We might say—to extend this theory to some characters he does not mention—that an anxious Othello will give birth to an Iago, a Tom Jones will inevitably generate a Blifil, and a Joe Christmas will propagate a Percy Grimm. Yet in speaking of the allegorical hero himself as a "highly imaginative projector," and in saying that Redcrosse "imagines" a Sansfoi, Fletcher detours the realm of author psychology. He skirts the assumption, though he presumably would not quarrel with it, that the primary generator or creator of a literary character is the author, not the character himself, so that while Redcrosse may legitimately be said to imagine a Sansfoi and others, we should not forget that Spenser imagined them all.[7]

Fletcher discusses allegory allegorically in using that most allegorical creature, the demon, to explain how allegory works. To be sure, Northrop Frye points out that "all commentary [on literature] is allegorical interpretation, an attaching of ideas to the structure of poetic imagery."[8] C. S. Lewis goes even further in contending that "we cannot speak, perhaps we can hardly think, of an 'inner conflict' without a metaphor; and every metaphor is an allegory in little."[9] Yet in spite of the allegorical flavor of Fletcher's generative hypothesis, it makes an important contribution by disabusing us of our simplistic notions concerning the monolithic nature of the allegorical hero and the seeming autonomy of the subcharacters he encounters. What needs looking into is the relationship between the fragmented allegorical hero and the fragmented psychological one.[10]

The explanation itself will be tainted by allegorical modes of expression. As the statement of C. S. Lewis implies, and as modern linguists are well aware, the problem of utilizing allegorical language in communication cannot be avoided. Essentially the same argument was made in connection with such phrases as "fragmentation of the mind." Even Freud could not eliminate allegorical illustrations from his work. Despite all attempts to adhere to the precise language of science by substituting nonemotive terms like "affect" for "emotion" and "libido" for (roughly) "lust," allegorical terminology keeps creeping in. A geographical analogy like that of fixation resembling the forces stationed by an army at various points during penetration of a foreign country and an architectural one like the doorkeeper-to-the-anteroom analogy in describing the topographical system cs-pcs-ucs—these have an unmistakable allegorical quality. A still more conspicuous example would be the Eros-Thanatos formulation. With this linguistic difficulty in mind, then, we may turn to a matter related to the fragmented nature of literary characters, the problem, in fact, of determining what constitutes a literary character.

Is the subordinate buffoon who attends the hero in Attic Comedy an autonomous character? Cornford suggests that he has "no independent existence." He is, in effect, a fragment or double of the hero. Even the antagonist, strictly speaking, has no independent existence because he is a double of the hero or agonist. Can the heroine of the *Romance of the Rose* be called a literary character according to normal usage of the term? In his perceptive discussion of the psychological realism of the work C. S. Lewis maintains that Guillaume de Lorris "practically abolishes the hero, as one of his dramatis personae, by

142

reducing him to the colourless teller of the tale. The whole poem is in the first person and we look through the lover's eyes, not at him."[11] As for the heroine, he removes her entirely: "Her character is distributed among personifications." Lewis says that Guillaume knows what he is doing, that we cannot have the lady and the lady's Pride strolling about on the same stage, and he adds, "A man need not go to the Middle Ages to discover that his mistress is many women as well as one, and that sometimes the woman he hoped to meet is replaced by a very different woman." If a mere "type" character from comedy like the buffoon or an allegorical agent like Feminine Pride seem incomplete characters, parts of a larger composite, we may ask by way of contrast if the kind of flat, stereotyped personifications of virtue and vice such as we encounter in Prudentius' *Psychomachia* enjoy any "roundness," any significant measure of psychological realism. Perhaps they do. We can discern, half buried in the stilted and artificial language (at least in the Loeb translation), metaphors and symbols which are psychologically appropriate to make the allegorical agents "come alive" to a surprising extent. Lust's weapon, naturally enough, is fire. Chastity disarms Lust with a stone (which may be handy in the field of battle but which is also a common castration symbol), cuts her throat (castration again), and treats her dying antagonist to an emasculating comparison with the beheaded Holofernes lying soaked in his Assyrian chamber with his own "lustful blood." Thus seemingly autonomous characters like the buffoon in Attic Comedy are splinters of the hero while flat personifications of allegory may be far more complex than they appear. Given the wide, almost indiscriminate usage of the term "character" by critics, the limits of the label remain ill-defined.

The "characters" analyzed earlier confirm what consideration of allegorical features of literary characters, be they major heroes or minor abstractions, would seem to imply, namely that complex, composite ones occur which seem complete but are not, while simple, component ones occur which are not complete either, being fragments of a whole. This distinction is fairly obvious when we encounter manifest doubles of the protagonist, as in Poe's second William Wilson or Dostoevsky's second Golyadkin. When we meet with transitional doubles like Conrad's Leggatt, the distinction begins to blur. And when we read about Dostoevsky's Myshkin and Rogozhin we lose sight of the paradoxical fact that one and one do not necessarily make two. Analysis shows that in *Othello* the conflict among several of the dramatis personae is really, psychologically speaking, an endopsychic one. In *The Portrait of a Lady* all of the major characters can be thought of as projections of aspects of the author. The last two chapters demonstrate that several representatives of the psychological father, mother, or mistress may appear on stage simultaneously, as in the case of the host of father figures in "My Kinsman, Major Molineux." Beside these examples of the ambiguity pertaining to the seeming singleness of many literary characters, one can point to the phenomena of autoscopic vision and multiple personality for analogs from real life of the potential divisiveness of the self.

If a character is not what he seems to be in the sense of being a fragment rather than a whole, it may be asked if he is *real*. Which, for example, is the real Macbeth? Ignore for the moment the naiveté of the question in order to reconsider Fletcher's assumptions when he states that the allegorical hero "is not so much a real person" as he is a "generator" of secondary personalities, partial aspects of himself. Just recently Norman N. Holland has done for Shakespeare's Mercutio roughly what Fletcher does for Spenser's Redcrosse. In reviewing, with special reference to Shakespearean criticism, the time-bedraggled question of characters being real persons, he shows Mercutio to be a most unreal, formalized, artificial, and implausible "person" or a very real one depending on how one regards him.[12] The gist of Holland's analysis is that Mercutio has great potential realism for the reader identifying with him, that is, the reader who experiences his own drives and defenses as they are manifested in Mercutio's words and actions. To illustrate the processes involved Holland cites an experiment conducted at Smith College in 1944 by two psychologists. A group of undergraduates were shown an animated cartoon which presented the adventures of

a large black triangle, a small black triangle, and a circle, the three of them moving in various ways in and out of a rectangle. After the short came the main feature: the psychologists asked for comments, and the Smith girls "with great uniformity" described the big triangle as "aggressive," "pugnacious," "mean," "temperamental," "irritable," "power-loving," "possessive," "quick to take offense," and "taking advantage of his size" (it was, after all, the larger triangle). Eight percent of the girls even went so far as to conclude that this triangle had a lower I.Q. than the other. Now if Smith girls can see that much in a triangle, how much more they—or we—are likely to see in Mercutio.

Psychomachia: The Soul Battle

Holland provides an excellent account of the controversy over whether a literary character can be treated as a real person, as A. C. Bradley is famous (or infamous) for doing, or whether we have to do only with what is really there, that is, words on the page, as the New Critics are inclined to do.

My own pluralistic view of the shape-shifting nature of the literary character might be summarized this way. Macbeth is not a "real person," but a fictive character in a play by Shakespeare. As a dramatis persona he is whole, single, indivisible (the orthodox, simplistic, or grammar-school conception of a character). But Macbeth is real to me subjectively because he seems real, behaves as if he were a real, complex human being, and so forth (reader psychology). Macbeth is also real in the sense that his personality must necessarily reflect aspects of Shakespeare's own, however difficult it may be to determine in just what way this is true (writer psychology, anathema to many orthodox critics). Macbeth is none of the entities just mentioned in the sense that he is but a fragment of a theoretical psychological whole and also simultaneously a composite character, a name under which other characters in the play may be subsumed (decomposition). Finally, when we speak of Macbeth we are really just alluding to a name which by convention might be said to constitute the locus of reference of a number of words (or letters, or syllables) seen on the printed page or heard in a theater (this might be called the "artifact view," one favored, though not exclusively, by formalist critics). In short, the alleged reality or unreality of a literary character is not so much a false issue as a misleading one.

An understanding of allegory helps us to comprehend not only the psychological realism of demonic agency in the case of psychological doubles, it aids even more in our appreciation of one of the most important formal (or esthetic) aspects of decomposition. This function of doubling will be referred to as "doubling for dramatic conflict." In essence, doubling of characters does not simply make the representation of intrapsychic conflict possible; it allows for the potential development of that conflict in the most dramatic way possible. The amount of emphasis psychoanalysis lays on the dynamic nature of mental processes must be kept in mind. Neurosis, properly speaking, cannot occur without mental conflict. Since there is every reason to believe that some of the highest achievements of mankind also have their origin as well in modes of dealing with mental conflict, there is nothing very revolutionary in the suggestion that a dynamic opposition of psychic forces permeates practically all modes of literature. Shaw's dictum, "No conflict, no drama," goes right to the heart of the matter for the genre he was most interested in. It is impossible to think of any play deserving the name drama which is without sharp conflict. What obviously holds for the drama might not seem to obtain for so-called nondramatic literature; but to say so is to mistake conventional label for literal fact. Even the lyric poem can be found to have its "symbolic action" and its wellsprings of conflict, as passing attention to almost any Shakespearean sonnet will show. These opening lines of sonnet 146 are an instance: "Poor soul, the center of my sinful earth,/Lord of these rebel powers that thee array."

Allegory, because of its well-known structural device of the battle, provides convenient examples of this nearly universal feature of literature. Sometimes the battle in allegory takes the subtler conventional forms of the debate, the dialogue, and the complaint. A poem which might be said to encompass all three is Marvell's "A Dialogue between the Soul and Body." This pugnacious property of allegory can be seen more clearly in such works as Spenser's *Faerie Queene,* Swift's *Battle of the Books,* Čapek's *War with the Newts,* or—best of all for our purposes—Prudentius' *Psychomachia,* in which the battle *for* Mansoul represents the battle *in* Mansoul.[13]

While discussing the representation of intrapsychic conflict in daydreams, Hanns Sachs remarks that "this conflict, when fought out in the realm of fantasies and within a limited psychic area, can be made attractive and interesting like a tourney or a sham battle."[14] What is true for daydreams and sham battles holds for the sham or fictive battles of literature, though these battles seldom involve knights in the lists with lances in hand, as perhaps the following analysis of Melville's *Billy Budd* will help to illustrate.[15]

No visible blemish mars the masculine beauty of Melville's Handsome Sailor. Billy Budd's only noticeable flaw is an occasional "vocal defect," a stutter which develops "under sudden provocation of strong heart-feeling." Melville regards this defect as "a striking instance that the arch interferer, the envious marplot of Eden, still has more or less to do with every human consignment to this planet." In mentioning Billy's defect Melville contrasts it to the visible blemish which appears in the shape of a tiny hand on Georgiana's cheek in Hawthorne's story,

"The Birthmark." A passage in that story describes the birthmark as "the fatal flaw of humanity" which nature stamps on all her productions, a crimson hand expressing "the ineludible gripe in which mortality clutches the highest and purest of earthly mould."

Most of the critics of the novel politely ignore Billy's stutter. Instead of taking it seriously they are inclined to seize upon allegorical paraphernalia in the work, such as the phrase "envious marplot of Eden." This emphasis on allegory is understandable because there is a great deal of it in the novel. The three main branches of allegorical elaboration to which the critics attend are the moral, political, and religious. Viewed in terms of moral dialectics, Billy stands for Innocence and Claggart for Evil, and one of the main issues of the trial and punishment is Absolute Morality versus Temporal Expediency, as in the Plinlimmon tract in *Pierre*. Richard Chase offers an eloquent version of the moral theme when he compares *Billy Budd* with *Antigone*: "Both works are concerned with the defeat by abstract legality of an individual who possesses in more than usual measure certain timelessly precious human attributes." Political allegory in the novel has a historical context, the human rights issue tying in with the French Revolution, the English monarchical system, and such practices as the impressment of seamen. The novel begins with a politically oriented preface (in the Freeman edition) in which Melville says that "Revolution itself became a wrongdoer" and yet the "outcome" to "some thinkers" seemed "a political advance along nearly the whole line for Europeans." Commentators seem to give most of their attention to the rich fabric of religious allegory. Billy can easily be seen as pre-lapsarian Adam, as an "angel of God," and as a Christ-figure. With respect to the last, the foundling hero's ambiguous answer, "God knows, Sir," when he is asked who his father is, can be taken as a hint that God is his Father, and the hanging of the "innocent" hero can be regarded as a crucifixion scene: "It chanced that the vapory fleece hanging low in the East, was shot through with a soft glory as of the fleece of the Lamb of God seen in mystical vision and simultaneously therewith, watched by the wedged mass of upturned faces, Billy ascended; and ascending, took the full rose of the dawn." Claggart makes a suitable satan, of course, and the significance of the *Indomitable* [the *Bellipotent* in the Hayford and Sealts edition] being sunk by the *Athéiste* is unmistakably religious. When autobiographical considerations are linked with the religious allegory, *Billy Budd* becomes either Melville's

147

"last testement of acceptance" of Christianity or the final, slashing rejoinder in his undying quarrel with God.

These readings conflict as often as they complement each other. The interpretation to follow, which combines genre criticism with "Freudian allegory," may possibly manage to resolve some of the many critical dilemmas which have developed, especially the deadlocked controversy with respect to Billy's innocence or guilt. Whether it succeeds in doing so or not, it will at least illustrate the resonance which results from doubling for dramatic conflict in the novel.

Billy would seem to fulfill the classic Aristotelian requirements for the tragic hero: in brief, that he be a morally imperfect though basically good man of noble or heroic stature, possessed of hubris (or as Fletcher might say, by the demon Pride), who precipitates his downfall by his own actions. To view Billy as a conventional tragic hero is to assume that he takes a tragic stance—that he maintains a typical posture with respect to the gods or the idea of moral order in the universe. Therefore it is crucial that all conflict in *Billy Budd* relates to the concepts of law, order, and authority. If the psychological father is one repository of authority, then we must heed the pervasive search-for-the-father motif in Melville's writing, the presence of which may be accounted for partly because Allan Melville died when his son was only thirteen years old. Newton Arvin considers this occurrence the most decisive event in Herman Melville's early life and says that the author "was to spend much of his life divided between the attempt to retaliate upon his father for this abandonment and the attempt, a still more passionate one, to recover the closeness and confidence of happy sonhood." *Pierre* furnishes one biographical parallel: the hero's father dies when Pierre is twelve. The protagonist of the more autobiographical *Redburn,* having heard that sea captains are "fathers to their crew . . . severe and chastising fathers, fathers whose sense of duty overcomes the sense of love [like Captain Vere]," responds to Captain Riga's initial friendliness with "tenderness and love" only to find himself rejected by Riga after the ship puts to sea. Redburn's obsession to retrace his father's footsteps in Liverpool by the aid of an old guidebook provides the most transparent example of this theme in Melville. F. O. Matthiessen gives a compelling statement of the motif in *Billy Budd* when he compares the relationship of Vere and Billy with the story of Abraham's willingness to sacrifice Isaac: "Here the search for a father, if latent in all Melville's Ishmaels, and in all the questings of his homeless spirit for authority, is enacted in an elemental pattern. . . . If Billy is young Adam before the Fall, and Claggart is almost the Devil Incarnate, Vere is the wise Father, terribly severe but righteous."[16]

Vere is not the only father surrogate in the novel, however. With a Protean-like dexterity Melville sketches a pageant of them, the father appearing in no less than eight different guises. Captain Graveling, the aging "ploughman of the troubled waters" who skippers the *Rights-of-Man* from which Billy is impressed, functions as a gentle father who, during Billy's presence aboard, governs "a happy family" on the *Rights*. On H. M. S. *Indomitable* the ancient, wizened, gruff old Dansker manifests a streak of "patriarchal irony touching Billy's youth and athletic frame"; he persistently refers to Billy as "Baby Budd"; and he serves as an adviser by warning him that "Jemmy Legs" Claggart is "down" on him. The chaplain, both as man and priest, plays a paternal role. He comes to Billy as he lies manacled on the gun deck, looking like "a slumbering child in the cradle," and after endeavoring to minister to the "young barbarian's" spiritual needs—an act ironically gratuitous for the Christ-like Billy—the chaplain stoops over to kiss the sailor's cheek with paternal gentleness. Though Billy does not come in contact with him, Admiral Nelson, who is transferred to the *Theseus* after her participation in the Great Mutiny on the theory that his charisma will win over the disgruntled sailors, represents an idealized nautical patriarch. The ample attention that critics have accorded to Captain Vere's paternal relation to Billy makes further comment unnecessary, though it might be noted that Vere is "old enough to have been Billy's father," speaks to him in a "fatherly tone," and as Captain of the ship represents a higher father, His Majesty the King. One need not belabor, on the religious and psychological levels, how God fulfills the role of father. Finally, John Claggart figures to some extent as a father by virtue of the authority vested in him as master-at-arms, a minor police officer in the service of the King.

That this extraordinary multiplication of father images is fraught with significance will be clear only in the light of Billy's relationship to them. He obviously views such men as the old Dansker with filial respect and devotion. But how does he relate to the father as an embodiment of authority? Is he rebellious or loyal? The consensus of critical opinion represents him as completely loyal. Newton Arvin says that "Billy is no rebel against divine justice, and he is not guilty, even symbolically, of disobeying some transcendent will. He is an unwitting, impulsive offender against the Mutiny Act."[17] For Milton R. Stern, Billy is "the childlike barbarian, the pure creature whose only experience is just the experience of his own inner purity and idealism."[18] E. L. Grant Watson insists that in his last novel Melville is no longer a rebel, arguing that Billy has not, "even under the severest provocation, any elements of rebellion in him."[19] The defenders of Billy's innocence, after discussing his ingenuous, naïve, and virgin heart, invariably quote the statement he makes during the court martial: "I have eaten the King's bread and I am true to the King." The advocates of Billy's innocence at the critical bar plead that he is Christ-like, that he is Adam before the Fall, and that—as Melville states—he has "not yet been proffered the questionable apple of knowledge" (ignoring the fact that the last quotation refers in context to Billy's illiteracy and that in the same paragraph Melville declares that while Billy shows no trace "of the wisdom of the serpent" he nevertheless is not "yet quite a dove"). On the other hand, attorneys for the prosecution adduce little evidence in support of their brief that Billy should be considered a rebel. They just assume it.

If Billy is entirely innocent, then the rebel who bulks so large in Melville's other works is conspicuous by his absence in this one. Where are the Tommos, Tajis, Pierres, Steelkilts, Ahabs, Jack Chases, and White Jackets, all of whom—like Melville himself in real life—are deserters or mutineers or both, either in deed or desire? White Jacket, for instance, is ready to murder Captain Claret rather than submit to being flogged, and Ishmael's "splintered heart and maddened hand" are turned against "the wolfish world." Certainly Claggart, as an allegorical satan, cannot fill the role of rebel in *Billy Budd* as some commentators seem to believe. Structural and other considerations, among them that Claggart is not the protagonist, forbid it. Only Billy can be the rebel, if there is one. Only he is accused. Only he is punished. And we know he is guilty. His stutter, amounting to a *lapsus linguae,* betrays him, for the stutterer's tongue involuntarily conspires with his psychic censor to block the expression of hostility.[20]

As I said, most of the critics politely ignore Billy's stutter. The only one to point out its hostile implications is Richard Chase, and he, recognizing the fact that the stutterer represses his impulses out of castration fear, ends by stressing the act of repression rather than what is repressed with the result that Billy is seen as "fatally passive," the hermaphroditic Christ submissive to his fate. If it can be demonstrated that Billy's "ineludible gripe" does reflect hostility, however, the reader will then perceive that Billy conforms to the role of the rebellious tragic hero.

That he does repress unconscious hostility can easily be seen when the only three occurrences of stuttering in the novel are correlated. In each episode someone challenges Billy's submissiveness to authority. In every case his stutter betrays repressed hostility, specifically toward the King and by extension toward God and other parental figures. The first instance takes place when the afterguardsman, a "catspaw" for Claggart, tries to implicate Billy in mutiny by offering him money. Even though he fails to comprehend the situation, Billy recoils in disgust from the overture and threatens to throw the sailor overboard (what matters psychologically is not the nature of an idea or action so much as the amount of psychic energy with which it is invested). In this case Billy feels the mere imputation of disloyalty to be an overwhelming threat. The second instance of stuttering occurs when an authoritarian figure, the master-at-arms, challenges Billy's loyalty in the presence of a higher authority and father figure, Captain Vere, who in turn represents still higher authority, the King. Billy's inability to articulate his denial verbally causes him to express it physically with the fatal blow to Claggart's skull. The third and last time Billy stutters is in court just after he affirms that he is true to the King. When Captain Vere says with suppressed emotion, "I believe you, my man," Billy replies, "God will bless you for that, your honor," stammering as he speaks. Again, the authoritarian context is manifest.

Melville tells us that Billy stutters "under sudden provocation of strong heart-feeling." That the impediment crops up under very special circumstances, depending on the kind of stress involved, is corroborated by Melville's assertion that "in the hour of elemental uproar or peril Billy is everything a sailor should be." In the execution scene, a specific instance of what must be called strong heart-feeling but where the question of loyalty to authority no longer obtains (having in effect been answered by the sentence of the court martial), Billy issues at the penultimate moment his dying benediction: "God bless Captain Vere!" Melville emphasizes the fact that Billy's words are "wholly unobstructed in the utterance." Billy's articulation at this fateful moment is so perfect that the syllables are described as "delivered in a clear melody of a singing-bird on the point of launching from the twig."

Thus Billy stutters only when his anxiety is mobilized by the insinuation that he hates authority. His antagonism is unconscious. Like Oedipus, he denies with vehemence his deepest urges.

A full understanding of the complex role of authority in the novel requires insight into Claggart's "Pale ire, envy, and despair," the phrase from *Paradise Lost* which Melville so artfully applies to Claggart's malady, his "depravity according to nature." To comprehend this depravity we must perceive Claggart's emotional relationship to both Billy and Captain Vere, which requires some knowledge of the nature of homosexuality.

Few critics mention Claggart's homosexuality. Those who do tend to slight it or else deny it, alleging that the words "the depravity here meant partakes nothing of the sordid or sensual" prove the absence of any sexual pathology. Not necessarily. The quotation indicates only the absence of any overt pathology and possibly shows Melville's unawareness of the underlying sexual problem. More important, it points to Claggart's own lack of awareness. The essence of his sickness lies in his elaborate paranoid defenses against his sexual impulses, not in the impulses themselves; in other words, his remedy is worse than his disease. Because of these paranoid defenses he cannot possibly understand his own depravity. In fact there is no reason to doubt that Claggart really believes Billy to be a mutineer and that he tempts Billy through the offices of the afterguardsman not to "frame" him but in order to verify his own smoldering suspicions.[21]

Melville provides ample textual evidence of Claggart's homosexual orientation (one which, by the way, he shares with some other notable literary villains, such as Shakespeare's Iago, Dostoevsky's Smerdyakov, Mann's Cipolla, and Faulkner's Jason Compson). Despite the profound ambiguity of style Melville uses when discussing the master-at-arms, Claggart emerges as physically effeminate, as the sobriquet "Jemmy Legs" (O.E.D.: "dandified, foppish, effeminate") corroborates. Melville hints at "something defective or abnormal in the constitution and blood" and indirectly compares Claggart to "the promiscuous lame ducks of morality" which find in the navy a "convenient and secure refuge." Submissive to authority, Claggart shows "a certain austere patriotism" and behaves with great obsequiousness to Captain Vere. He avoids wine, which might endanger his defenses. He looks at the handsome Billy with melancholy expression,

> . . . his eyes strangely suffused with incipient feverish tears. . . .Yes, and sometimes the melancholy expression would have in it a touch of soft yearning, as if Claggart could even have loved Billy but for fate and ban.

His paranoid symptoms damn him more than anything else: he makes "ogres of trifles," as when he thinks Billy spilled the soup on purpose; and in contrast to Billy's feeble intellect and large heart Claggart reveals the paranoid's desperate reliance on reason, though Melville, not without humor, leaves it an open question whether he suffers from "mania in the brain or rabies of the heart" (Freeman edition, chap. 12; deleted in the Hayford and Sealts edition). Thus Melville shows deep insight in remarking that Claggart employs reason "as an ambidexter implement for effecting the irrational." A look at two of Claggart's prototypes further substantiates the presence of homosexual impulses. Bland, the "neat and gentlemanly villain" in *White Jacket,* breaks his biscuit with a dainty hand, possesses a "wickedly delicate" mouth and a "snaky black eye," and shuns all indelicacy, such as swearing.[22] Jackson, the villain in *Redburn,* appears to be fond of boys. He is a "clever, cunning man" with a "cold, and snaky, and deadly" eye. (In the accusation scene Claggart's "first mesmeric glance" at Billy is one of "surprised fascination" and "the last was as the lurch of the torpedo-fish.") Though Jackson tries to tyrannize over others, he befriends the handsome orphaned young Lancashire lad; but when the boy instinctively shrinks from him, Jackson's love changes to hatred. Much the same thing happens on the *Indomitable:* Claggart envies and therefore desires Billy's beauty; he recognizes the healthiness and robustness of Billy's masculinity and therefore despairs of possessing it; and he responds to what amounts to a rejection of his advances with "pale ire."

Thus far Billy and Claggart have been discussed as though they were separate and autonomous psychological entities; but they may be regarded as a composite character, each representing different aspects of the psychological son. Billy and Claggart as fictional representatives of these two sides of a decomposed single character engage in a sort of sexual dialectic or *agon,* a veiled but dramatic struggle between the normal and abnormal. In terms of their psychological kinship, both are sons to Captain Vere. One infers the existence of this relationship on several grounds: first, psychological (the complementary psychosexual orientations to the father); second, allegorical (Claggart-Satan, the Bad

Angel of God; Billy-Christ-Adam, the Good Angel of God); third, relation to authority (Captain Vere as father to all of his crew, like Captain Riga); fourth, the mystery common to both their backgrounds (the family romance); fifth, the complementary nature of most of their attributes (e.g., Claggart as head, Billy as heart). Finally, both are as sons to Jacob. As he speaks before the mainmast, Claggart regards Captain Vere with "a look such as might have been that of the spokesman of the envious children of Jacob deceptively imposing upon the troubled patriarch the blood-dyed coat of young Joseph," that is, Vere is Jacob, Billy is Joseph, and Claggart is one of his brothers. While Richard Chase—and only Chase—perceives that both Claggart and Billy are sons to Vere, he reverses their psychological relationship to him by stating that Claggart assumes the aggressive and hostile role of the father and Billy the passive one of the mother. Quite the opposite is true.

The crucial accusation scene in Captain Vere's cabin dramatizes the psychosexual dialectic between Claggart and Billy. Claggart's indictment, if false on the story level, is ironically true on the symbolic level. Rightly surmising the rebellion lurking behind Billy's placid exterior, Claggart charges him with it. He accuses Billy not of any crime but of the only one Billy can possibly be guilty of (for the narrator certainly does not blame Billy for frolicking on "fiddler's green" along with the rest of his sex-starved shipmates). In effect he says to Vere, "I am your good, loyal, passive, obedient, submissive son, but Billy is your rebellious sexual rival, a potential parricide and mutineer." To be sure, Claggart appears aggressive enough in this scene, for his thwarted lust has turned to hostility; but it is directed at his alter ego, not at his father, toward whom he is passive to the point of obsequiousness. Accused of rebellion, Billy predictably manifests acute castration anxiety—precisely the appropriate, normal response. He stands like one "impaled and gagged." His face, "a crucifixion to behold," reminds Vere of a schoolmate whom he had seen "struck by much the same startling impotence." Billy's expression resembles "that of a condemned vestal priestess in the moment of being buried alive, and the first struggle against suffocation." Yet it must be insisted that while gagging, suffocation, and fear of being buried alive may represent fear of castration, as Chase points out, it does not necessarily follow that a person who endures castration anxiety, a universal phenomenon for males, desires castration or considers himself impotent. In this scene, furthermore, Billy reveals his virile power through action, while Claggart succumbs without resistance, static and symbolically limp in death. Billy's arm, "quick as the flame from a discharged cannon at night," proves potent enough. The assertion that lifting Claggart's "spare," "flexible," "inert" body is "like handling a dead snake" demonstrates beyond cavil that it is Claggart who figures as the flaccid, impotent, castrated son—not Billy.

But since Billy's blow unveils his repressed antipathy for authority, he is guilty and must be punished. He is *de facto* guilty, and Vere's warnings to the drumhead court that leniency will be construed by the sailors as pusillanimous behavior, thus tempting them to mutiny, should not be read solely as an ironic counterpoint to Billy's "innocence." After the crime "the father in him" which Vere has thus far "manifested toward Billy" is "replaced by the military disciplinarian." This disposition predominates until the court condemns Billy, after which time Vere reverts to his role as the tender, compassionate father. The affection between Vere and Billy during this period symbolizes the peaceful father-son love which follows the resolution of oedipal conflict, and finds its principal expression during Vere's private interview with Billy after the court martial and in Vere's dying words: "Billy Budd, Billy Budd."

After the death blow to Claggart's head (Billy's blow is symbolically directed to the forehead, the "mind"), there appears to be little dramatic action in the novel. Members of the drumhead court differ with the captain, but not openly. Due to the secrecy and expeditiousness of the trial, the anger of the crew does not become aroused. Even the execution scene has little of the dramatic about it in the ordinary sense of the term, and the potential mutiny of the crew in support of Billy never materializes because Vere's shrewd observance of the "forms, measured forms" of ordered military life keeps them in check. Nothing could be more "peaceful" than the scene in which the chaplain administers his benediction to the hero as he lies asleep in manacles on the gun-deck with "the look of a child slumbering in the cradle." It is symptomatic of the subtle orchestration of action in the work that one of the more conflictful scenes occurring after the hanging amounts only to an allegorical debate between the Purser and the Surgeon as to whether the absence of spasmodic tremors in the body of the hanged man signifies a species of what the Purser calls "euthanasia."[23] Equally symptomatic of how action is treated is the perfunctory way in which the wounding of Vere is described in the battle of the *Indomitable* with the *Athéiste*. And few readers will even remember that just before Claggart speaks to Captain Vere at the mainmast, the *Indomitable* gives chase to an enemy frigate. Melville obviously makes no effort to resort to crude physical action as a source of dramatic intensity.

But once we divest our minds of the habit of thinking of action in Aristotelian terms (a tragedy as an imitation of an action . . . in the form of action) *Billy Budd* can be seen as jammed to the hatches with action—if by that we mean conflict, a dynamic opposition of themes, forces, ideas, values, and so forth. To cite but a few examples, there is the contrast between ships, the *Indomitable* versus the *Athéiste,* and the man-of-war versus the *Rights-of-Man*. Vere's conservative politics contrast with libertarian innovation: "His settled convictions were as a dyke against those invading waters of novel opinion." He opposes radical social change not because it is inimical to the aristocracy of which he is a member but because the changes seem incapable of embodiment in lasting institutions and are "at war with the peace of the world and the true welfare of mankind." Much conflict in the novel has to do with that between loyal subordinates, the officers of the drumhead court, and the authoritarianism of a captain who seems, if not mad indeed, "yet not quite unaffected in his intellect." Vere speaks to them of "the clashing of military duty with moral scruple—scruple vitalized by compassion," of the conflict between "warm hearts" and heads which should be cool. He even voices the idea of a conflict between nature and society, arguing that the uniforms they wear attest that their allegiance is not to "nature" but to "the King"—a formulation of the conflict between individual conscience and the social juggernaut which still rages in our own time, as the Nuremberg trials indicate. These examples, when added to the psychosexual conflict of Billy and Claggart, demonstrate the novel to be full of drama, of conflict presented in an ambiguous, fragmentary, and diffused manner such that parallels between psychological action and other modes are not always apparent. We are told, for instance, that for the officers composing the court "to argue his [Vere's] order to him would be insolence. To resist him would be mutiny." Here, in miniature, we have a precise analog to Billy's psychic rebelliousness.

Without question, I think, the main source of drama in the novel is mental conflict, all other sources being correlative with, and perhaps subordinate to, that mental conflict. It seems strange, therefore, that a perceptive critic of Melville should insist that "what is wrong with Billy Budd as tragic hero" is that "there is no 'palatial stage' in his personality, no conscious structure, *no mind* whose disintegration we should watch with pity and terror rather than merely with bewilderment and an obscure sense of loss."[24] Ironically, the "palatial stage" which Richard Chase refers to comes from one of the scenes in the novel which shows Melville's genius for psychological drama to its best advantage. Melville prefaces the scene by saying,

> Passion, and passion in its profoundest, is not a thing demanding a palatial stage whereon to play its part. Down among the groundlings, among the beggars and rakers of the garbage, profound passion is enacted. And the circumstances that provoke it, however trivial or mean, are no measure of its power. In the present instance the stage is a scrubbed gundeck, and one of the external provocations a man-of-war's man's spilled soup.

Perhaps only Melville or Conrad might have picked so drab a setting for so deep a drama. More important, we have to do, in this humble setting, not with overt conflict presented on the histrionic boards but the most profound kind of passion taking place unseen within the mind. And there is a mind in question. Chase does not perceive the mind at odds with itself because of the way in which that mind is fragmented. One of the minds involved is the author's. Another mind at work is the reader's, which transmutes the elements of the story—every event, metaphor, and allusion—into a drama of drive and defense which he experiences as he reads. Still another mind, one present in the work itself, is the composite mind of Billy-Claggart whose parts (one that of the rebellious, heterosexually-oriented son and the other that of the loyal, homosexually-oriented son) may be said to be enacted on an oedipal stage before the eyes of the father, Vere, who combines both the tender and punishing aspects of the psychological father in a way that has confused commentators inclined to see him as either a mad martinet or a compassionate man who nevertheless feels obliged to do his duty.

We may also speak, with reservation, of the minds of Billy and Claggart as though they were independent without forgetting that they form a composite one. Claggart's mind we understand to be busy with its paranoid delusional operations when Melville tells us, with respect

157

to the "greasy fluid streaming before his feet," that Claggart "must have taken it—to some extent willfully—perhaps not for the mere accident it assuredly was, but for the sly escape of a spontaneous feeling on Billy's part more or less answering to the antipathy of his own." For the most part we are not privy to Claggart's thoughts the way we are to Iago's (in the soliloquies), and what "affectual activity" he may be said to be experiencing is distilled, with great indirection, into such allusions as that to the phrase "Pale ire, envy and despair" which Milton uses to depict Satan's ambivalent feelings as he first looks upon Adam and Eve in the Garden of Eden.

So much does Melville stress the opposition of head and heart that Billy seems all heart, with hardly any mind at all. He is light-hearted, unintellectual, not introspective. He can only be imagined as virtually inarticulate during his private interview with Vere after the trial. The limits of his mental activity might seem to be expressed in the vague, bewildered perturbation he experiences in trying to reconcile Claggart's pleasant words to him with the Dansker's opinion that Jemmy Legs is down on him. Judged by Henry James's concept of the literary character as a "vessel of consciousness," Billy does not seem capacious. The agents of any drama, says James, "are interesting only in proportion as they feel their respective situations," and he argues that "their being finely aware—as Hamlet and Lear, say, are finely aware—*makes* absolutely the intensity of their adventure":

> Edgar of Ravenswood, for instance, visited by the tragic tempest of "The Bride of Lammermoor," has a black cloak and hat and feathers more than he has a mind; just as Hamlet, while equally sabled and draped and plumed. . .has yet a mind still more than he has a costume.

Though we are told Billy Budd sings like a nightingale, we cannot imagine him articulating his feelings in such words as "Oh, that this too too solid flesh would melt,/ Thaw, and resolve itself into a dew!" Even Billy's dying benediction, "God bless Captain Vere," seems stereotyped. Yet Billy, in his simple sailor costume, does feel "finely aware" on at least one occasion. He feels "horrified" at the sight of a seaman being flogged and resolves that "never through remissness would he make himself liable to such a visitation." While Billy's resolve seems natural, the intensity of his concern suggests not physical cowardice, but a spiritual pride so great that he could never submit to such a punishment, that he would rebel—like White Jacket—before submitting to the lash. In any case, the difficulty of even attempting to talk about Billy's mind remains insurmountable simply because Melville has perpetrated an extreme diffusion in the novel of all mental activity which pertains to individual characters.

Fletcher contends that fragmentation of the allegorical hero enables a writer to deal with a highly complex moral world by creating a protagonist (the composite one) who is by no means so restricted as he might at first seem to be. Melville achieves just this sort of flexibility in dealing with life, particularly the life of the mind, by effecting a fragmentation of his hero in all the senses that have been mentioned.

He thereby not only represents the complex life of the mind in conflict with itself, he manages to do so in the most dramatic manner possible. That conflict of the most strenuous sort pervades the novel has been demonstrated only in a selective fashion. That the degree or intensity of conflict would not have been as great without the presence of decomposition must be appealed to the judgment of the reader. Since the novel cannot be rewritten, it is doubtless idle to speculate that (given exactly the themes which have been stressed in this analysis, such as the search for an ideal father and the conflict in psychosexual orientation) the story might have seemed more dramatic to the reader if no villainous Claggart appeared and the story began, without digressions, with a rebellious and highly articulate Billy agonizing over whether to allow himself to be impressed, having words with Lieutenant Ratcliffe, behaving in surly fashion aboard the *Indomitable,* and gradually working himself up to the stage of fomenting a mutiny. The hypothetical result might read more like *Mutiny on the Bounty.* It can only be suggested that Billy and Claggart, as doubles in dynamic opposition to each other, provide in Melville's understated tragedy all the dramatic intensity of an Othello gulled, debauched, and undone by an Iago. Conflict makes drama. Psychological conflict probably makes the best drama. And psychological conflict portrayed in such a fashion that the reader achieves a maximum involvement or identification with the characters with a minimum awareness that he is involved (latent decomposition being one way, though not the only way, in which such esthetic distance between reader and text can be induced) will give rise to an optimum amount of pleasurable tension between the reader's conscious response to the work and his unconscious immersion in it.

What psychological decomposition has in common with the allegorical mode is conflict. Allegory tends to portray battles of one kind or another, some literal and some figurative. Even the typical journey of the allegorical hero involves a quest so perilous or difficult, like that of Bunyan's Christian, that sub-battles occur along the way. Similarly, some form of battle or mental conflict will ensue whenever psychological decomposition takes place, though often the struggle will be as veiled as in *Billy Budd*. Decomposition operates allegorically, even in works which do not appear to be allegories in the conventional sense, and decomposition may be said to occur in all cases where the fragmentation of the allegorical hero has psychological coordinates.

Baroque Doubles

Jorge Luis Borges numbers the double (along with the voyage in time, the contamination of reality by dream, and the work within the work) as one of the four fundamental devices of fantastic literature.[1] He plays vertiginous variations on the theme of doubling in his own work with artful deliberateness. In a tale called "Three Versions of Judas," Borges' scholarly protagonist realizes that an apostolic betrayer is gratuitous, that Judas "reflects Christ," that Christ *was* Judas (or Judas was Christ), and the protagonist ends by sacrificing his own life, like Christ, for a mysterious truth after being betrayed and damned by his fellow theologians for betraying Holy Writ. Two parables by Borges present highly conscious variations on the theme of the division between author and man. "Everything and Nothing" begins, "There was no one in him; behind his face . . . and his words . . . there was only a bit of coldness, a dream dreamt by no one." After learning to simulate being someone so that no one will discover he is no one, and after being many men as an actor on the stage, this man becomes the many characters in his works. Either "before or after dying" he tells God that he wants to be "one and myself." The piece ends with the Lord saying,

> Neither am I anyone; I have dreamt the world as you dreamt your work, my Shakespeare, and among the forms in my dream are you, who like myself are many and no one.

161

"Borges and I" begins, "The other one, the one called Borges, is the one things happen to." We learn that the speaker lets himself go on living "that Borges may conceive his literature" and that "this literature justifies me." The speaker says, "I shall remain in Borges, not in myself (if it is true that I am someone)," and he concludes his confession by declaring, "Thus my life is a flight and I lose everything and everything belongs to oblivion, or to him. I do not know which of us has written this page."

The dazzling virtuosity with which Borges deals so knowingly in doubles brings us back to a consideration raised early in this book. Should decomposition be employed by an author as a conscious device?

Little has been said about contemporary fiction which utilizes the manifest double in a relatively unambiguous fashion. Several instances, some of them minor, might be mentioned. Short stories like "The Echo and the Nemesis" by Jean Stafford and "Miriam" by Truman Capote make orthodox use of doubles. A recent story in *Playboy* portrays a suburbanite Negro accountant who meets his white alter ego on a commuter train.[2] Ihab Hassan calls attention to Howard Nemerov's employment of the doppelgänger in *Federigo, Or, The Power of Love.*[3] In an article subtitled "The Conscious and Unconscious Use of the Double," Claire Rosenfield follows her brief examination of the significance of doubles in literature from Plautus to Henry James with commentary on such modern authors as Thomas Mann, Flannery O'Connor, John Knowles, William Faulkner, and Vladimir Nabokov.[4]

The reader of Rosenfield's paper should remember that almost all of the doubles she discusses are manifest. Thus, though she tries to distinguish between conscious and unconscious *use* of doubles, she ends by assuming almost all doubles to be consciously used because she does not discriminate between manifest and latent ones. Since no modern author at all conversant with literature can possibly avoid knowing something about manifest double figures, perhaps our question ought to be rephrased. How can the post-Freudian author who resorts to decomposition in a conscious way transcend the limitations of representing doubles in an overt manner? One way of generating a measure of compensating ambiguity, as Rosenfield seems to recognize, is to complicate technique, to make the formal features of the work as intricate as possible. What Borges and others have done, though this feature of their work has to do with more than just their employment of doubles, is to elaborate their technique to the point of self-parody.

Baroque Doubles

"Baroque" is the term which Borges applies to such technique: "The Baroque is that style which deliberately exhausts (or tries to exhaust) its possibilities and borders on its own caricature."[5]

One recent novel which employs doubles in such baroque convolutions that the necessary degree of ambiguity is sustained is Leslie Fiedler's delightful farce, *The Second Stone*. Clem Stone, the novel's seedy protagonist, has a brief love affair in Rome with Hilda Stone, wife of Clem's old friend and subject double, Mark Stone. Mark is in Rome playing impressario for an international conference on love, a pretentious convention which hopes to enjoy the presence of Martin Buber and among whose delegates is moneybags Irwin Magruder, a man engaged in "the confection of chemical contraceptives" who delivers a paper entitled "The Emancipation of Eros: Technology and Love." Mark himself, a rabbi, presents a paper called "Bundling, Necking, *Amor Purus* and *Coitus Interruptus:* A Theological Interpretation." Thus Mark is a cuckold, a phony, a rabbi, a Jew, an academician, a public personality, and a great success. In contrast, Clem is a cuckolder; superficially a freeloading writer who isn't doing any writing but underneath a sincere and passionate man who plays *eiron*-buffoon to Mark's *alazon*-buffoon; a goy who declares, "I am the real Jew,"; a private man; and a failure.

Indicative of the exuberant games which Fiedler may be supposed to be playing with his identity in this book, which also embodies uproarious satire on the entire contemporary scene, are the comic complexities involved in splitting his characters. Mark's mother's suitor mistakes Clem for Mark. They look alike, of course, and their last name is the same because Mark has translated his Jewish-sounding name from Stein to Stone. When Mark is stoned by a mob during a communist riot, Clem casts "the second stone." Clem's real name is Marcus Stone but he changed his name to Clem because people confused him with Mark Stone ("We used to get each other's letters, each other's grades."). Clem's choice of his name involves a joke about Samuel Clemens, alias Mark Twain, another writer concerned about his identity whose fiction is full of doubles (as in "Those Extraordinary Twins"). Hilda (a sort of "literary double" of Hawthorne's Hilda in *The Marble Faun*) goes to bed with Clem because he claims to be the real author of a poem which led Hilda to fall in love with Mark, who claimed he had written it. By virtue of writing the poem, Clem thinks later, "he had been Mark, had been Hilda's husband before he became her lover." To make matters even more complicated, Clem's wife—also a writer—signs her letter "Slem," which alludes to "Clem-Slem," their joint name. Clem thinks, "He was Slem, *was* Selma." And Hilda, whom Clem calls a femme fatale disguised as a snowmaiden and a snowmaiden disguised as a femme fatale, ultimately becomes confused in Clem's mind with Selma, a double of Hilda. Related to the double motif in the novel is the weighty theme of stones—symbols of love and death. None are left unturned as the author of *Love and Death in the American Novel* showers the reader with all kinds: Biblical second stones, stepstones, cobblestones, flagstones, tombstones, gall stones, stone *Pietàs,* and what Clem describes as a "tombstone-dealer's wet dream" (the monument of Victor Emmanuel). Clem even pretends that his great-great-grandmother was a Negress raped by Stonewall Jackson. These are but a few of the highjinks which generate enough ambiguity in *The Second Stone* to offset its otherwise blatant use of manifest doubles.

Even more baroquely self-conscious in its treatment of doubles— and constituting what amounts to a tour de force on the subject—is Vladimir Nabokov's *Despair,* a story in which a German chocolate manufacturer named Hermann believes he encounters his physical double in a vagabond, Felix ("the happy one"); plots to obtain his life insurance money by substituting Felix's body for his own; and learns to his amazement that he has been foiled by his foil: Felix does not resemble him in the least. Like the scholar-narrator of *Pale Fire,* another book littered with shadows and Shades and mirrors and doubles and whatnot, Hermann is insane—insane in the paradoxically rational mode of the paranoid personality. Unfortunately, psychoanalysis must lay down its arms before the problem of creative foolery in *Despair* because, as Nabokov patiently informs us in his foreward, "The attractively shaped object or wienerschnitzel dream that the eager Freudian may think he distinguishes in the remoteness of my wastes will turn out to be on closer inspection a derisive mirage organized by my agents."

The pun in "mirage" is not accidental. Hermann, for one thing, suffers from catoptricophobia. Symbolic of his fear of mirrors is this passage from a digression on mirrors: "Then, too, there are crooked ones, monsters among mirrors: a neck bared, no matter how slightly, draws out suddenly into a downward yawn of flesh, to meet which there stretches up from below the belt another marchpane-pink nudity and both merge into one." Inveterate punster, Nabokov even has his narrator toy with the idea of calling the memoirs which constitute the novel (so that Hermann as author may be said to mirror Nabokov) by the title of *Crime and Pun*—though he also considers calling it *The Mirror, Portrait of the Artist in a Mirror, The Likeness,* and *The Double.* Another typical pun occurs when the narrator tries to escape from a hotel: "I attempted to go out into the garden, but at once was *doubled up"* (italics added, here and immediately below). Vain about his literary prowess, the narrator firmly believes that "the loss of a single *shade* or inflection" would hopelessly mar his work. When he shoots Felix, the body swings before him in jest, "as before a *mirror."* Mocking his readers, the narrator swears he has made a fool of someone: "Who is he? Gentle Reader, look at yourself in the *mirror,* as you seem to like *mirrors* so much." Even leaves of trees have alter egos as they fall to the mirroring surface of still water: "When a slow leaf fell, there would flutter up to meet it, out of the water's *shadowy* depths, its unavoidable *double."*

Related to the double motif are the many castration and anal images. When Hermann first encounters Felix the "opened flap" of the latter's shabby knapsack reveals "a pretzel and the greater part of a sausage with the usual connotations of ill-timed lust and brutal amputation." Hermann's associations are projective, as are those which Hermann makes with another wienerschnitzel sort of object he finds upon returning the next day to the scene of his first encounter with Felix. On the ground lies a double turd: "one large, straight, manly piece and a thinner one coiled over it." Whether Nabokov intended it or not, the remains on the ground, one masculine and one emasculate, are doubles of the doubles in the book and all of a piece with other anal imagery which flecks the narrative's surface (samples: "the world, you know, is dirt"; "I'm silent before eyes in mire and mirorage"; "that drivel and dirt" [psychoanalysis]; " . . . from old Dusty's great book, *Crime and Slime.* Sorry: *Schuld und Sühne."*). Nor should it be forgotten in this context that Hermann is a manufacturer of chocolate.

The psychopathic narrator is a latent homosexual and pathological liar suffering from a castration complex and paranoid delusions of persecution and grandeur. These matters are mentioned as background to a scene from the novel which illustrates to perfection the baroque

features of Nabokov's handling of the double motif and which dramatizes how the impacted narcissism of a dissociated personality precludes
any satisfactory heterosexual relationship.

Throughout the book Hermann wonders why he married his wife,
whom he despises but of whom he is paradoxically jealous. "Probably
the truth was that I loved her because she loved me. To her I was the
ideal man: brains, pluck. And there was none dressed better." The
scene in question occurs when Hermann learns with pleasure that he
can "split off" in such a way as to observe his body as it copulates with
his wife:

> Not only had I always been eminently satisfied with my meek
> bedmate and her cherubic charms, but I had noticed lately, with grati-
> tude to nature and a thrill of surprise, that the violence and the sweet-
> ness of my nightly joys were being raised to an exquisite vertex owing
> to a certain aberration. . . .I am referring to a well-known kind of
> "dissociation." . . .For example, I would be in bed with Lydia, winding
> up the brief series of preparatory caresses she was supposed to be en-
> titled to, when all at once I would become aware that imp Split had
> taken over. My face was buried in the folds of her neck, her legs had
> started to clamp me, the ashtray toppled off the bed table, the universe
> followed—but at the same time, incomprehensibly and delightfully, I
> was standing naked in the middle of the room, one hand resting on the
> back of the chair where she had left her stockings and panties. The
> sensation of being in two places at once gave me an extraordinary kick;
> but this was nothing compared to later developments. In my impatience
> to split I would bundle Lydia to bed as soon as we had finished supper.
> The dissociation had now reached its perfect phase. I sat in an armchair
> half a dozen paces away from the bed upon which Lydia had been
> properly placed and distributed. From my magical point of vantage I
> watched the ripples running and plunging along my muscular back, in
> the laboratorial light of a strong bed-lamp. . . .The next phase came
> when I realized that the greater the interval between my two selves the
> more I was ecstasied. . . .Eventually I found myself sitting in the
> parlor—while making love in the bedroom. It was not enough.

Though he longs to be so far removed as to need "opera glasses, field
glasses, a tremendous telescope," the best he can manage is "to have the
bed reflected in the oblique speculum or *spiegel*" on the wardrobe. It
comes as something of a shock to the voyeuristic narrator when, ready
one evening to watch the spectacle from the fifteenth row of his private
theater, his wife calls from the bedroom to ask when he is coming to

bed. We learn later that Hermann's lovemaking lapses after this episode.

The admirable virtuosity with which writers such as Borges, Fiedler, and Nabokov complicate their presentation of doubles unquestionably generates enough ambiguity to avoid such boring stereotypes as the criminal-superego composite in Poe's "William Wilson." In part the ambiguity results not so much because they deliberately complicate their technique as because their complex formal effects reflect the intricacy of their general artistic vision. Besides, the mere fact that manifest doubles are presented in overt fashion does not necessarily mean that the psychological significance of such doubles is so transparent as to deprive the responding reader of all of the buffering obscurity which enables him, as he must, to identify with the various characters without experiencing undue anxiety. Yet the advantages of depicting manifest decomposition are almost invariably outweighed by the disadvantages.

Albert Guerard suggests the contrary when he says of the decomposition in Dostoevsky's *The Double,* "It [the resultant ambiguity] also permits a mature reader to enjoy the two levels of the story—to enjoy the story of a troubling human relationship without losing sight of the fact that we are dealing with a sick man, and to enjoy a story of neurotic behavior without ceasing to see not one physical being but two." Similarly, Guerard sees as a gain the fact that Stevenson's *Dr. Jekyll and Mr. Hyde* "makes so explicit a meaning latent in other double stories."[6] Psychoanalytic criticism, with its awareness that the dynamics of literary response necessitate unconscious as well as conscious participation by the reader, takes a seemingly paradoxical position: the more patently bizarre or neurotic a character, the more likely the reader will be alienated by him. Applied to decomposition, this paradox implies that endopsychic conflict is better portrayed by latent doubles than by manifest ones, all other things being equal. A concluding illustration of this assumption involves a brief consideration of latent doubles in John Barth's *End of the Road.*

Barth exhibits his fascination with twins, doubles, and the nature of selfhood most notably in *The Sot-Weed Factor* and *Giles Goat-Boy.* A choice example of his interest in twins is found in a chapter of *The Sot-Weed Factor* entitled "A Layman's Pandect of Geminology Compended by Henry Burlingame, Cosmophilist," but the supreme instance of baroque intricacy in Barth's handling of the twin motif appears in "Petition," a story in *Lost in the Funhouse*. A Siamese twin, joined belly-to-back with his brother, petitions the king of Siam for help in achieving separation. Among the complaints he makes are these: "He obscures my view, sits in my lap (never mind how his weight impedes my circulation), smothers me in his wraps. What I suffer in the bathroom is too disgusting for Your Majesty's ears." These mortifications are as nothing, however, to the misery the petitioner experiences when he and his brother make love to a pretty contortionist named Thalia, at times in positions beyond imagining in their complexity. Personality differences parallel the physical complications. The petitioner is refined and ascetic, his brother gross and lecherous, making it clear that the twinship symbolizes conflicting inclinations in a single nature.

As for *End of the Road,* much attention is devoted to the multiple selves of the protagonist, Jacob Horner, whose identity shifts with his moods, like the weather, or else corresponds to the role he decides to play while practicing Mythotherapy—a technique for adopting whatever role or personality best suits the exigencies of one's situation of the moment. In contrast to this emphasis on the kaleidoscopic variations at the surface of Jacob Horner's personality, there are almost no overt indications that the antagonist, Joe Morgan, is a complementary double of Jake Horner, no more than one finds, say, that Myshkin and Rogozhin of *The Idiot* constitute a psychological composite. The indications are so few and so veiled, in fact, as to make it reasonable to assume the decomposition was unintended by the author.

Unlike as they are at bottom, Jake and Joe have some things in common. Both were educated at Johns Hopkins. Both are brilliant. Rennie (Joe's wife) tells Jake, "In a lot of ways you're *not* totally different from Joe: you're just like him. . . . You work from a lot of the same premises." For reasons somewhat analogous to Hamlet's argument for calling Claudius "dear mother" ("Father and Mother is man and wife,/ Man and Wife is one flesh, and so my mother"), Jake's adultery with Rennie joins Jake and Joe, just as Velchaninov and Pavel Pavlovich become psychologically united in Dostoevsky's *The Eternal Husband,* a work with which *End of the Road* has much in common. Obvious differences between Jake and Joe exist as well. Indecisiveness, of which Jake is the epitome, is foreign to Joe, who feels certain about everything pertaining to his personal life, while Jake feels certain of nothing. Some allegorical touches in the novel point up other differences. Rennie tells Jake that she dreams Joe has made friends with the devil, for the fun of it, in order to test his own strength. "He told me that the Devil wasn't real, and that he had conjured up the Devil out of his own strength, just like God might do." Later in the book Jake dramatizes the situation as being

> part of a romantic contest between symbols. Joe was The Reason, or Being (I was using Rennie's cosmos); I was The Unreason, or Not-Being; and the two of us were fighting without quarter for possession of Rennie, like God and Satan for the soul of Man. This pretty onto-logical Manichaeism would certainly stand no close examination, but it had the triple virtue of excusing me from having to assign to Rennie any essence more specific than The Human Personality, further of allow-ing me to fornicate with her with a Mephistophe lean relish, and finally of making it possible for me not to question my motives, since what I was doing was of the essence of my essence. Does one look for intro-spection from Satan?

Ironically, it is Joe who turns out to be the diabolical one.

Given the metaphysical bravura which informs this novel, any attempt to define with precision the relationship between Jake and Joe must prove hazardous, but one way of tackling the problem is to scrutinize the psychological defenses which the two characters employ.

The principal symptom of Jake's problem is mental paralysis, symbolized by his prolonged physical immobility on the railway station bench. He cannot decide where to go because he has run out of motives, "as a car runs out of gas." Victim of what he calls *cosmopsis,* the cosmic view, Jake says that his eyes are "sightless, gazing on eternity, fixed on ultimacy, and when that is the case there is no reason to do anything—even to change the focus of one's eyes." His limbs are bound like Laocoön's by "the twin serpents Knowledge and Imagina-tion." In short, he entertains so complex a *Weltanschauung* that there remain for this modern Everyman no simple questions, no simple answers, no simple identities to assume, no simple values. Freud may be "caller of the whole cosmic hoedown," but Jake cannot dance because the steps seem too intricate and the orchestra seems to be playing polkas, waltzes, foxtrots, marches, tangoes, and calypso all at the same time. Though life cannot be said to be less complex than Jake sees it as being, most ordinary people perform modestly well in the cosmic hoedown by simplifying some of the steps, ignoring some of the music, picking a partner, adopting provisional identities, and—like

Joe—appropriating some relative absolutes. For Jake the complexity of the outside world reflects a paralysis-provoking chaos within. More than that, the Hamlet-like complexity of his intellectual vision of the world serves as a perfect rationalization for avoiding commitment, especially any kind of emotional commitment. Like Hamlet, he may be said to suffer from what psychology calls aboulia—paralysis of the will; unlike Hamlet, his aboulia is more general than specific and involves inhibitions in the sphere of the emotions as much as the will. His exaggerated self-observation, hyperintellectualization, depersonalization, and aboulia place him in a category recognizable enough to warrant the assumption that his world view, however realistic, serves the ulterior purpose of enabling him to defend against impulses felt to be intolerable.[7]

Jake's cranky genius of a doctor—no psychoanalyst he—cares nothing about the origins of Jake's problem and treats the symptoms instead of getting at the causes like the good behavioral therapist that he is. He counsels his patient to act impulsively and prescribes Information Therapy to quiet his uncertainties. Just where the causes of Jake's problems lie is hard to say. The adulterous triangle hints at early oedipal difficulties, but we know nothing about Jake's childhood, and his symptom formations take on the characterological intricacy typical of the modern analysand, so that all we can say is what the basic problem is and what the characteristic defenses are.

The sources of Joe Morgan's problems are equally obscure, but the problems themselves are almost transparent as compared to Jake's. There can be no question that Joe subtly encourages Rennie and Jake to commit adultery. Joe's "reasoned" façade about taking marriage seriously (the relative value of marital fidelity adopted as an absolute) masks sadistic, masochistic, voyeuristic, and homosexual proclivities, as his fanatical probing of the intimate "facts" of Jake's sexual relationship with Rennie reveals plainly enough. Yet he is so clever he can fool himself, like Faulkner's Flem Snopes. He remains completely unconscious of his complicity, casting himself (in his own little game of Mythotherapy) as victim rather than villain. Reason undoes him, not because he is rational but because, as a defense, it proves inadequate. Far from representing Reason battling Unreason for The Human Personality, as Jake playfully casts him in the miniature allegory, Joe is literally insane, as Jake well understands and repeatedly states. A paranoid personality, Joe employs reason in much the same way as

Melville's Claggart does—"as an ambidexter implement for effecting the irrational." The dramatic psychological difference between Jake and Joe, then, is that Jake uses reason as a device for calling all in doubt, especially any kind of deep emotional involvement, whereas Joe uses reason as a massive dyke to hold back whole seas of perverse sexual and aggressive impulses which threaten to engulf him. Jake must be certain of nothing. Joe must be certain of everything, including what brand of condoms his cuckolder uses and who was on top of whom during the first session. Considered as a pair, they dramatize some of the problematic aspects of the synergistic relationship between man's intelligence and his emotions.

At the cost of oversimplifying the philosophical, moral, formal, and other coordinates of *End of the Road,* I have stressed some of the psychological dimensions of the work in an effort to suggest the dramatic potential of representing endopsychic conflict in terms of the confrontation of seemingly autonomous characters. By comparison, *End of the Road* incorporates the kind of dramatic tension one associates with works like *Othello,* whereas a book like *Despair,* despite the ingenuity it displays, reads more like an analyst's case history. The richness of the psychological implications in *Despair* and its scintillating verbal texture are marvels to behold, but as literature it seems niggling, coy, bizarre, extravagant, precious, posturing, and—to sum up what could be a long list of complaints—ultimately not very satisfying.

If the term baroque, in Borges' sense, is applied specifically to the doubles of a novel like *Despair,* we may then distinguish between manifest and baroque doubles. Both are overt, and the reader is aware in each case that he is confronted by a division of the self, but the baroque double is at once more ambiguously and more self-consciously treated than the ordinary manifest double. Regardless of chronology, *Steppenwolf* might be called a forerunner of the contemporary baroque rendering of the double, and *Despair* the epitome of this mode. Dostoevsky's *The Double,* given the ambiguity and intricacy of its presentation, could be described as baroque. Baroque doubles succeed better than the ordinary manifest ones because the treatment bedazzles, befuddles, or drugs the reader into a state of confusion in which the reality-testing functions of the ego are in abeyance, allowing him to participate in the situations portrayed in a less critical fashion. In contrast to baroque doubles, latent ones do not necessitate these essentially defensive techniques on the part of the artist. Having no call to disarm his reader beforehand, the creator of latent doubles has more freedom in his characterization and can take us down to the depths without our knowing we have left the surface.

These remarks should not be construed as advice to novelists. The question posed earlier—should decomposition be employed by an author as a conscious device?—is really a rhetorical one. If contemporary writers deploy doubles overtly, they know what they are doing and will probably tend toward a baroque treatment of the double. It is possible that a writer may sense, dimly, that some characters he creates are latent doubles, but the chances are that he will make no attempt to analyze them as such and that the less awareness he has of this process, the better it will work. Neither should my remarks be supposed to recommend complete abandonment of the double as a manifest device. It depends on what the writer wants to express. One of the most fruitful themes in the modern novel is that of attempting to discover personal identity, as in Ellison's *Invisible Man* and Barth's *The Sot-Weed Factor*. Such a theme lends itself to self-conscious treatment of the double, especially in the comic, ironic novels typical of our age.

The functions of doubling may be summarized according to six categories. Some of these functions are primarily psychological, some are primarily literary (or formal), and some are as much one as the other. In all cases the various functions overlap.

Where the conflict portrayed in a literary work is intrapsychic in nature, the splitting up of a composite character tends to enhance the dramatic qualities of that conflict. The value in this case is primarily formal. A classic instance of the formal gains involved can be seen in *Othello,* universally regarded as Shakespeare's most dramatic work. Inextricably linked with doubling for dramatic conflict is the function of representation. Freud's remarks about regard for representability in connection with dream symbolism, which has to do with the way in which wishes, fears, thoughts, and associations find concrete expression, apply as well to the concept of decomposition. If an "ego-split" or some kind of endopsychic conflict is being pictured, what better mode offers itself than the portrayal of such conflict in terms of interpersonal relationships? The gain here is also primarily formal.

A third potential function of doubling lies in the opportunity it offers for making a balanced appeal to the reader's psychological makeup. In terms of Freud's structural model of the psyche, decomposition of a literary character is apt to involve a coordinated appeal to the reader's id, ego, and superego. One example would be Kafka's "In the Penal Colony." In the course of reading a narrative like this one the reader tends to make multiple identifications, to associate himself with various figures each of which corresponds roughly to one aspect of the mind. As Lesser suggests, inferior literature often makes one-sided appeals to the psychological man; the best literature makes a more balanced appeal. The gain here is primarily psychological. Similarly, literature mobilizes defenses as well as drives. Hence a fourth function of decomposition is to stimulate defensive adaptions. These defenses may be those of author, reader, and even those of the literary character. A character may be said, for example, to defend against an inner drive or conflict by projecting the unwanted "thing" onto another character, just as people do in real life. Much the same process holds for author and reader. Melville was said to defend against certain anxieties at a particular period in his life by representing the conflict involved in terms of the relationship between Bartleby and the lawyer. The reader defends against his identifications with one character by unconsciously associating himself with the values or behavior of another character. He plays off the Sancho Panza side of himself against the Don Quixote side, let us say.

A fifth function of decomposition, that of distortion, relates closely to the functions of representation and defense. In essence, the author must distort, or censor, his own productions. He cannot—perhaps should not—be fully cognizant of all of their psychological implications. By the same token, the reader (at least the nonanalytic one) should receive a large portion of the work's "meaning" unconsciously, and the distortion of the fantasy content of a work by a host of defensive techniques (displacement, reversal, projection, and so forth), of which decomposition is an important and complex one, enables him to register unconsciously what he could not easily confront in all its naked glory any more than Semele could be allowed to see her lover in the fullness of his might. A sixth function of decomposition is the establishment of esthetic distance. As a result of the distorting features embedded in a literary work and the way in which it makes a balanced appeal to the reader's mind, the kind of detachment—in both artist and reader—deemed necessary for the production and appreciation of the putative "beauty" of art is induced. The intimate becomes distanced. A kind of equilibrium becomes established such that the reader may introject the potentially disturbing elements of the work without experiencing undue anxiety. Decomposition is but one of many defensive features present in literature which tend to promote such a distancing of the intimate (to adapt a phrase which Ralph Maud applies to the syntactical strategies of Dylan Thomas' poetry). Thus the reader of Dostoevsky's *The Idiot* may remain comfortably disengaged at the conscious level while the *inner* warfare of his sadistic and masochistic impulses explodes into action as a result of his identifications with Myshkin and Rogozhin.

Notes

All references to the work of Freud in the following notes are to *The Standard Edition of the Complete Psychological Works of Sigmund Freud,* trans. James Strachey, Anna Freud, Alix Strachey, and Alan Tyson, ed. James Strachey (London, 1966), 24 vols., referred to hereafter as *SE,* or else to Sigmund Freud, *Collected Papers,* trans. under the supervision of Joan Riviere, ed. Ernest Jones (London, 1953), 5 vols., referred to hereafter as *CP.*

Chapter 1

1. From Guerard's editor's introduction to a special issue, The Perspectives of the Novel, in *Daed.,* XCII (Spring 1963), 204.

2. Henry Lowenfeld, "Psychic Trauma and Productive Experience in the Artist," in *Art and Psychoanalysis,* ed. William Phillips (New York, 1963), p. 302.

3. René Wellek and Austin Warren, *Theory of Literature* (2nd ed.; New York, 1956), p. 78.

4. "The Role of Unconscious Understanding in Flaubert and Dostoevsky," *Daed.,* XCII (Spring 1963), 363–82.

5. *The Creative Unconscious* (2nd ed.; Cambridge, Mass., 1951), pp. 343–44.

6. "Two Modern Incest Heroes," *PR,* XXVIII (1961), 648.

7. Doubling by multiplication of similar psychological entities would be an exception to the rule.

8. John Skinner, "Lewis Carroll's Adventures in Wonderland," in *Psychoanalysis and Literature,* ed. Hendrick M. Ruitenbeek (New York, 1964), p. 226.

9. *Sex in History* (New York, 1954), pp. 122–24; Reference is made in chap. 8 below to Freud's analysis of the devil as a father figure in "A Neurosis of Demoniacal Possession in the Seventeenth Century," *CP,* IV, 436–72.

10. *Ibid.,* p. 124.

11. Sir James George Frazer, *The Golden Bough* (abr. ed.; New York, 1951), pp.

206–25. The information in the next two paragraphs is based on Frazer's chap. 18, "The Perils of the Soul."

12. *Ibid.,* chap. 66, "The External Soul in Folk-Tales," and chap. 67, "The External Soul in Folk-Custom," pp. 773–812.

13. Crawley, "Doubles," in *Encyclopaedia of Religion and Ethics,* ed. James Hastings (London, 1908–26), IV, 853–60.

14. Ralph Tymms, *Double in Literary Psychology* (Cambridge, England, 1949), pp. 17–18; 23. Tymms's pioneering study was of considerable use to me. For psychoanalytic comment on golim and robots, see Robert Plank's "The Golem and the Robot," *LP,* XV (Winter 1961), 12–28. Plank mentions, incidentally, that Paracelsus boasted that he could make an homunculus "and prescribed that it should be produced from human sperm and nurtured in horse dung."

15. Robert Rogers, "Plato and Psychoanalysis," *LP,* XI (Winter 1961), 4–5.

16. James R. Wilson, "Comment," *LP,* X (Winter 1960), 2–3.

17. *SE,* IV, 322–23. Note that even as late as the *Outline of Psychoanalysis* (1938; first published 1940) Freud uses "ego" in the sense of "self."

18. *CP,* IV, 180. It might be noted here that Maud Bodkin asserts, "Perhaps the most important contribution that has been made by the Freudian theory of dream interpretation to the understanding of the emotional symbolism of poetic themes is that concerned with the 'splitting' of type figures," *Archetypal Patterns in Poetry* (New York, 1958), p. 12.

19. (New York, 1959).

20. *Ibid.,* p. 65.

21. James Schroeter, "The Four Fathers: Symbolism in *Oedipus Rex,*" *Criticism,* III (Summer 1961), 186–200.

22. "The Oedipus-Complex as an Explanation of Hamlet's Mystery: A Study in Motive," *Am. J. Psych.,* XXI (1910), 105. A more available source of the same discussion is chap. 7, "Hamlet's Place in Mythology," in Jones's *Hamlet and Oedipus* (Garden City, 1954).

23. *Hamlet and Oedipus,* p. 140.

24. See Marie Bonaparte, *The Life and Works of Edgar Allan Poe* (London, 1949), pp. 648, 650.

25. Newton Arvin's critical biography, *Herman Melville* (New York, 1957), pp. 143–93, discusses many of these points.

26. In this connection it would seem especially curious—and relevant—that the two most important characters in the novel are never portrayed as speaking to, or coming in direct contact with, each other; it follows that there is no need for them to be so portrayed if they are doubles, though of course various other explanations might possibly account for the anomaly.

27. For an exception to this rule, see Mortimer Ostow, "The Metapsychology of Autoscopic Phenomena," *International J. Psycho-Analysis,* XLI (1960), 619–25, which gives an account of two patients in analysis who experienced autoscopy.

28. *Der Doppelgänger,* published originally in *Imago,* III (1914); *Der Doppelgänger, psychoanalytische Studie* (Leipzig, 1925); *Don Juan: Une étude sur le Double,* tr. S. Lautman (Paris, 1932) [contains *Le Double,* first published in 1914, and *Le Personnage de Don Juan,* first published as *Don Juan-Gestalt* in *Imago,* VIII (1922)]; and "The Double as Immortal Self," chap. 2 of *Beyond Psychology* (published privately, 1941), pp. 62–101.

29. *Beyond Psychology,* p. 66.

30. "Psychological Analysis and Literary Form: A Study of the Doubles in

Dostoevsky," *Daed.*, XCII (Spring 1963), 345–62. Kohlberg seems to have the *manifest* double in mind. His argument that awareness of a double self is not characteristic of paranoia naturally does not hold for instances of the *latent* double; in fact, latent doubles like Shakespeare's Iago and Melville's Claggart turn out to be classic paranoid personalities. Projection, the defense mechanism so basic in paranoia, is only one typical characteristic and by itself not a defining feature; i.e., projection can be seen in other syndromes and even in "normal" psychology.

31. John Todd and Kenneth Dewhurst, "The Double: Its Psychopathology and Psychophysiology," *J. Nervous and Mental Diseases*, CXXII (1955), 47–55. Note that by "archetypic thinking" Todd and Dewhurst have in mind the kind of "thought" which has been discussed in connection with primitive conceptions of the soul. The comparable psychoanalytic term is primary process thinking.

32. Compare the "vastation" experienced by Henry James, Sr., the day-nightmare of sensing an invisible figure squatting in his room "raying out from his fetid personality influences fatal to life." See Leon Edel, *Henry James: The Untried Years* (Philadelphia, 1953), pp. 29*ff*.

33. N. Lukianowicz, "Autoscopic Phenomena," *Archives of Neurology and Psychiatry*, LXXX (1958), 199–220.

34. Morton Prince, *The Dissociation of a Personality* (New York, 1908); Corbett H. Thigpen and Hervey Cleckley, *The Three Faces of Eve* (New York, 1957).

35. "The Phantom Double: Its Psychological Significance," *Brit. J. Med. Psych.*, XIV (1934), 254–73.

36. Freud, *CP*, II, 58.

37. Angus Fletcher, *Allegory: The Theory of a Symbolic Mode* (Ithaca, 1964), pp. 35–36.

38. *SE*, XXII, I, 59.

Chapter 2

1. *SE*, XXII, 58 (*New Introductory Lectures*).

2. "On Narcissism: An Introduction," *CP*, IV. See especially pp. 31, 39–40, 46.

3. *Ibid.*, p. 52.

4. Specific citations are provided only for nonliterary works.

5. "On Narcissism," *CP*, IV, 33.

6. Compare with Rank, *Don Juan*, pp. 118–19: "A ce narcissime, se joint un magnifique égoisme, une incapacité à l'amour et une vie sexuelle anormale." ("To this narcissism is joined a grandiose egotism, an inability to love, and an abnormal sexual life.") Wilde's novel serves Rank as a prime example of the relationship between narcissism and decomposition.

7. Todd and Dewhurst (p. 49) record the following scene which occurred just after Musset had walked through a cemetery: "Suddenly, in the moonlight, de Musset caught sight of a man running towards him. As the stranger drew nearer, the poet saw that his face was haggard, his clothes torn, and his hair dishevelled. The man was drunk; as he lurched past, his face contorted in a leer of hatred. At that instant the poet was overwhelmed with terror for the mysterious stranger was *himself,* twenty years older, with features ravaged by debauchery, mouth agape, and eyes aghast with fear."

8. Coleman, p. 267, makes essentially the same inference: "In Maupassant . . . the hallucinated double is a projection mechanism, the result of repression and amnesia concerning a constellation of ideas centred about the feared results of sexual excesses."

9. Bonaparte, chap. 41. Bonaparte points out the disparity between the severity of the schoolmaster depicted in the story and the mild, much-loved principal of the same name who was Poe's principal in England as evidence that Poe's conception of his foster father is projected onto both the schoolmaster and the double.

10. *Ibid.,* p. 553.

11. Tymms, p. 16, n. 2. Tymms remarks that Jean Paul's typical doppelgänger "are pairs of friends (in the original sense of 'fellows, two of a pair') who together form a unit, but individually appear as 'half,' dependent on the *alter ego.*" (p. 29) In Jean Paul's *Siebenkäs* two such friends, dressed alike, stand before a mirror, thus making four doubles. "Not content with this, however, Leibgeber (with baroque ingenuity) squeezes his eye so as to see double, and thus increases the total of *Doppelgänger* to five!" (p. 30).

12. *Ibid.,* p. 28.

13. *Tales of Hoffmann,* ed. Christopher Lazare (New York, n.d.), p. 30.

14. "The 'Uncanny,'" *CP,* IV, 368–407.

15. *Ibid.,* esp. pp. 396 and 403.

16. *Ibid.,* p. 387.

17. Todd and Dewhurst, pp. 51–52.

18. For a description of primary process mentation, see Otto Fenichel, *The Psychoanalytic Theory of Neurosis* (New York, 1945), pp. 45–51.

19. This case history and the ones which follow are taken from Lukianowicz, "Autoscopic Phenomena."

20. Todd and Dewhurst, p. 50.

21. For the concept of shifts in psychic distance, see Ernst Kris and Abraham Kaplan, "Aesthetic Ambiguity," chap. 10 of Ernst Kris's *Psychoanalytic Explorations in Art* (New York, 1952). See esp. pp. 255–59.

22. A discussion of the symbolic equation matricide-incest can be found in Henry A. Bunker, "Mother-Murder in Myth and Legend," *PQ,* XXIII (1944), 198–207.

23. For some valuable comment on decomposition in Gide's work, see Mark Kanzer's "André Gide: Acting Out and the Creative Imagination," in *Acting Out—Theoretical and Clinical Aspects* (New York, 1965).

24. Simon O. Lesser, *Fiction and the Unconscious* (New York, 1962), p. 112.

25. "Dostoevsky and Parricide," *CP,* V, 222–42.

26. I say "in veiled form" because this ambiguous behavior is not necessarily abnormal in slavic culture.

Chapter 3

1. *Biographia Literaria,* ed. George Watson (London, 1965), pp. 173–74: "The poet, described in ideal perfection, brings the whole soul of man into activity, with the subordination of its faculties to each other, according to their relative worth and dignity. He diffuses a tone and spirit of unity that blends (as it were) fuses, each into each, by that synthetic and magical power to which we have exclusively appropriated the name of imagination."

2. Frederick C. Crews, *The Sins of the Father: Hawthorne's Psychological Themes* (New York, 1966), chap. 3, offers an informative analysis of the tale. In a footnote Crews points out that Elizabeth, Hawthorne's sister, took particular interest in the alleged incest of Byron with his sister.

3. *Ibid.,* pp. 161–62, 206, Crews discusses Cloverdale and Westervelt in *The Blithdale Romance* and Fanshawe and Edward Walcott in *Fanshawe* as being what I call subjective doubles.

4. Albert J. Guerard, *Conrad the Novelist* (Cambridge, Mass., 1958), pp. 27–29.

Notes

Another autobiographical parallel can be found in the killing at sea by Conrad's admired friend, Dominic Cervoni, of Cervoni's nephew.

5. *Ibid.*, p. 3.

6. See Bonaparte, *Poe*, pp. 237, 653.

7. *Fiction and the Unconscious*, pp. 110–12; "Saint and Sinner—Dostoevsky's *Idiot*," *MFS*, IV (Autumn 1958), 211–24; "Unconscious Understanding," 363–82.

8. *Fiction and the Unconscious*, pp. 111–12. Lesser remarks in "Saint and Sinner," p. 213, that "the complete man would perhaps be an amalgam of the three men whose destinies become interlocked in the first chapter of the novel—idealistic, sensual, prudent [Myshkin, Rogozhin, and Lebedyev, respectively]. The amalgam is unlovely, but it is man. Anyone who, like Myshkin, tries to deny, or simply lacks, some of the components is doomed, more surely than the mixed and imperfect ordinary man, to defeat and destruction by society."

9. "Some Character-Types Met with in Psycho-Analytic Work," *CP*, IV, 331–32.

10. *Ibid.*, pp. 332–33.

11. It is Macbeth himself, by the way, who calls the crime "parricide" in pretending that Malcolm and Donalbain have killed their father (III.i. 29ff.).

12. "The Riddle of Shakespeare's *Macbeth*," in *Psychoanalysis and Literature*, pp. 142–67; reprinted from Ludwig Jekels, *Selected Papers* (London, 1952). Note that Jekels composed this paper *after* Freud applied Jekels' earlier suggestion that Shakespeare sometimes creates composite characters.

13. "The Babe that Milks: An Organic Study of *Macbeth*," *AI*, XVII (Summer 1960), 132–61. With respect to the feeding situation, Barron states: "Infantile rage at interference with feeding is a basic motive of Macbeth, and is projected in several violent images: First and foremost of course is the instance of Lady Macbeth speaking of plucking out her nipple and dashing the brains out. The murder of Duncan is described as an obstruction of liquid flow: the fountain is stopped. Banquo's bloody ghost appears to Macbeth to interrupt him in the midst of drinking wine. The extent of Macbeth's rage is revealed in his imprecation: 'But let the frame of things disjoint, both the worlds suffer, ere we will eat our meal in fear,' etc." (p. 148). See as well the excellent study by L. Veszy-Wagner, *"Macbeth:* 'Fair is Foul and Foul is Fair,' " *AI*, XXV (Fall 1968), 242–57.

14. Norman N. Holland, *Psychoanalysis and Shakespeare* (New York, 1966), p. 277.

15. *The Diaries of Franz Kafka: 1910–1913*, trans. Joseph Kresh, ed. Max Brod (New York, 1948), p. 278. For passages relating to "The Judgment," see also pp. 275–80 and 296.

16. My interpretation of this story differs from Peter Dow Webster's—"Franz Kafka's 'In the Penal Colony,' " *AI*, XIII (Winter 1956), 399–407—in several respects. The major difference is that Webster regards the conflict as basically preoedipal, whereas I see it as primarily oedipal. See also Gordon G. Globus and Richard C. Pillard, "Tausk's *Influencing Machine* and Kafka's *In the Penal Colony*," *AI*, XXIII (Fall 1966), 191–207, an article called to my attention after completion of the manuscript. The authors of this insightful paper find essentially the same structural configuration in Kafka's story as I do, though their interpretation varies from mine in many particulars because of our different emphases.

Chapter 4

1. Lesser, *Fiction and the Unconscious*, p. 202, mentions Don Quixote and Sancho Panza—among others—as representing "component parts of one person." In "Saint

and Sinner," p. 211, he suggests that the fundamental conflict between them is that of superego and ego.

2. *Jacques the Fatalist and His Master* (New York, 1962), p. 79. I am in debt to Leonard and Eleanor Manheim for calling my attention to this example of decomposition.

3. No allusion to Lionel Trilling's volume of essays entitled *The Opposing Self* is intended. In selecting this title Trilling had in mind a quite different "opposing self," the modern self of the writer as it stands indignant in its opposition to and alienation from "culture."

4. Personal communication. The pursuer-pursued doubles we can expect will symbolize superego-id splits.

5. The sensitive study of Alex Page, "A Dangerous Day: Mrs. Dalloway Discovers Her Double," *MFS*, VII (1961–62), 115–24, does not emphasize this sexual dichotomy in quite the same way, as the following passage—well worth quoting at length—will make clear: "What I have tried to show is that Septimus' character is in all essentials Clarissa's, but taken to a deadly extreme. Both spend the day wandering, but he to his death; both react vigorously to the world around them, but he in dire anguish; both mean to shape their lives, and they succeed—she with a workable compromise, he by defying his compellers; both live on a kind of border, but his is by far the more exposed; both can 'feel,' but his feelings become a torture chamber; both are creators, she of the possible, he of the extravagantly far fetched; failure of communication throttles him, whereas it frustrates her. One way of looking at him, then, is as a warning, the warning that beneath Clarissa's regulated shiny life lies an abyss, that her extraordinary gifts contain the seeds of poison . . .

A more clinical way of putting it is this: she recognizes that he is the id to her ego. In that sense I take him as her double and see them 'merge' at the end."

6. *The Origin of Attic Comedy* (Garden City, 1961), especially the chapter entitled "The Imposter."

7. *SE*, V, 339–49, 507; Bonaparte, *Poe*, pp. 645, 653, cites Freud's principle of "representability" in this connection. She adds that "such splittings-off [of the "ego"] enable specific aspects and qualities of the ego to be personified and made concrete and visual."

8. Lukianowicz, "Autoscopic Phenomena," pp. 213, 215.

9. Fenichel, *Psychoanalytic Theory of Neuroses*, p. 157. The examples he gives involve both subjective decomposition and, in the case of ambivalence, objective decomposition.

10. *Don Juan*, p. 120. The original reads: "Dans la psychoanalyse, on considère ces altérations comme un méchanisme de défense où l'individu se sépare d'une partie de son Moi contre lequel il se défend, auquel il voudrait échapper."

11. See "Fetishism," *CP*, V, 202–203; "Splitting of the Ego in the Defensive Process," *CP*, V, 372–75; *SE*, XXIII, 201–204 (in *An Outline of Psychoanalysis*).

12. Cornford, pp. 130–31, 183.

13. Frazer, *Golden Bough*, p. 449.

14. "I have left weaving at the loom for greater things—for hunting wild beasts with my bare hands," she declaims. It is also significant, by the way, that Agauë plans to eat the lion cub during the ritual feast; since it is the Dying God or his surrogate who is eaten in the totem feast, this intention of Agauë provides still another link between Pentheus and Dionysus.

15. His mother's presence at the rites makes it the more likely a primal scene is involved. As for scoptophilia, which in itself has defensive elements, the Vellacott

Notes

translation gives verbs like "see" and "spy" again and again during this part of the play; for example, Pentheus: "I am not eager to see them drunk; that would be a painful sight." Dionysus: "Yet you would be glad to see a sight that would pain you?" Pentheus: "I would, yes; if I could sit quietly under the pine trees and watch."

16. The tragic hero is always a scapegoat figure, I think, a thesis not original with me, but one which I have argued at some length elsewhere: "Prometheus as a Scapegoat," *LP*, XI (Winter 1961), 6–11.

17. *Selected Tales and Poems by Herman Melville,* ed. Richard Chase (New York, 1950), p. viii.

18. "Melville's Bartleby as a Psychological Double," in *The Dimensions of the Short Story,* ed. James E. Miller, Jr. and Bernice Slote (New York, 1965), pp. 539–45.

19. To interpret the conflict of the story in psychological terms, with emphasis on the writer-allegory, is not by any means to imply that because the work has a personal matrix it does not, for the reader, embody some such broad metaphysical theme as the antagonism of realism and idealism. On the contrary, the psychodynamic underpinnings of the story support and energize the nonpsychological import, as may always be the case in fiction.

20. *The Art of the Novel* (New York, 1934), the Scribner Library edition, pp. 257–58; originally in the preface to vol. XVII of the New York edition.

21. "The Beast in Henry James," *AI*, XIII (Winter 1956), pp. 427–54.

22. Saul Rosenzweig, "The Ghost of Henry James," in *Art and Psychoanalysis,* pp. 89–111; pub. orig. in *Character and Personality* (Durham, N.C., 1943). Leon Edel, *Henry James* (Philadelphia, 1953), I, 75, 180. Edel links the antagonist figure in James's dream of the Galerie d'Apollon, whom the dreamer "turns the tables on" by switching from passive defense to active aggression, with Henry's father and brother.

23. Fenichel, p. 144, regards fainting as a quintessential instance of "the pattern according to which all other pathogenic defenses are formed: fainting is a complete cessation of the functions of the ego; other defense mechanisms consist of a partial cessation of certain functions of the ego."

24. *Psychoanalysis and Shakespeare,* pp. 338–39.

25. Francis Fergusson, *The Human Image in Dramatic Literature* (Garden City, 1957), pp. 126–43. Reading this play as an essay on government seems a lot like reading *Moby Dick* as a whaling story.

26. Surprisingly, even the interpretation of Hanns Sachs fails to discern that the crimes are specifically sexual in nature—*The Creative Unconscious* (Cambridge, Mass., 1942), chap. 3. He calls it "a comedy without 'gayety'" and takes its moral to be "they are all sinners."

27. A more complete version of this analysis of the play, with full documentation, appears in *SQ*, XX (Spring 1969), 205–15.

28. *Ulysses* (New York, 1934), p. 210. An Argus-eyed colleague, Professor Herbert Schneidau, called my attention to this passage.

29. "Diabolic Intellect and the Noble Hero," *Scrutiny*, VI (December 1937), 264.

30. "The Modern Othello," *ELH*, II (1944), 292.

31. "Othello: The Tragedy of Iago," *PQ*, XIX (1950), 202–12.

Chapter 5

1. "A Case of Double Personality," *J. Mental Science*, LVIII (1912), 236–43.

2. *The Three Faces of Eve.*

3. *The Dissociation of a Personality.*

4. "A Case of Multiple Personality," *PR*, XIII (1925), 344–45.

5. "The Conception of Dissociation," *Brit. J. Med. Psych.*, VI (1926), 241.

6. For an historical critique of changing metapsychological concepts, see Merton M. Gill, *Topography and Systems in Psychoanalytic Theory*, III, No. 2, *Psych. Issues* (New York, 1963).

7. Prince, p. 75.

8. *Ibid.*, p. 3. Italics added. At this point Prince is trying to make a distinction between "insanity" and multiple personality.

9. Hart, p. 47.

10. *SE*, XIX, 30–31 (*The Ego and the Id*).

11. W. S. Taylor and Mabel F. Martin, "Multiple Personality," *J. Abnormal and Social Psychology*, XXXIX (1944), 292.

12. *Doubles in Literary Psychology*, pp. 44ff.

13. "Multiple Personality," pp. 286–87.

14. *Love's Body* (New York, 1966), p. 82. Chaps. 3 and 4 entitled "Trinity" and "Unity" are especially relevant.

15. "A Portrait of the Artist *as Friend*," in *Joyce's Portrait: Criticism and Critiques*, ed. Thomas E. Connolly (New York, 1962), p. 99.

16. *The American Novel and Its Tradition* (Garden City, 1957), p. 79.

17. Francis Reitman, *Psychotic Art* (London, 1950), pp. 84–88.

18. See *Psychoanalytic Explorations in Art*, chap. 4.

19. *The Notebooks of Henry James*, ed. F. O. Matthiessen and Kenneth B. Murdock (New York, 1955), p. 364.

20. Edel, *Henry James*, II, 428. Hereafter cited in the text as *James*, with volume and page reference.

Chapter 6

1. "The Phantom Double," p. 271.

2. See chap. 4 of this book concerning Virginia Woolf. Claire Rosenfield notes that in *Wuthering Heights* "Cathy and Heathcliff are themselves exact Doubles differing in sex alone"—"The Shadow Within: The Conscious and Unconscious Use of the Double," *Daed.*, XCII (Spring 1963), 329.

3. "Psycho-Analytic Notes upon an Autobiographical Account of a Case of Paranoia (Dementia Paranoides)," *CP*, III, 390–472.

4. After analyzing this fairy tale I encountered Erich Fromm's somewhat similar interpretation of it in *The Forgotten Language* (New York, 1957), in chap. 7, which the reader might wish to consult.

5. Bonaparte, *Poe*, 650–51. Her remarks on this story are part of several pages in chap. 45 which deal with the mechanism of decomposition in the works of Poe.

6. Howard Wolf, "Forms of Abandonment in Henry James" (unpublished dissertation, University of Michigan, 1967), chap. 5. Wolf also perceives Chad Newsome to be, in some respects, a double of Strether. I should add that this sensitive, insightful discussion of the novel does not actually focus on doubling, which is ancillary to Wolf's concern for the way the novel portrays "the abandoned child as spectator."

7. *"Death in Venice* by Thomas Mann: A Story about the Disintegration of Artistic Sublimation," in *Psychoanalysis and Literature*, pp. 282–302. See especially pp. 294–96.

8. As an example I might cite Irving Malin's paper, "Mark Twain: The Boy as Artist," in *LP*, XI (Summer 1961), 78–83, in which the author convincingly argues that Twain portrays good and bad father figures in the riverboat pilots, Mr. Bixby and

Notes

Mr. Brown, in *Life on the Mississippi*, but maintains—quite unconvincingly, I think—that Jim plays good father to Pap's bad father in *Huckleberry Finn*. There can be no question that Pap is a decomposed bad father figure, one quite unlike Twain's own father; yet unless one nominates Judge Thatcher as a good father figure I think we must remain content with the assumption that the novel represents only one side of the child's view of the father.

9. "The Personal History of David Copperfield," *AI*, IX (April 1952), 21–43.

10. Manheim offers further comment on the splitting of female figures in "Floras and Doras: The Women in Dickens' Novels," *Texas Studies in Literature and Language*, VII (Summer 1965), 181–200.

11. I base this commentary on an unpublished undergraduate paper of one of my former students, Jack Shapiro. The words are mine; the analysis, which I give in abbreviated form, is entirely his.

12. Many of the observations I make have already been pointed out by Frederick Crews, *Sins of the Father*, and Simon O. Lesser, *Fiction and the Unconscious*, in their perceptive analyses of the tale.

13. "The Four Fathers," pp. 187–89.

14. Kris, *Psychoanalytic Explorations in Art*, Chap. 12.

15. It could be said that Agamemnon's return from Troy with a mistress leaves him with a trace of concupicence; however, it might be argued that possession of Cassandra flatters Agamemnon's vanity, being a prize won, more than she excites him as a sexual object. Her presence in the play is a matter of concern to Clytemnestra rather than to Orestes.

16. "Mother-Murder," pp. 198–207.

17. *CP*, V, 105–106.

Chapter 7

1. Taylor, *Sex in History*, p. 21.

2. As for Tristan's psychosexual impotence with Isolde of the White Hands, it is well established that when men are impotent in the arms of some women but not others, the former are associated with the mother. Tristan's impulse to remain sexually faithful to Isolde the Fair reflects a mother fixation so strong that sexual loyalty must be maintained. Note, by the way, that toward the end of the romance Isolde becomes endowed with the healing powers which her mother was famous for and which signify the mother's ability to protect the helpless, ailing child.

3. *Love and Death in the American Novel* (Cleveland, 1962), p. 197.

4. See Bonaparte's analysis, *Poe*, pp. 224–36.

5. For a general discussion of the sentimental heroine, with special reference to the works of Henry James, see William Wasserstrom, *Heiress of All the Ages* (Minneapolis, 1959).

6. "A Special Type of Choice of Object Made by Men," *CP*, IV, 198–99. Alberto Moravia's *Agostino* offers a brilliant and very explicit rendering of the adolescent's dawning awareness of his mother's sexual nature.

7. Steven Marcus, *The Other Victorians* (New York, 1966), p. 29.

8. Theodor Reik tells of a case in which a man overcame his impotence not by going to prostitutes but by addressing a preamble of vulgar and obscene words to his wife before intercourse, words he imagined would be appropriate for a streetwalker. *Of Love and Lust* (New York, 1957), p. 446.

9. Both his mother and father have Helena under their protection; moreover, the

countess says, "You know, Helen, I am a mother to you," at which way of putting the relationship Helena balks, saying, "Or were you both our mothers,/ I care no more for than I do for Heaven / So I were not his sister" (I.iii.144; 169ff.).

10. My own reading of *Pierre,* an incomplete one because it focuses on object doubling without attempting to treat the novel comprehensively, corresponds closely to Leslie Fiedler's. His rhetoric, emphasis, and purposes are such that his readers might easily be lured into supposing that he does not value the work highly; the statement just quoted above proves that he does.

As I do, Richard Chase regards Pierre, like Taji in *Mardi,* as being "torn between two women who symbolize two aspects of the mother" (*Herman Melville,* pp. 104, 137). But Chase's discussion follows quite different lines from mine because he concerns himself with the conscious allegorical elements of the work, those intended by Melville, so that Chase ends by defining the "two aspects of the mother" in Biblical terms: Lucy is the New Jerusalem; Mrs. Glendinning is "the Bride promised to Christ in Revelation"; and Isabel is "haughty Daughter of Zion chided by the Prophets for moral corruption" (p. 133).

In the introduction to the edition of *Pierre* which he edits (New York, 1949), Henry A. Murray offers useful insights but goes far astray in his remarks about Lucy and Isabel and their relation to Pierre. He sees no qualitative, only a quantitative difference between them ("Isabel's power being greater," p. xlix), and insists that Isabel falls into the Jungian category of the anima figure (lii ff.). He finds her to be "the personification of Pierre's unconscious." Though he does not use my terminology, it is evident that Murray regards Isabel as a subject double of Pierre, whereas I am convinced that she is an object double, along with Lucy, of the psychological mother.

11. Chase gives a good account of the name symbolism.

12. Compare with *Moby Dick,* chap. 36: The Quarter-deck.

13. *Herman Melville,* p. 121: "Etymologically, we perceive, Pierre Glendinning and Glendinning Stanly are the same name, since 'Stanly' comes from a Germanic word for 'stone' and 'Pierre' comes from a Greek word meaning the same."

Chapter 8

1. *Dark Conceit: The Making of Allegory* (New York, 1966).

2. *Allegory: The Theory of a Symbolic Mode,* pp. 35–36. My argument has been much influenced by Professor Fletcher's study, particularly by chap. 1 entitled "The Daemonic Agent."

3. Emil Schneweis, *Angels and Demons According to Lactantius;* quoted from Fletcher, p. 43.

4. *CP,* IV, 436–72. See Mark Kanzer, "Freud and the Demon," *J. of Hillside Hospital,* X (July–October 1961), 190–202, for a fascinating study of Freud's tendency to describe his struggles during the creative period of the Fliess correspondence in terms of an encounter with demonic agents.

5. *Doubles in Literary Psychology,* p. 42.

6. See Fletcher, p. 185.

7. Perhaps because of his formalist orientation, Fletcher eschews consideration of any genetic or psychobiographical elements in favor of noting patterns regardless of what origins they may have in the mind of the individual author. Nor does he care to consider the realm of reader psychology, what the individual succeeds in making of the patterns and characters he finds on the printed page. See *Allegory,* pp. 12–13, 301–302.

Notes

8. *Anatomy of Criticism* (Princeton, 1957), p. 89.

9. *The Allegory of Love* (New York, 1958), p. 60.

10. My explanation applies equally to both author and reader psychology. Fletcher mentions the term "decomposition" only twice, and his use of the term "doubling" refers more often to double plots than double characters. His main application of psychoanalysis, involving the development of analogs between allegory and obsessional neurosis, is not particularly germaine to the matter at hand.

11. *Allegory of Love*, p. 188.

12. *The Dynamics of Literary Response* (New York, 1968), chap. 10, "Character and Identification."

13. I borrow Fletcher's examples here. He emphasizes, by the way, that the progress, or journey, ranks alongside of the battle as a typical structuring principle of allegory, which is true but should not be taken as negating the fact that even the progress will have its fair share of "battle scenes."

14. *The Creative Unconscious*, p. 218.

15. This commentary reproduces portions of an article—"The 'Ineludible Gripe' of Billy Budd," *LP*, XIV (Winter 1964), 9–22—which focused on Billy's stutter as a symbol of his inner conflict against authority; various interpolations and extrapolations have been added to shift the emphasis to the present context.

16. *American Renaissance* (New York, 1941), p. 509.

17. *Herman Melville*, p. 297.

18. *The Fine Hammered Steel of Herman Melville* (Urbana, 1957), p. 26.

19. "Melville's Testament of Acceptance," in *Melville's Billy Budd and the Critics*, ed. William T. Stafford (San Francisco, 1961), p. 76.

20. An indication that Melville knew something about the implications of slips-of-the-tongue can be found in *Pierre* where the hero playfully accuses his mother of making a *lapsus-lingua* in suggesting that Lucy had also been in a hurry to marry; it is no accident on Melville's part that Pierre, in the same paragraph, makes a slip of his own when he says (with Isabel in the back of his mind): "she—I mean Lucy—has never been in the slightest hurry to be married."

There are many other theories of the etiology of stuttering in the literature of aphasia, and no doubt the phenomenon can result from more than one cause; the psychoanalytic theory is adopted here as a working hypothesis. According to Fenichel, *The Psychoanalytic Theory of Neurosis*, pp. 311–17, stuttering is a conversion symptom "exacerbated in the presence of prominent or authoritative persons, that is, paternal figures against whom the unconscious hostility is most intense." When a patient is particularly eager to prove a point, he has concealed behind his apparent zeal "a hostile or sadistic tendency to destroy his opponent by means of words, and the stuttering is both the blocking of and the punishment for this tendency." Fenichel also remarks that when occasional (as distinct from habitual) stuttering "occurs regularly as a response to a specific stimulus, knowledge of the stimulus can be used as a starting point for an analysis of the disturbing factor." Billy, be it noted, stutters only occasionally and then only under specific circumstances, as will be shown.

21. Melville makes it quite clear in chap. 14 (Freeman text) that Claggart's understrappers, sensing their superior's antipathy for Billy, make false reports to the master-at-arms, the veracity of which he never questions.

22. Hayford and Sealts in their edition of the novel, pp. 31–32, suggest that Melville based Bland on a corrupt master-at-arms (described by William McNally in *Evils and Abuses in the Naval Merchant Service* [Boston, 1839]) named Sterritt, who was castrated by his shipmates.

23. Since such spasms normally involve ejaculation of sperm, the "digression"—as the chapter is labeled—has psychological relevance to the castration motif.

24. Chase, *Herman Melville*, pp. 271–72. Italics added.

Chapter 9

1. *Labyrinths* (New York, 1964), p. xviii.

2. Evan Hunter, "The Sharers," *Playboy*, XIV (November 1967), 90–92; 206–10.

3. *Radical Innocence* (Princeton, 1961), p. 73.

4. "The Shadow Within," pp. 326–44.

5. *Labyrinths*, p. xxii. Compare with John Barth, "The Literature of Exhaustion," *Atlantic*, CCXX (August 1967), 29–34.

6. Albert J. Guerard, ed., *Stories of the Double* (Philadelphia, 1967), pp. 8–9. Though I disagree with Guerard on this point, I find his introductory essay of great merit.

7. See Otto Fenichel, section entitled "Inhibitions of Sexualized Functions," pp. 179–84, especially p. 182, and Freud, *CP*, III, 372–83, the portion of "Notes Upon a Case of Obsessional Neurosis" which deals with neurotic needs for uncertainty and doubt.

Index

Index

Robert Rogers received the A.B. degree (1950) from the University of Michigan and the A.M. (1954) and Ph.D. (1961) degrees from Columbia University. He is associate professor of English at State University of New York at Buffalo.

The manuscript was edited by Linda Grant. This book was designed by Donald Ross. The type face used is Mergenthaler's Granjon designed by George W. Jones based on original designs cut by Claude Garamond. The display face is Melior, designed by Hermann Zapf in 1952.

The book is printed on Warren's Olde Style Antique paper and bound with Columbia Mills Linen cloth over binder's boards. Manufactured in the United States of America.